Secular Surge

American society is rapidly secularizing – a radical departure from its historically high level of religiosity – and politics is a big part of the reason. Just as, forty years ago, the Religious Right arose as a new political movement, today secularism is gaining traction as a distinct and politically energized identity. This book examines the political causes and political consequences of this secular surge, drawing on a wealth of original data. The authors show that secular identity is in part a reaction to the Religious Right. However, while the political impact of secularism is profound, there may not yet be a Secular Left to counterbalance the Religious Right. Secularism has introduced new tensions within the Democratic Party while adding oxygen to political polarization between Democrats and Republicans. Still, there may be opportunities to reach common ground if politicians seek to forge coalitions that encompass both secular and religious Americans.

DAVID E. CAMPBELL is the Packey J. Dee Professor of American Democracy at the University of Notre Dame. He is the co-author of *American Grace: How Religion Divides and Unites Us* and *Seeking the Promised Land: Mormons and American Politics*, as well as numerous other publications on religion, civic engagement, and American politics. Campbell is a nationally recognized expert in the study of religion's role in American politics.

GEOFFREY C. LAYMAN is Professor of Political Science at the University of Notre Dame. He is the author of *The Great Divide: Religious and Cultural Conflict in American Party Politics* (2001) and has published widely on religion and politics, party politics, public opinion, and voting behavior. He is currently the co-editor of the journal *Political Behavior*.

JOHN C. GREEN is Emeritus Director of the Bliss Institute of Applied Politics at the University of Akron. He is the author of *The Faith Factor: How Religion Influences the Vote*, and co-author of *Seeking the Promised Land: Mormons and American Politics* and *Mr. Chairman: The Life and Times of Ray C. Bliss*, in addition to published articles on religion and politics, American political parties, and campaign finance.

Cambridge Studies in Social Theory, Religion, and Politics

Editors

David E. Campbell, University of Notre Dame
Anna M. Grzymala-Busse, Stanford University
Kenneth D. Wald, University of Florida, Gainesville
Richard L. Wood, University of New Mexico

Founding Co-Editor

David C. Leege, University of Notre Dame

In societies around the world, dynamic changes are occurring at the intersection of religion and politics. In some settings, these changes are driven by internal shifts within religions; in others, by shifting political structures, institutional contexts, or by war or other upheavals. *Cambridge Studies in Social Theory, Religion, and Politics* publishes books that seek to understand and explain these changes to a wide audience, drawing on insight from social theory and original empirical analysis. We welcome work built on strong theoretical framing, careful research design, and rigorous methods using any social scientific method(s) appropriate to the study. The series examines the relationship of religion and politics broadly understood, including directly political behavior, action in civil society and in the mediating institutions that undergird politics, and the ways religion shapes the cultural dynamics underlying political and civil society.

Gary J. Adler Jr., *Empathy Beyond US Borders: The Challenges of Transnational Civic Engagement*

Mikhail A. Alexseev and Sufian N. Zhemukhov, *Mass Religious Ritual and Intergroup Tolerance: The Muslim Pilgrims' Paradox*

Luke Bretherton, *Resurrecting Democracy: Faith, Citizenship, and the Politics of a Common Life*

David E. Campbell, John C. Green, and J. Quin Monson, *Seeking the Promised Land: Mormons and American Politics*

Ryan L. Claassen, *Godless Democrats and Pious Republicans? Party Activists, Party Capture, and the "God Gap"*

Darren W. Davis and Donald Pope-Davis, *Perseverance in the Parish? Religious Attitudes from a Black Catholic Perspective.*

Paul A. Djupe and Christopher P. Gilbert, *The Political Influence of Churches*

Joel S. Fetzer and J. Christopher Soper, *Muslims and the State in Britain, France, and Germany*

François Foret, *Religion and Politics in the European Union: The Secular Canopy*

Jonathan Fox, *A World Survey of Religion and the State*

Jonathan Fox, *Political Secularism, Religion, and the State: A Time Series Analysis of Worldwide Data*

Anthony Gill, *The Political Origins of Religious Liberty*

Brian J. Grim and Roger Finke, *The Price of Freedom Denied: Religious Persecution and Conflict in the 21st Century*

Kees van Kersbergen and Philip Manow, editors, *Religion, Class Coalitions, and Welfare States*

Ramazan Kılınç, *Alien Citizens: The State and Religious Minorities in Turkey and France*

Secular Surge

A New Fault Line in American Politics

DAVID E. CAMPBELL
University of Notre Dame

GEOFFREY C. LAYMAN
University of Notre Dame

JOHN C. GREEN
University of Akron

CAMBRIDGE
UNIVERSITY PRESS

University Printing House, Cambridge CB2 8BS, United Kingdom

One Liberty Plaza, 20th Floor, New York, NY 10006, USA

477 Williamstown Road, Port Melbourne, VIC 3207, Australia

314–321, 3rd Floor, Plot 3, Splendor Forum, Jasola District Centre,
New Delhi – 110025, India

79 Anson Road, #06–04/06, Singapore 079906

Cambridge University Press is part of the University of Cambridge.

It furthers the University's mission by disseminating knowledge in the pursuit of
education, learning, and research at the highest international levels of excellence.

www.cambridge.org
Information on this title: www.cambridge.org/9781108831130
DOI: 10.1017/9781108923347

First published 2021

A catalogue record for this publication is available from the British Library.

Library of Congress Cataloging-in-Publication Data
NAMES: Campbell, David E., 1971– author. | Layman, Geoffrey C., 1968– author. |
Green, John Clifford, 1953- author.
TITLE: Secular surge : a new fault line in American politics / David E. Campbell, Geoffrey C.
Layman, John C. Green.
DESCRIPTION: Cambridge ; New York, NY : Cambridge University Press, 2021. | Series:
Cambridge studies in social theory, religion and politics | Includes bibliographical references
and index.
IDENTIFIERS: LCCN 2020023978 (print) | LCCN 2020023979 (ebook) | ISBN
9781108831130 (hardback) | ISBN 9781108926379 (paperback) | ISBN 9781108923347
(ebook)
SUBJECTS: LCSH: Secularism – Political aspects – United States. | Religion and politics –
United States. | Religion and state – United States. Campbell, David E., 1971– | Layman,
Geoffrey C., 1968– | Green, John C., 1953–
CLASSIFICATION: LCC BL2760 .S43 2021 (print) | LCC BL2760 (ebook) |
DDC 201/.720973–dc23
LC record available at https://lccn.loc.gov/2020023978
LC ebook record available at https://lccn.loc.gov/2020023979

ISBN 978-1-108-83113-0 Hardback
ISBN 978-1-108-92637-9 Paperback

David Campbell:
  To Kirsten, Katie, and Soren

Geoffrey Layman:
  To Amy, Caroline, Grace, and Kate

John Green:
  To Lynn Green, Brendan Green, and Darcy Lutz

Contents

Figures

Tables

A Closer Look

Preface

Students of the politics of personal beliefs – religious and secular – operate in an uncertain time frame. Dramatic changes regularly loom large in the short run, but have little lasting impact, while changes modest in the moment often have consequences years hence. One of your authors (Green) remembers researching the politics of the New Christian Right circa 1980 with colleague James Guth. Guth and Green reminded each other: "we need to work fast because everybody knows these things don't last." Forty years later, Christian conservatives are a staple of national politics. Similarly, the New Christian Right was deeply worried about the progressive politics of "secular humanists," a fear ridiculed by nearly everybody. Forty years on, this book is about the politics of Secularists – humanist and otherwise. Perhaps ironically, our analysis suggests that it is the stridency of the New Christian Right over those forty years that has accelerated the emergence of Secularists as a political force to be reckoned with. While we are no more prescient than anybody else, we suspect that, like the New Christian Right, secular progressives will matter for decades to come.

Many of the details of our analysis, as well as documentation of the survey instruments we have employed, are available in an online appendix. Readers interested in consulting the online appendix will find it at secularsurge.com.

Acknowledgments

Our study of the secular surge has spanned a decade, during which time we have collected a lot of data, delivered many lectures, written numerous papers, and revised countless drafts. Along the way, we have had cause to be grateful to many organizations and individuals.

This work began with a grant from the National Science Foundation, a reminder that federal funding plays a vital role in supporting political science research.[1] We are grateful to the NSF – its program officers and reviewers – for investing in what was then a nascent idea.

We also thank the American Humanist Association, particularly executive director Roy Speckhardt, for allowing us to survey the AHA membership. We particularly appreciate the many colleagues who worked with two of us (Green and Layman) to both fund and conduct the surveys of 2016 state and national party convention delegates that play a key role in our chapters on secularism and party politics. Our colleagues on the survey of national convention delegates – the latest iteration of the Convention Delegate Study series of national delegate surveys begun by Warren Miller, Kent Jennings, and their colleagues in 1972 – were Mark Brockway of Syracuse University, Kimberly Conger of the University of Cincinnati, Rosalyn Cooperman of the University of Mary Washington, Richard Herrera of Arizona State University, Ozan Kalkan of Eastern Kentucky University, and Gregory Shufeldt of Butler University. On the survey of state convention delegates, Green, Layman, and Mark Brockway were joined by Rachel Blum of Miami University (Ohio) and Hans Noel of Georgetown University. In addition to funding from the universities of our colleagues, we received funding for these delegate surveys from the Ray C. Bliss Institute of Applied Politics at the University of Akron and from the

[1] NSF Grant SES-0961700.

Institute for Scholarship in the Liberal Arts and the Rooney Center for the Study of American Democracy at the University of Notre Dame.

We have also benefitted from the work of multiple research assistants. At Notre Dame, they include Mark Brockway, Maura Bailey, Jeremy Castle, Patrick Schoettmer, and Nate Sumaktoyo. At the University of Akron, the students and staff of the Bliss Institute have been instrumental, especially Janet Bolois and Jenni Fitzgerald.

We are grateful to the pastors and congregation of Christ the King Lutheran Church in South Bend, Indiana for allowing us to take the photos for our "Clerical Campaign Experiment" on their campus, and to Todd Adkins and Dan Hubert for superbly portraying our two candidates in that experiment. We owe Jennifer Smith a debt of gratitude for creating the news stories we used in that and various other experiments.

In the course of this project, each of us has "road tested" our ideas and analysis in talks given to a wide variety of audiences. A partial list includes panels at the annual meetings of the American Political Science Association and Midwest Political Science Association; Harvard's Kennedy School of Government; Princeton University; University of Michigan; University of Texas-Austin; University of North Carolina at Chapel Hill, Cornell University, Indiana University, Vanderbilt University, Temple University, Virginia Tech, University of Colorado Boulder, University of Iowa, St. Louis University, the Rooney Center for the Study of American Democracy (University of Notre Dame), and the Notre Dame Institute of Advanced Study.

We have also received assistance from multiple colleagues who have offered advice and criticism, including Chris Achen, Daniel Cox, Brendan Green, Patricia Hallam Joseph, Robert Jones, Jane Mansbridge, David Nickerson, Bob Putnam, Ben Radcliff, Tom Tweed, and Christina Wolbrecht. Over the course of this project, the discipline lost one of the pioneers in the study of religion and politics, Ted Jelen, who contributed to our earliest thinking on this project. Thanks, Ted. We also received helpful insights from the late Tom Carsey, whose untimely passing was a tremendous loss. We miss you, Tom.

In June of 2019, we gathered a group of leading scholars in both political science and sociology to critique the manuscript. And critique it they did! Their thoughtful commentary improved the book immensely. This group includes Bethany Albertson, Kraig Beyerlin, Paul Goren, Diana Mutz, Laura Olson, David Sikkink, Greg Smith, D. Sunshine Hillygus, Ken Wald, and Clyde Wilcox. In addition, John Sides and Michele Margolis provided extensive written comments. We are grateful to them all.

At Cambridge University Press, we thank editor Sara Doskow and the coeditors of the Studies in Social Theory, Religion, and Politics series, Ken Wald particularly. Thanks also to two anonymous reviewers for their insightful comments. You know who you are.

DAVID CAMPBELL ADDS:

I am grateful to the Carnegie Corporation for awarding me a Carnegie Fellowship in 2017–2018, which allowed for the essential ingredients of time and data. Their generous support was critical to this project, as it came at precisely the right time. At a time when federal support for social science is constantly under threat, I applaud Carnegie for recognizing its value.

In addition, I am thankful to my children, Katie and Soren, and my wife, Kirsten. It is because of their love and support that I dedicate this book to them.

GEOFFREY LAYMAN ADDS:

I am grateful to my parents, Barbara and Rod Layman, for dragging me to political conventions and rallies in Virginia in the 1970s and 1980s, despite my vigorous complaints at the time, thereby inspiring my love of politics. I am also grateful to my dear friend Tom Carsey for helping me become a political scientist and supporting me from grad school to tenure and beyond. Sadly, we lost both my dad and Tom in 2018 and they will be sorely missed.

I, of course, am deeply thankful to my wife, Amy, and my children Caroline, Grace, and Kate. Their love and support helped make this book possible and make life a whole lot happier.

JOHN GREEN ADDS:

I owe a special thanks to many colleagues and associates across the country, but especially at the Pew Research Center and the University of Akron, and of course, to my wife and children, without whose support my scholarly work would not have been possible.

I

The Secular Surge

Barack Obama's first presidential inaugural address was historic for many reasons. Among the least noticed is one word: *nonbelievers*. As is expected of American presidents, Obama's address was rife with religious references. He cited the biblical passage that "the time has come to put aside childish things," noted the "God-given promise that all are equal," spoke of "the knowledge that God calls on us to shape an uncertain destiny," invoked God's grace, and – as has become customary – closed his historic speech with "God bless you. And God bless the United States of America." He also highlighted America's religious diversity, calling it a strength. Obama's precise formulation made history: he described the United States as a "nation of Christians and Muslims, Jews, and Hindus, and *nonbelievers*" (Obama 2009). It was the first time ever that a presidential inaugural address mentioned Americans who were not religious.[1]

In the midst of that history-making day, many secular Americans took note. Ed Buckner, at the time the president of American Atheists, said that "President Barack Obama finally did what many before him should have done, rightly citing the great diversity of Americans as part of the nation's great strength and including 'nonbelievers' in that mix" (Waldman 2009). A blog post by the Center for Inquiry also drew attention to Obama's mention of nonbelievers, but it is the comments from those who read the post that best underscore its significance. One commenter wrote, "Thank you, President Obama, for realizing that there are many of us that do not believe with blind faith, and for understanding that we, too, are patriotic Americans" (Grothe 2009).[2]

---

[1] It is worth noting that in less prominent ways previous American presidents had also acknowledged nonbelievers, including George W. Bush (Gerson, Cannon, and Cromartie 2004) and Gerald Ford (Baker and Smith 2015).

[2] Some secular activists went so far as to suggest that Obama was one of them:
Cheryl K. Chumley, "Bill Maher on Obama: 'He's a Drop-Dead Atheist,'" *The Washington Times*, June 24, 2014; www.washingtontimes.com/news/2014/jun/24/bill-maher-obama-hes-drop-dead-atheist/; Gina Meeks, "Richard Dawkins Confident President Obama Is an Atheist," *Charisma News*, October 29, 2013, www.charismanews.com/us/41553-video-richard-dawkins-confident-president-obama-is-an-atheist.

Almost four years later, thousands of nonbelievers gathered on the Washington Mall for the Reason Rally.[3] In the words of its organizers, the 2012 rally was designed to "show the American public that the number of people who don't believe in a god is growing into a force to be recognized and reckoned with." David Silverman, who succeeded Buckner as president of American Atheists, addressed the rally's participants with these words: "We are here and we will never be silent again … In years to come, the Reason Rally will be seen as the beginning of the end of the Religious Right's grip on American life."[4]

In 2016, thousands of nonbelievers again gathered in the nation's capital for a second Reason Rally. According to an article by CNN, the "standout favorite" among the participants was US Senator Bernie Sanders (Mellen 2016), who at the time was in the waning days of his unsuccessful bid for the Democratic presidential nomination. It is not surprising that Sanders would gain favor among the self-proclaimed "secular American voting bloc." During the race, Sanders did something no other serious presidential candidate had ever done: openly describe himself as "not actively involved with organized religion" (Sellers and Wagner 2016). However, he pointedly denied the claim that he is an *atheist*, as was suggested in leaked emails from Democratic National Committee officials, in which they discussed deploying his alleged atheism against him (Boorstein and Zauzmer 2016; "Sanders: 'I'm Not Atheist … It's an Outrage'" 2016).

The public presence of nonbelievers has also expanded outside the glare of national politics. A good example occurred in December 2018, when people entering the County-City Building in South Bend, Indiana were met by a traditional crèche, complete with small statues of Joseph, Mary, and baby Jesus in a manger. Less traditionally, right next to that nativity scene was a display featuring another version of the scene, only this one featured the Statue of Liberty, flanked by George Washington, Thomas Jefferson, and Benjamin Franklin. In the center was a manger holding not the Christ child but instead the Bill of Rights. Right next to this display is a banner with the messages "Oh Come All Ye Faithless" and "Even Heathens Celebrate the Season!"[5]

The president of the group responsible for the banner and alternative "nativity," the Northern Indiana Atheists, told the *South Bend Tribune* that after repeated calls to the county board of commissioners their application for the holiday installation was eventually approved. County Commissioner Andy

---

[3] The US Parks Service does not provide estimates of crowd size for events on the Mall but the *Washington Post* wrote that there were "several thousand" present (Aratani 2012).

[4] See "2012 Reason Rally: Atheists and Secularists Gather," Reason Rally (website), https://reason-rally.org/2012-reason-rally.html.

[5] The Freedom From Religion Foundation placed similar displays in the state capitols of Wisconsin, Iowa, Illinois, California, Washington, and New Hampshire (Freedom From Religion Foundation 2018).

Kostielney, a Republican, indicated that "This was a pretty simple decision. If we allow one, then we would allow others" (Booker 2018). His understanding of the law is correct, and so visitors to this government building in the American heartland were greeted with dueling holiday messages: one a celebration of Christianity, the other a celebration of the Constitution.

Each of these stories illustrates the recent "secular surge" in the United States: the expanding size, increased political engagement, and emerging collective identity of secular Americans.[6]

When Obama referred to "nonbelievers," he was acknowledging a demographic reality. Although the precise contours of the secular population are debated, there can be no denying that its ranks are large and growing. One common metric is the share of Americans who report having no religious affiliation, or to use the term of art, are religious "Nones." As Figure 1.1 shows, roughly 23 percent of Americans made this claim in 2018, up from 5 percent in 1972, 14 percent in 2000, and 18 percent in 2010 (Norpoth 2019). And this increase parallels declines in worship attendance and belief in God.[7] At roughly 70 million adults, there were more Nones in the United States than mainline Protestants or Roman Catholics (Pew Research Center 2015), and they were more numerous than either Latinos or African Americans.[8] But as with religion, ethnicity, and race, there was considerable diversity within the secular population, with self-identified atheists being a small portion of the total.

The Reason Rally underscores that the secular surge is more than just demographics: secular activists have become increasingly prominent in politics, seeking in part to build a cohesive electoral constituency out of the diverse nonreligious population. These efforts are led by the expansion of existing secular organizations, such as the American Humanist Association, American Atheists, and the Freedom From Religion Foundation (founded in 1941, 1963, and 1978, respectively), and the creation of new groups, such as the Center for Inquiry (1991), the Military Association of Atheists and Freethinkers

---

[6] For an earlier use of the term "secular surge," see Haught (2018).

[7] These figures are from the General Social Survey. In the GSS dataset:

> No religion: religious preference is "None" (RELIG)
> Never attend worship: frequency of attendance at religious services is "Never" (ATTEND)
> Nonbeliever: "I don't believe in God" or "I don't know whether there is a God and I don't believe there is any way to find out" (GOD)
> Data are weighted (WTSSALL)

Other data sources, such as the American National Election Study, American Religious Identification Survey, Gallup, and the Pew Research Center, all show exactly the same trend. Note that given the social desirability of religious attendance in the United States, the number of nonattenders is probably higher (Brenner 2011; Hadaway, Marler, and Chaves 1993).

[8] "Quick Facts: United States: Population Estimates, July 1, 2019," United States Census Bureau (website), www.census.gov/quickfacts/fact/table/US/PST045216.

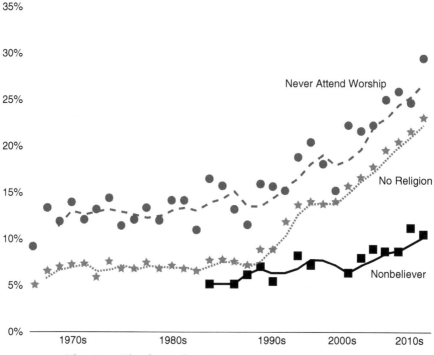

FIGURE I.I The rising tide of nonreligiosity
Source: General Social Survey

(1998), the Secular Student Alliance (2001), and the Secular Coalition for America (2002). Taken together, these organizations engage in litigation, lobbying, coalition building, and campaigning as well as publicizing secular perspectives on a wide range of issues (Kettell 2013).[9] And by 2013, seculars had a political party to call their own – the National Secular Party. Beyond such organizations, secular activists are engaged in many political venues, especially the Democratic Party. But as the experience of the not-particularly-religious-but-not-an-atheist Bernie Sanders reveals, secular people still have an uncertain place within American politics. Indeed, it is notable that Obama chose the word "nonbelievers" rather than "atheists" in his first inaugural address.

The holiday display by the Northern Indiana Atheists demonstrates that Secularists are increasingly a presence in the public square. This presence includes legal advocacy over the public role of religion – and irreligion. Secular organizations have brought many legal battles over the always-fraught relationship between church and state. Can prayers be said at town

---

[9] For a sense of the wide variety of political activities of secular activists, see the American Humanist Association "What We Do" page: https://americanhumanist.org/what-we-do/.

council meetings? Can places of worship receive a government subsidy? Can a cross be displayed as a public war memorial? Secular advocacy has also included seeking legal protection under nondiscrimination statutes. For example, both Portland, Oregon and Madison, Wisconsin include the rights of nonbelievers in their municipal civil rights codes, alongside the protected characteristics of race, religion, gender, and national origin (Simmons 2019).

Secularist organizations also promote a sense of secular community by celebrating secular "holidays," such as Darwin Day and the National Day of Reason.[10] Nor are they limited to serving the needs of fellow Secularists, as some secular groups engage in the sort of charitable work long associated with religious organizations. In the case of the Northern Indiana Atheists, the organization's website mentions its charitable activities, including a clothing drive for the homeless and a program to adopt a family in need for the holidays. As one secular leader argues, Secularists "need to do more than just pry people out of religion … We need to develop secular and atheist communities, to replace the ones people often lose when they let go of their religion" (Christina 2012). In building this sense of community, some Secularists are forming a new collective identity.

The goal of this book is to describe and explain the consequences of the secular surge in American politics. To the extent that the three key elements of the secular surge – growing size, increased engagement, emerging identity – reinforce each other, a self-conscious secular community could field a cadre of secular activists to mobilize a corps of secular citizens in pursuit of common political objectives. If so, the fault line between the religious and secular populations could deepen, reinforcing the high levels of political polarization in the United States. However, we also suggest that the secular surge is not *destined* to lead to greater political conflict. Perhaps many religious and secular Americans will find common cause. Politics, after all, makes for strange bedfellows.

SECULARITY AND ITS COMPLEXITIES

As suggested by Bernie Sanders's denial that he was an atheist, the very language used to describe the secular population is fraught. The variety of commonly used terms reads like a thesaurus entry: Nones, atheists, agnostics, nontheists, humanists, skeptics, freethinkers, brights. Moving forward, we will use "secular" to refer to anyone within this diverse population, and "secularism" to reference beliefs, identities, and activities that distinguish Secularists from

---

[10] For good examples of these services, see the American Humanist Association: Education Center (http://cohe.humanistinstitute.org/) and the Humanist Society (www.thehumanistsociety.org/); Darwin Day (https://americanhumanist.org/what-we-do/darwin-day/) and National Day of Reason (https://americanhumanist.org/what-we-do/national-day-of-reason/), and Humanist Disaster Relief (https://americanhumanist.org/what-we-do/humanist-disaster-recovery/).

other Americans – including those who are simply nonreligious as well as those who combine secularism and religiosity. From time to time, we will also use the term "secularity" to describe the combination of all these societal currents, as an analog to "religiosity." When necessary, we also use more specific terms, such as Nones (people without a religious affiliation) and atheists (people who believe there is no God) – two groups that are not identical, as we will illustrate below.

In this vein, we should be clear that in describing seculars and secularism we are referring to individuals' own *personal* beliefs, identities, and activities, and not public policy or law. The term "secularism" often refers to a state's constitutional structure, and whether it mandates what Americans commonly call a "separation between church and state." By such a constitutional standard, the United States would be considered to have a secular *state* – the first amendment to the United States Constitution prohibits both the establishment of religion and government-imposed limitations on individuals' free exercise of their religion, while Article VI prohibits a religious test for public office.

Despite having a secular state, the United States can also be described as a religious *nation*. Indeed, a plurality of Americans say the United States "has always been and is currently a Christian nation" (Cox and Piacenza 2015). This pattern helps account for numerous examples of public endorsement of religion, usually of a Christian – and specifically Protestant – variety. Some are a matter of custom, such as the aforementioned references to religion in presidential speeches and the addition of "so help me God" to close the presidential oath of office. Others have an official governmental imprimatur, like the phrase "In God We Trust" on US currency and "one nation under God" in the Pledge of Allegiance, and the references to the divine found in every state constitution (Sandstrom 2017b). In short, while Americans often subscribe to the principle of a secular state, what that means in practice remains a matter of often-heated debate. We will call these attitudes *public secularism*.

It is worth noting that personal opinions on public secularism are not necessarily a reflection of an individual's own level of religious devotion. This pattern follows from the long arc of American history, where many proponents of a strict nonestablishment of religion have themselves been highly religious people (Hamburger 2002). Likewise, some secular people have also been staunch defenders of the free exercise of religion (Kurtz, Bullough, and Madigan 1993). Of course, we expect public secularism and levels of religious devotion to be related, but precisely how is an empirical question (which we will address in Chapter 3).

To date, the empirical literature on the American secular population has focused almost entirely on the decline of personal religiosity – the absence of religious identities, beliefs, and activities. By this definition, "secular" is not a commitment to distinctly secular beliefs, identities, or activities, but simply a lack of commitment to things religious. While there is value in this approach, it obscures important differences among secular people, much as there are important differences among religious people. The rise of the Nones is a case in point: there is a great deal of diversity within this group. Some Nones are best described as "liminals," that is, their lack of affiliation is ambiguous and changes easily (Hout 2017; Lim, MacGregor, and Putnam 2010). Others are "nominals," as their lack of affiliation is unrelated to their beliefs and practices (Hout and Fischer 2002). Still others are "spirituals." Their lack of affiliation is a disinclination toward organized religion (Fuller 2001).

Nones should not be equated with atheists, as many people who do not affiliate with a religion nonetheless believe in God. According to the General Social Survey, roughly 20 percent of the Nones say that they are certain God exists, while another 31 percent believe in a higher power, even if not a personal God. We will call the absence of religion *personal nonreligiosity*, recognizing that there are as many ways to depart from religion as there are ways to be religious. Put another way, people we describe as nonreligious are defined primarily by what they are *not*.

Some Nones add to the absence of religion an embrace of secular beliefs, identities, and activities. Such people often believe in scientific naturalism, rationalism, humanism, or freethinking; they may also identify themselves as atheists, agnostics, or humanists; and they may seek guidance from secular sources, belong to a secular organization, or celebrate secular holidays. Many such individuals partake of a secular worldview. We refer to this affirmative position as *personal secularism*, recognizing that there are likely many ways to be secular.[11] People who are personally secular, therefore, are defined by what they *are*.

Measuring personal nonreligiosity empirically is straightforward. It is simply the inverse of how religiosity is measured: *not* affiliating with a religion, *not* attending religious services, *not* praying, *not* believing in scripture, and so forth (Kellstedt et al. 1996). In contrast, measuring personal secularism empirically presents more of a challenge because it requires affirmation of secular beliefs, identities, and activities. To this end, we have developed new measures of personal secularism, drawing on elements associated with secularity.

Although related empirically, personal nonreligiosity and personal secularism are not simply two sides of the same coin. Instead, these concepts represent differences in *kind* rather than differences in *degree*. Table 1.1 offers a simple illustration of the overlap of these two concepts. Personal nonreligiosity is arrayed vertically down the side of the figure, divided into "low" and "high" categories, while personal secularism is arrayed horizontally across the top of the figure, and also divided into "low" and

---

[11] In earlier work, we used slightly different terms for these concepts. Instead of "personal nonreligiosity" we referred to "passive secularism" because individuals fell into the category by virtue of doing nothing – that is, being passive in religious terms. "Personal secularism" was labeled "active secularism," as it refers to doing something – that is, being active in secular terms (Campbell et al. 2018; Campbell and Layman 2017).

TABLE I.I *Overlap of personal nonreligiosity and personal secularism*

	Personal Secularism	
	Low	High
Personal nonreligiosity		
High	Non-Religionists	Secularists
Low	Religionists	Religious Secularists

"high" categories. For now, we present these four secular–religious categories for illustration. We get into specifics in Chapter 2, where we introduce our measures of both personal nonreligiosity and secularism.

We label the top left-hand combination *Non-Religionists* because they score high on personal nonreligiosity but also low on personal secularism. These are ideal-type Nones – in two senses of the word – combining the lack of religiosity with the absence of secularism. In contrast, we label the top right-hand combination as *Secularists*, scoring high on both personal nonreligiosity and personal secularism. They combine a lack of religiosity with the presence of secularism. The bottom left-hand combination we label *Religionists*, scoring low in nonreligiosity (high in religiosity) and low on secularism. They embrace religion but eschew secularism.

The remaining combination, in the lower right-hand of the figure, is intriguing. The *Religious Secularists* score low on personal nonreligiosity (high in religiosity) but high on personal secularism. It may seem counterintuitive for "religious" people to also be "Secularists." But many religious traditions have space for beliefs that come from the natural realm. A good example are religious modernists, who believe in God but also in science and reason (Hutchison 1992). This mixed combination fully reveals the conceptual distinctiveness of nonreligiosity and secularism. Indeed, this combination resembles the contemporary distinction between "religion" and "spirituality" (Baker and Smith 2015). One person can be "spiritual but not religious," while another can be "spiritual and religious" – just as a person could partake of various combinations of personal nonreligiosity and personal secularism.

Although often unrecognized, the distinction between nonreligiosity and secularism has a long history. It can be seen in the shifting meaning of the term "atheist." The word derives originally from ancient Greek, where it meant "without god(s)" (Whitmarsh 2016). This broad sense of the word fits well with our concept of personal nonreligiosity. However, during the Enlightenment, the term "atheist" took on a narrower meaning: one who was an adherent to "atheism," understood as the opposite of theism. If theism is a belief in the existence of God (or gods), atheism was the affirmative belief that god(s) do not exist (Rowe 1998). This understanding was further narrowed by critiques of religion from the perspective of a secular worldview (Armstrong 1998), which fits with our concept of personal secularism.

Our concepts align with the types of secularity Charles Taylor describes in his magisterial book *A Secular Age* (2007). First there is secularity 1, or the withdrawal of religion from public spaces, what we call public secularism. Next is secularity 2, or the individual-level decline in religious belief and behavior, or what we refer to as nonreligiosity. In Taylor's words, these are both "subtraction stories," as they refer to religion having been removed either from public life or an individual's mind. Taylor then describes a third conception of secularity, which he defines as a society in which religious belief has become "one option among others" (3) as it competes with nonreligious influences, each of which is "something in itself" (Warner, VanAntwerpen, and Calhoun 2010, 8). This kind of secularity is an "addition story."

There are many kinds of secular alternatives in the United States, most defined with reference to religion, largely because these alternatives arose from various critiques of religion. One type is a religion without a focus on theistic beliefs, such as the American Ethical Union.[12] Another type is a life stance with clear parallels to aspects of religion – congregational life, rituals, and celebrants – but with explicitly nontheistic beliefs, such as "religious humanism."[13] Yet another type is an explicitly nontheistic belief system that offers practical and moral guidance for individual and social life – for example "secular humanism."[14] Another alternative is a consistent nontheistic worldview, such as some versions of atheism.[15]

---

[12] The AEU's motto is "deed before creed." It describes itself as "a religious movement because for us the ethical quest has the depth of a religious commitment, and because we recognize the value of a community of support, celebration, and action." See "Mission and Vision," https://aeu.org/who-we-are/mission-vision/.

[13] Examples include the "UUHumanists," part of the Unitarian Universalist Association (www.huumanists.org/); the Humanist Society, an affiliate of the American Humanist Association (www.thehumanistsociety.org/history); and Sunday Assembly (for one example see https://sundayassemblysiliconvalley.org/).

[14] The Center for Inquiry defines the term this way: "Because no transcendent power will save us, secular humanists maintain that humans must take responsibility for themselves ... Far from living in a moral vacuum, secular humanists 'wish to encourage wherever possible the growth of moral awareness and the capacity for free choice and an understanding of the consequences thereof'" (https://secularhumanism.org/what-is-secular-humanism/secular-humanism-defined/). However, there has been considerable debate over whether secular humanism is in fact a religion. Many critics want to define it as a religion, while many adherents do not.

[15] American Atheists define atheism as "the comprehensive world view of persons who are free from theism and have freed themselves of supernatural beliefs altogether. It is predicated on ancient Greek Materialism ... Atheism involves the mental attitude that unreservedly accepts the supremacy of reason and aims at establishing a lifestyle and ethical outlook verifiable by experience and the scientific methods, independent of all arbitrary assumptions of authority and creeds" (www.atheists.org/about/our-vision/).

These secular alternatives suggest a functional counterpart to religion in one way or another, much like the distinction John Dewey (2013) drew between "religion" (organization of particular faiths) and the "religious" (the experience of faith common to all religions). His concept of a "common faith" underlying alternative religions could now include secular alternatives as well, which exist alongside a host of religious alternatives in American society – some long-standing, some newly arrived, and some newly minted.

While our concepts mesh with Taylor's, we have a different objective. He blends philosophy and history to trace the historical arc and normative implications of a society in which religion is a choice. We provide an empirical examination of how individuals who partake of different combinations of personal nonreligiosity and personal secularism make political choices in the contemporary United States.

Despite our focus on the secular surge, it is important to remember that Americans as a whole are far from abandoning religion. The United States remains a highly religious nation, especially when compared to its international peers.[16] For example, recent studies by the Pew Research Center find that 53 percent of Americans say that religion is very important in their lives, as compared to 11 percent of Western Europeans. Similarly, while 63 percent of Americans believe in God with absolute certainty, only 15 percent of Western Europeans do.[17] Indeed, it is the rapid growth of personal secularism within such a religious population that sets the stage for a secular–religious fault line in American politics.

SECULARITY, SECULARIZATION, AND POLITICS

America's recent secular surge has turned the tables in the long-standing debate within the sociology of religion between advocates for and critics of what is loosely called secularization theory. Going back to the seminal social theorists, such as Marx, Weber, and Durkheim, many scholars have argued that secularization is inevitable: as societies modernize, religion fades in importance – because, to paraphrase Walter Lippmann (1982), the acids of

---

[16] In fact, the Pew studies show that in terms of religiosity, Nones in the United States are actually quite comparable to Western Europeans who identify themselves as Christians. For example, 13 percent of Americans with no religion and 14 percent of Western European Christians say religion is very important in their lives. Twenty percent of Nones in the United States and 18 percent of Christians in Western Europe pray daily. Twenty-seven percent of unaffiliated Americans and 23 percent of Western European Christians believe in God with absolute certainty (Pew Research Center 2018).

[17] See Angelina E. Theodorou, "Americans Are in the Middle of the Pack Globally When It Comes to Importance of Religion," Pew Research Center, December 23, 2015, www.pewresearch.org /fact-tank/2015/12/23/americans-are-in-the-middle-of-the-pack-globally-when-it-comes-to-importance-of-religion/ and Griffin Paul Jackson, "Western Europe's Christians Are as Religious as America's 'Nones,'" *Christianity Today*, May 19, 2018, www.christianitytoday.com/news/ 2018/may/pew-western-europe-christians-religious-practice-us-nones.html.

modernity corrode the pillars of faith. In truth, secularization is not a single theory but a family of theories, as scholars vary in the precise mechanisms by which they argue that secularization comes about. Like a family tree, some of these causal mechanisms share more DNA than others.

Regardless of the specifics of various theories of secularization, they have all had to grapple with the case of the United States, widely seen as a glaring exception to the rule. While Western European nations fit the pattern of secularization following in the wake of modernization, the United States stood apart as a modern, economically advanced, and democratic nation in which religiosity levels were high. Thus, there has long been a debate over whether the case of the United States can be explained by any branch of secularization theory. Reviewing these theories reveals that politics plays a role in each of them. Indeed, all these insights are helpful for describing political aspects of the secular surge. Some interpret the secular surge as caused by politics, others as an effect, and still others as a bit of both.

Some scholars see secularization as driven, at least in part, by a backlash to the politicization of religion. In a theory that we will take up in greater detail in Chapter 6, Michael Hout and Claude Fischer (2002, 2014) argue that many Americans are moving away from religion "as a symbolic statement against the Religious Right." Or as one secular activist put it: "The Religious Right all too often seems to dominate our national dialogue ... They want to run your life, mine, and everyone else's as much as they possibly can" (Lynn 2006, 17–18). This backlash has not happened in a vacuum, as the end of the Cold War is likely an enabling condition. The United States is no longer squaring off against the godless Communists but instead facing a threat from militant Islamists, lessening the stigma of disclaiming a religious affiliation. Thus, the religious landscape has been altered by political activity itself (Djupe, Neiheisel, and Conger 2018; Margolis 2018b; Patrikios 2008). This hypothesis is a story of the *displacement* of the pillars of faith, caused by the acids of faith-based politics.

Other scholars argue that the United States was an exception but is no longer: secularization simply arrived later in America than in other comparable societies (Stolz 2019). David Voas and Mark Chaves (2016) argue that a key factor is generational change, with a succession of cohorts that each become less religious than the preceding one. In part, this generational shift may reflect changes in marriage customs, including delayed family formation and greater numbers of interfaith marriages (Riley 2013). This shift also coincides with the rise of progressive cultural movements in American politics, beginning with civil rights for African Americans, followed by the emancipation of women, and the recognition of homosexuality. Thus, cultural politics contributed to the secular surge, principally through its impact on younger citizens. This would be the *subtraction* of the pillars of faith, mediated by the acids of youth-based politics.

Still other scholars believe that the United States could and still can be explained by their branch of secularization theory. For example, Pippa Norris and Ronald Inglehart (2011) see the high levels of religiosity in the modern United States as consistent with a theory of existential security. Where economic security is low (i.e. risk is high), people are more likely to turn to religion. With great risk comes great religiosity. Ergo, as a nation with a weak social safety net and high income inequality, the United States is also highly religious. Of course, social welfare policies arise from politics, and during roughly the same time frame, the more religious US population opted for weaker social welfare policies than did its more modern counterparts. Thus, the secular surge reflects a new version of this pattern, with the growing number of nonreligious citizens supporting progressive social welfare policies. This theory is a *realignment* of the pillars of faith, mediated by the acids of class-based politics.

Another point of view sees the United States not as an outlier per se but as just exhibiting another kind of secularity, now and in the past. Steve Bruce (2011) acknowledges the high self-reported religiosity of modern Americans, but argues that the United States is more secular than generally recognized – if secularization is defined as a diminished role for exclusively religious arguments in the public sphere and religious institutions that deemphasize the supernatural. One reason for this situation is the extraordinary diversity, dynamism and decentralization of religion in America, which regularly brings different religions into contact with one another (Kaufmann 2010). In this context, the tensions between modernity and religiosity are worked out largely within key institutions of civil society – in science, medicine, technology, law, journalism, education – and within religious organizations themselves (Smith 2015). Various kinds of "secular" professional elites, distinguished by their high levels of education, have sought control of these institutions (Smith 2003). Thus, the secular surge is a result of the loss of religious influence due to the power of well-educated professionals within these institutions. This theory of secularization is about the *transformation* of the pillars of faith, due to the acids of profession-based politics.

Another school of thought rejects secularization theory altogether. Roger Finke and Rodney Stark (2005) have argued that there has been a long-term rise in religiosity over the course of American history – the exact opposite of what secularization theory predicts.[18] In this theory, the key mechanism is the supply of religious goods provided by competition among rival faiths. This situation has been fostered by a religious marketplace largely unregulated by a secular state. But politics has played an important role in determining the exact contours and characteristics of this marketplace. Thus, the secular surge in part reflects changes in such regulation, which disadvantage some religious competitors and/or advantage new secular competitors. The religious markets theory is about the *addition* of new pillars of "faith," aided by the acids of public secularism.

---

[18] See also Stolz et al. (2015).

THE POLITICS OF SECULARISM

It is one thing for a demographic group, like the secular population, to become larger over a relatively short period of time, as President Obama noted in his first inaugural address. But it is quite another thing for its members to develop a distinctive politics. Considerable evidence suggests that as a group, secular voters are a growing component of the Democratic Party coalition. By some accounts, they strongly support Democratic candidates and tend to have progressive views on cultural issues (Hansen 2011). But other evidence suggests that some, perhaps many, nonreligious Americans do not strongly identify as Democrats, are not particularly active in political or civic affairs, and have more diverse views on noncultural issues (Green 2007).

Our distinction between personal nonreligiosity and personal secularism helps to reconcile these seemingly inconsistent conclusions. Because Non-Religionists are defined by the absence of both religiosity and secular values, they are unlikely to share a distinctive worldview that in turn informs their politics. To foreshadow our more detailed discussion later on, Non-Religionists are generally "civic dropouts." Their disconnection with religion is one symptom of a larger syndrome, as they are often disengaged from political and civic life as well. They generally do not have a consistent political ideology, nor do they identify strongly with a political party. In contrast, Secularists affirmatively embrace a distinctive secular worldview; they are likely to have well-formed political opinions and the motivation to be politically engaged.

Indeed, contemporary accounts of Secularist politics (Kettell 2013) note a strong and consistent reaction to the Religious Right as a motivation for mobilization, just as we heard from the organizers of the Reason Rally. In the context of a society with many religious people, nontheistic beliefs add elements of identity politics, including staunch opposition to a privileged position for religion in public life as well as to discrimination against secular people. For example, consider these words from the website of the American Humanist Association. "We do take philosophical issue with beliefs of religious followers. However, what concerns us even more is when religious believers attempt to use the power of the government to force their beliefs upon the rest of society. As it has been shown throughout history, no one benefits when religious belief and government power mix."[19]

Related to these reactions are progressive attitudes on cultural issues, especially on controversies that involve traditional morality. A common Secularist saying is "One can be good without god."[20] Such views are self-

---

[19] American Humanist Association. "Frequently Asked Questions." https://americanhumanist.org/about/faq/.

[20] For an example see American Humanist Association, "Millions Are Good Without God, Moscow, ID, Billboard Declares." Press Release, September 17, 2009. https://americanhumanist.org/press-releases/2009–09-millions-are-good-without-god-moscow-id-billboard-dec/.

consciously linked with progressive views on social welfare and foreign policy, where the authority of secular perspectives, especially those of science and philosophy, plays a major role. We again turn to the words of the American Humanist Association: "Advocating for equality for nontheists and a society guided by reason, empathy, and our growing knowledge of the world, [secularism] promotes a worldview that encourages individuals to live informed and meaningful lives that aspire to the greater good."[21] This combination of identity and ideological politics supports strong identification with the Democratic Party and a high level of political and civic engagement. While this phenomenon has become more prominent in recent times, it is hardly new in the United States (Jacoby 2004).

If these expectations hold, then Secularists could well be a strong base constituency of the Democratic Party, while Non-Religionists would be a more peripheral constituency. The key to this possibility is the work of Secularist political activists in mobilizing secular citizens of all kinds on behalf of progressive causes and into the Democratic Party. In this regard, Democratic activists are already more likely to be Secularists than the population as a whole, and Democratic identifiers in general (Layman and Weaver 2016).

The prominence of this constituency could grow if, over time, Non-Religionists become Secularists by embracing a secular worldview. This might result from the work of Secularist activists in making "converts" to personal secularism – an example is the "evangelism" of Northern Indiana Atheists described at the beginning of this chapter. In this regard, an overarching goal is building a distinctive, cohesive, and attractive collective identity among secular people. A secular activist described such aspirations this way:

The "first wave" of atheism were the traditional philosophers, freethinkers, and academics. Then came the second wave of [atheism] …, whose trademark was their unabashed public criticism of religion. Now it's time for a third wave [of atheism] … that cares about how religion affects everyone and that applies skepticism to everything, including social issues like sexism, racism, politics, poverty, and crime. (Kettell 2013, 67)

This aspiration for "third-wave" secularism suggests that for many secular people their collective identity as such is nascent, if an identity at all, while for others it is affirmative membership in a community with "a strong sense of group commitment, clear identity markers and a collective sense of relative deprivation" (Reicher, Spears, and Haslam 2010). It is possible that in the future, the secular population will develop a collective superordinate identity that unites its diverse components, not unlike the way that "Latino" has come to refer an array of nationality groups, or "people of faith" is used to reference a range of religious groups (Niose 2013).

---

[21] "Frequently Asked Questions." American Humanist Association (website), n.d. https://americanhumanist.org/about/faq/.

Secularists are poised to be more tightly integrated into the Democratic Party, bolstering its progressive ranks and expanding its resources. Today, evangelical Protestants are just such a tightly integrated constituency for the Republican Party, so much so that nearly all Republican candidates feel compelled to actively court evangelical leaders and voters. When a group becomes a major component of one party's coalition, it tends to become a formidable presence in American politics (Frymer 2010).

There are, however, potential costs to the development of a strong Secularist constituency. For one thing, it is likely to bring new tensions into the Democratic coalition. One point of friction might be with African American and Latino Democrats, who are more likely than white Democrats to be strong Religionists; another flashpoint could be white religious progressives, whether they are Religionists or Religious Secularists.[22] Many of these voters and activists hold progressive policy positions *precisely* because of their religious worldviews. The dislike that many Secularists have for religion could inhibit strong and effective coalitions in party politics, campaigns, and policymaking. As one secular activist writes: "moderate and progressive religion still encourages the basic idea of faith; the idea that it's acceptable, and even virtuous, to believe in things you have no good reason to think are true" (Christina 2012). And on the other side, there is evidence that many religious people, including Democrats, distrust Secularists (Edgell, Gerteis, and Hartmann 2007; Franks 2017). This pattern raises doubts about the viability of frankly secular candidates for elective office. Many Democrats are no doubt wary of being branded as the "godless" party by Republicans – or even by other Democrats, as Bernie Sanders feared.

While Secularists are most active in Democratic Party politics, Republicans are part of the story too. There are pockets of the secular population who lean to the right (Hunsberger and Altemeyer 2006). One example is staunch libertarians, of the sort who rallied behind Ron Paul's bid for the Republican presidential nomination in 2012 (Layman and Weaver 2016). Although secular libertarians are a tiny slice of the general population – and are even a small share of Republican identifiers – they nonetheless comprised a sizable share of the delegates to the 2012 Republican National Convention. In 2016, Donald Trump found support among a very different type of secular voter: people who nominally identify with a religion but otherwise have no connection to a congregation or religious community and who do not exhibit much personal religious behavior. Joseph Baker and Buster Smith aptly refer to these people as being "culturally religious" (2015). One should not exaggerate the Trump leanings of the culturally religious, as on the whole they tend toward the

---

[22] For an example of such politics, see Daniel Bush, "Religious Liberals Want to Change What It Means to Be a Christian Voter," *PBS News Hour*, July 8, 2019. www.pbs.org/newshour/politics/religious-liberals-want-to-change-what-it-means-to-be-a-christian-voter.

political left. However, they represented an important part of Trump's base in the 2016 nomination and general election campaigns (see Chapter 9).

Needless to say, libertarian and culturally religious Republicans are in tension with the Religionists in the Republican coalition.

Thus, the secular surge has the capacity to deepen an existing political fault line in American politics between Religionists and Secularists. Such an extension of conflict could well intensify the high level of polarization in the United States. One result of these shifts and tensions might be the transformation of American politics into a "confessional" party system.[23] In confessional party systems, some or all political parties are organized around religion and/or secularism, sometimes *de jure* but usually *de facto*. In the American case, this would mean a "religious" Republican Party (Religionists of all kinds) and a "secular" Democratic Party (Secularists and most Non-Religionists), perhaps with Religious Secularists representing a new kind of swing voter. If such a confessional, or perhaps confessional-adjacent, system were to arise, it would institutionalize the religious–secular fault line in American politics.

PLAN OF THE BOOK

We acknowledge that the secular surge is a highly charged topic, even more so when one adds politics to the mix. We stress, therefore, that our efforts are empirical, not normative: we neither celebrate nor lament the secular surge and its political impact. Our role is to observe and explain. Accordingly, we rely not on conjecture but data. Much of that data we gathered ourselves, principally by means of the Secular America Studies (SAS). The first SAS was a four-wave panel survey of a nationally representative sample, fielded from 2010 to 2012. The second was a national survey fielded in 2017. By developing, fielding, and analyzing multiple rounds of data collection, we have been able to refine new measures of personal secularism – secular beliefs, identities, and activities. Importantly, as we show in Chapter 2, these measures of secularism are distinct from the absence of religiosity. They measure what people are, instead of what they are not.

We also surveyed the membership of the American Humanist Association (AHA), an organization that is explicitly secular, and which says its mission is "to advance humanism, and ethical and life-affirming philosophy free of belief in any gods and other supernatural forces."[24] Indeed, an alert reader may have

---

[23] On confessional parties and the American case, see Payam Mohseni, "Organizing Politics: Religion and Political Parties in Comparative Perspective." Belfer Center for Science and International Affairs (website), January 2016. www.belfercenter.org/publication/organizing-politics-religion-and-political-parties-comparative-perspective.

[24] "Humanist Common Ground: Atheism." American Humanist Association (website), n.d. https://americanhumanist.org/paths/atheism/.

noticed that we have already cited AHA statements earlier in this chapter. The data from the AHA members serve multiple purposes. For one, they enable us to validate our measurement of personal secularism. By including our secular measures on these surveys, we can see whether they resonate with "card-carrying" Secularists, and thus reflect a genuinely secular worldview. The AHA data, however, also enable us to learn about a highly secular slice of the American population for its own sake. While the AHA data instruct us in the politics of secular activists, we have collected other data to illuminate the secularism of political activists – specifically, surveys of delegates to the Republican and Democratic national conventions, as well as a unique survey of delegates to various state political conventions in 2016.

These surveys enable us to describe various groups of people in their natural habitat. In addition to these observational data, we have also conducted a series of survey experiments as more stringent tests of causation. Some of these experiments gauge how people react to the mixture of religion and politics, while others examine the connection between secularism and politics.

For a complete list of the datasets employed in this book, see the box labeled A Closer Look 1.1. You will find Closer Look boxes throughout the book. Each contains methodological or other technical information that will be fascinating to some of our readers and of little interest to others. If you fall into the uninterested category, you can skip these boxes without missing anything from our analysis or argument.

The chapters that follow center on four major conclusions.

All Secular People Are Not Alike

Chapter 2 digs deep into the distinction – central to the remainder of the book – between personal nonreligiosity and secularism. This chapter is where we introduce our new measures of personal secularism. We use a variety of methods, quantitative and qualitative, to validate these measures. In doing so, we show that American society is more secular than commonly thought.

Secularism Affects Politics – And Politics Affects Secularism

Chapter 3 then examines how personal secularism shapes public opinion where we would most expect it to matter: the line between church and state, or public secularism. We explore the nuances in Americans' attitudes on church–state separation, including how both personal secularism and nonreligiosity shape attitudes toward the twin religious protections guaranteed by the First Amendment, protection *of* religious free exercise, and protection *from* government establishment of religion. Our analysis speaks directly to the current debate over the meaning of religious liberty.

Chapter 4 examines how secularism affects the civic landscape. To what extent are Secularists civically engaged, including in nonpolitical activity (such

A Closer Look 1.1:
Original Datasets Used in This Book

Throughout this book we use original data from a number of different surveys and experiments, each of which is described below.

SURVEYS

Secular America Panel Study (SAS), 2010–2012

A four-wave panel study. The number of panel respondents was 2,635 in fall 2010, 1,909 in summer 2011, 1,541 in winter 2012, and 1,412 in winter 2012. The survey was done online by Knowledge Networks (now GfK).

Secular America Panel Study (SAS), 2017

A national survey conducted in the fall of 2017, with a total sample size of 3,000. The survey was done online by YouGov.

American Humanist Association Survey (AHA), 2018

A survey of the AHA's membership, employing a random sample of the group's membership list. It has a total sample size of 547. The survey was completed either by mail or online. This survey was built upon 2011 and 2002 mail surveys of the AHA. Data from the 2011 survey is also referenced in the text.

Convention Delegate Surveys (CDS), 2012 and 2016

These 2012 and 2016 surveys are a continuation of a long-running series of quadrennial surveys of delegates to the Democratic and Republican national conventions. The 2012 survey had a total sample size of 483 Republicans and 745 Democrats. In 2016, the total sample size was 307 Republicans and 806 Democrats. Both the 2012 and 2016 surveys were conducted online, with a handful of respondents choosing to complete the surveys by mail.

State Convention Delegate Study (SCDS), 2016

A survey of delegates to state party conventions in 2016: Democratic Party conventions in Texas, Minnesota, Washington, and Iowa, and Republican Party conventions in Texas, Illinois, and Utah. The total sample size is 2,837 Democratic delegates and 2,790 Republicans. The breakdown by state for the Democratic respondents is 1,740 from Texas, 236 from Iowa, 460 from Minnesota, and 401 from Washington. For Republicans, there are 1,578 respondents from Texas, 247 from Illinois, and 965 from Utah. With the exception of a handful of respondents who requested to take the survey by mail, respondents completed the survey online.

EXPERIMENTS

Each of the following three experiments has essentially the same design. Subjects completed a baseline survey that includes their religious identity, behavior, and beliefs. Roughly a week later they read a news story and again answered the same question as in the baseline survey.

Clerical Campaign Experiment

Conducted in 2012 by Knowledge Networks (GfK). The treatment (news stories) varied the degree to which local congressional candidates portrayed themselves as religious. Total N = 1,023.

Political Pastor Experiment

Conducted in 2017 by YouGov. In this experiment, the variation was in the degree to which a local pastor was portrayed as political. Total N = 1,000.

Transactional Religion Experiment

Conducted in 2017 by YouGov. The treatment varied the extent to which a politician is portrayed as making religious appeals as a political transaction or out of sincere convictions. Two of the treatments refer to Donald Trump and Mike Pence, respectively, while the other two describe fictional congressional candidates. Total N = 2,000.

In these two experiments, subjects were given a news story to read and then asked a series of questions immediately afterward.

Secular Candidate Experiment and Partisan Secular Candidate Experiment

Both experiments were conducted in 2018 by Qualtrics, using a quota sample of 40 percent Republicans, 40 percent Democrats, and 20 percent Independents. The treatments varied as to whether and how a local school board candidate discussed his secularity or religiosity. In the Partisan Secular Candidate Experiment, the candidate was identified with a party label; in the other experiment, the race was portrayed as nonpartisan. Total N for Secular Candidate Experiment = 1,252. Total N for the Partisan Secular Candidate Experiment = 2,523.

as community voluntarism) and explicitly political action (like working on a political campaign)? When it comes to engagement outside of politics, Secularists pale in comparison to Religionists but shine next to the Non-Religionists. Secularism, however, is a powerful predictor of political activity, and so Secularists are highly engaged in politics.

Chapter 5 extends the analysis of secularism's political importance by examining its connection to a wide range of political attitudes. The analysis draws on cross-sectional data to show how secularism is a potent predictor of public opinion in ways that, heretofore, have been undetected. It then digs deeper into the relationship between secularism, nonreligiosity, and politics. By employing the 2010–2012 panel version of the SAS, we test whether, over time, political views are more likely to lead to secular orientations or the other way around. The results show that politics drives nonreligiosity. But they also show that secularism drives political views, even on issues far removed from questions related to church and state. Secularists are firmly ensconced in the progressive wing of the Democratic Party.

A Secular–Religious Divide Is Becoming Embedded in Party Politics

Chapter 6 further examines whether there is a causal relationship between the political environment and the rise of the Nones. Specifically, the chapter tests the hypothesis that the recent rise in nonreligiosity has been caused, at least in part, by a political backlash against the Religious Right, and the infusion of religion into conservative politics more generally. Using a series of experiments, we put the backlash hypothesis to the test to see whether exposure to religion-infused politics causes people to disclaim a religious identity. (Spoiler alert: it does.)

Chapters 7–9 delve deeply into the relationship between secularism and party politics. In Chapter 7, we see how secularism is a dividing line *between* the parties, which suggests that the United States is indeed moving toward a confessional party system.

Chapter 8, however, demonstrates that secularism can also lead to *intra*party tension among Democrats. While many grassroots activists within the Democratic Party are highly secular (and predominantly white), the party also has a large contingent of Religionist activists (who are far more likely to be African Americans and Latinos). Not only do these two groups of activists have different worldviews, they often disagree on both policy and strategy. Secularists are farther to the left, and more interested in ideological purity than compromise. In short, there is potentially a secular–religious storm brewing within the Democratic coalition.

Chapter 9 then shows that although Secularists are concentrated in Democratic ranks, secularism and nonreligiosity both also matter within the GOP. Among Republicans, there is a small but vocal group of Secularist libertarians. Like the Secularists on the political left, they have sharply defined ideological views. Even larger is the number of Non-Religionists who found a political home with Donald Trump – less consistently ideological, perhaps, but no less passionate.

For Political Candidates, Secularity Is Not Necessarily Fatal

Given the political activism of Secularists, it seems likely, even inevitable, that more and more candidates will identify as secular in some way, shape, or form.

Chapter 10 thus explores how voters react to political candidates who describe themselves with varying degrees of secularity, from a hard-edged version such as "atheist" to a softer statement like "I'm not particularly religious." It is a political article of faith – supported by a number of empirical studies – that many voters react negatively to candidates described as atheists (Edgell, Gerteis, and Hartmann 2007; Franks 2017). Still, this self-description remains more a matter of theory than practice. The evidence of voters' wariness toward atheists still leaves open the question of how they react to candidates of varying gradations of secularity. Although voters' negative reaction to atheists is informative as a boundary condition, we are interested in a more nuanced, and thus realistic, test of voters' acceptance of candidates who come from the growing ranks of the secular population.

We conclude with Chapter 11, in which we consider the likely future of secularism as a fault line in American politics. The secular surge is likely to continue, suggesting that it will feed further political polarization, and perhaps even lead to a confessional party system based on religious–secular differences. We also speculate that the conditions may be right for the creation of a new political movement – a Secular Left to parallel the Religious Right. Such a movement is not a certainty, however. Whether it emerges depends on our politicians. Will strategic candidates seek to mobilize the growing secular population?

For all the talk that more secularism means more political division, there is another potential path, down which secularism does not fan the flames of polarization. Again, it depends on strategic politicians. While Secularists are an inviting political target, what if politicians forged a coalition of both Secularists *and* Religionists – emphasizing what brings them together instead of what pulls them apart? To the extent that Religionists and Secularists were to come together they could make formidable political allies. Such an alliance would be good politics. It would also be good for the nation's civic health.

2

America the Secular

To this point, most of the public discussion of America's secular surge has focused on the increasing number of Americans who report having no religious affiliation, better known as the rise of the Nones. However, there is more to the secular population than the Nones. The sudden rise of the Nones has received so much attention mostly, we suspect, because of the classic problem of the drunkard's search. The story goes that a police officer comes across an intoxicated fellow looking for his keys. The officer helps him search for a few minutes, without success. Eventually the cop turns to the drunk guy and asks if he is sure that this is where he dropped the keys. "No," he responds, "I think I lost them over there," and points down the street. "Then why are you looking here?" asks the officer. The drunkard answers: "Because this is where the light is good."

The light is good for tracing the rise of the Nones because they are simply people who do not identify with a religion, a readily available indicator on nearly every national survey. Yet while this trend is important, the focus on the Nones ignores the great diversity within the secular population. Understanding the size and scope of Americans' secularism requires distinguishing between those whose secularity is defined as the absence of religion and those who affirmatively embrace a secular perspective.

This chapter discusses measures of both personal nonreligiosity (which are not unique to our study) and personal secularism (which are).[1] The distinction between them will then be a recurring theme in the remainder of the book. In particular, personal secularism will take center stage in much of our analysis. So we describe it in detail. In addition to describing how we measure this concept, the chapter also provides both qualitative and quantitative validation of these measures, as well as the demographic characteristics of American Secularists. Along the way, the reader will become acquainted with the main source of data employed throughout the rest of the book, the Secular America Studies (SAS).

---

[1] For insightful discussion of the distinction between the nonreligious and the secular, see Lee (2017). Also see the online journal *Secularism and Nonreligion*, https://secularismandnonreligion .org/.

MEASURING PERSONAL NONRELIGIOSITY

In order to keep the focus on the absence of religion, we will refer to personal nonreligiosity, which will no doubt seem unfamiliar to readers accustomed to discussions of religiosity. Our measures simply flip the conventional measures of religious belief, belonging, and behavior around, so that our attention is now on the opposite of religiosity. Just remember that a statement like "a rise in nonreligiosity" is the exact inverse of "a drop in religiosity."

As noted above, the rise of the Nones is the best-known indicator of America's secular surge. Nones describe their religious affiliation as "nothing in particular," "no preference," or simply "none." In other words, it is the quintessential example of not being religious – the absence of a religious affiliation. In Chapter 1, we presented data on the growing number of Nones from the General Social Survey (GSS; see Figure 1.1), widely considered to be the leading national study of Americans' social attitudes and attachments. But the GSS is not alone, as other sources of data show precisely the same trend. Precise estimates vary according to the normal vagaries of survey research, but they are all within a comparable range.[2] When taken as a whole, the religiously unaffiliated share of the American population ranges somewhere between 18 and 25 percent, with people identifying explicitly as atheists and agnostics ranging between 7 and 12 percent.

Throughout this book, the core of our analysis is from our Secular America Studies (SAS), which we explicitly designed to measure secularism among the American population. The percentage of Nones in the 2017 SAS is on the higher end of comparable national surveys, as 24.7 percent of respondents are "nothing in particular," with another 5.7 percent identifying as atheists and 6 percent as agnostics. In addition to the rise of non-affiliation, the SAS parallel the GSS in finding that other indicators of nonreligiosity have increased between 2010 and 2017. This pattern includes people who say that religion provides no personal guidance, never attend religious services, are unsure about the existence of God, never pray, and believe the Bible is mere superstition and myth.[3]

---

[2] In 2016, the Public Religion Research Institute's American Values Atlas found that 24 percent of the US population was religiously unaffiliated (Cox and Jones 2017), while both the Gallup Poll (Gallup 2016) and the American National Election Studies put the Nones at 21 percent of Americans. In the 2016 Cooperative Congressional Election Study, 19 percent said that they were "nothing in particular," while another 6 percent reported being an atheist, and still another 6 percent said that they were agnostic, options not available on the American Values Atlas or the GSS. The 2014 Pew Religious Landscape Survey puts the percentage of Nones at 16 percent, plus another 3 percent who are atheists and 4 percent who are agnostics (Pew Research Center 2015).

[3] According to the SAS, in 2010, 31 percent of Americans said that they received no guidance from religion, compared to 44 percent in 2017. In 2010, about one in five Americans did not attend religious services, climbing to a third in 2017. There was a seven-point rise in the percentage unsure about the existence of God – from 13 percent in 2010 to 20 percent in 2017 (operationalized as those who chose a number below 50 on a 100-point scale on their

It is not clear why our study finds greater nonreligiosity within the population than some others. One explanation could be because internet surveys skew toward a more secular population, even when they are weighted to match known demographics of the US population. It could also be that cloaked behind the impersonal anonymity of an online survey, our respondents felt more comfortable reporting no religious affiliation than respondents to face-to-face or phone surveys. Because the two iterations of the SAS were done by different survey firms, some of these differences are no doubt due to "house effects," or the differences that result from the vagaries inherent to different companies' practices.

However, the differences between 2010 and 2017 are so substantial, and consistent with multiple other data sources, that it is only reasonable to conclude that the two versions of the SAS show an increase in nonreligiosity. One can debate whether these levels are objectively high or low but there can be no dispute on the trend – Americans are pulling away from religion.[4] This trend is unquestionably an important development in American society but, as we have argued, it only tells part of the story. It would be like tracing Americans' sporting preferences by focusing only on the declining interest in baseball without also acknowledging the growing popularity of soccer (Neil 2016).

MEASURING PERSONAL SECULARISM

With the proper measures, the United States is revealed to be a more secular nation than most observers think (Bruce 2011). If one takes nothing else from this chapter, remember that. We make this claim because in most empirical studies, the secular population has been poorly measured, leaving many secular Americans in the shadows. We agree with prominent scholars of secularism who criticize the extant literature for its inattention to the heterogeneity of the secular population. "The various forms, types, and shades of secularity are overlooked or ignored, and all manifestations of irreligion are lumped together. Yet secularity comes in many shapes and sizes, and this diversity needs to be better understood and better investigated" (Zuckerman, Galen, and Pasquale 2016).

Just as natural scientists need the right instruments to detect the phenomena they wish to study, so too do social scientists need the right instruments to

---

belief in God). The percentage saying that they never pray went from 11 percent in 2010 to 19 percent in 2017. The belief that the Bible is a "worthless book of superstition and myth" rose from 5 to 12 percent. In drawing on a longitudinal study that involved interviewing the same respondents three times over five years, Putnam and Campbell find comparable declines in religiosity (2012).

[4] As a validity check, examining the 2010 and 2017 editions of the SAS enables us to examine changes in the intervening seven years, and compare the observed changes to the results of other studies (e.g. GSS and ANES). Between 2010 and 2017, the percentage of Nones rose 5.5 percentage points – right in the middle of the range of other surveys over that same span of time.

measure social phenomena. In our case, the right instrument consists of questions asked on a public opinion survey designed to detect attitudes that heretofore had been unseen. If we know what to ask, American Secularists can come out of the proverbial shadows and into the scholarly sunlight.[5] In designing our instrument, we have been guided by a fundamental insight introduced in Chapter 1: secularism is not just the absence of religiosity – although of course nonreligiosity is an element of it. An equally important element is the presence of a secular worldview, as indicated by secular beliefs, identities, and activities.[6]

There is an extensive social science literature on the measurement of religious concepts, complete with healthy debate over which of those measures are most valid and reliable.[7] In contrast, until recently scholars have paid relatively little attention to the measurement of explicitly secular concepts and orientations. Just as the refinement of religiosity measures has enriched the public discussion of religion in America, secular concepts will enrich the public discussion of the secular population. We stress, however, that while our specific measures are new, we are not the first or only scholars to suggest that secularism is more than what someone does not believe or do.[8] For example, over forty years ago, Paul Pruyser noted that "Irreligion is not merely the absence of something" (1974, 195). More recently, Joseph Baker and Buster Smith have argued that "mapping the diversity of secular expressions and conceptualizing secularisms as assertive worldviews in their own right, rather than merely negated reflections of religion, stands as a crucial challenge for better understanding secularity and religion" (2015, 6). We have taken up this challenge.

Part of this challenge is the lack of a standardized vocabulary with which to do so. Religion has a deep and long-standing cultural prominence, and thus has a rich and nuanced lexicon. It is thus not surprising that secularism is typically defined by its relation to religion, partly the *absence* of religion and partly as an *alternative* to religion. This tendency is often reinforced by the antagonism of some Secularists to Religionists – in public and private life. By default, then,

---

[5] The social science literature is rife with comparable examples of instruments that have enabled researchers to identify people who hold particular views, with significant implications for civic and political life. These include postmaterialism (Inglehart 1977), symbolic racism (Tarman and Sears 2005), authoritarianism (Hetherington and Weiler 2009), and ethnocentrism (Kinder and Kam 2009).

[6] As mentioned in Chapter 1, and elaborated upon in Chapter 3, personal secularism is distinct from public secularism, which we define as attitudes regarding religion's role in society.

[7] See for example Djupe and Gilbert (2009); Kellstedt et al. (1996); Smidt, Kellstedt, and Guth (2009); Steensland et al. (2000); Wuthnow (2015). For an early look at the secular population in this context, see Kellstedt (2008).

[8] In recent years, there have been notable exceptions, as the study of secularism has exploded. For examples, see Baker and Smith (2015); Calhoun, Juergensmeyer, and VanAntwerpen (2011); Cimino and Smith (2014); Hunsberger and Altemeyer (2006); Lee (2017); Zuckerman, Galen, and Pasquale (2016). In addition, the Pew Research Center has been on the forefront of tracking the secular population: www.pewresearch.org.

secularism is thought of in terms of general concepts that derive from but are not limited to religiosity: beliefs, identifications, and activities. So, we begin by asking: what are distinctively secular counterparts to these elements of religiosity?

This territory is uncharted and so over the last decade we have developed and refined a set of measures of personal secularism. Like a portfolio of mutual funds, we do not rely on a single measure, but have instead combined a set of them into a Personal Secularism Index. We have validated these measures both quantitatively, using extensive statistical modeling, and qualitatively by interviewing people who have responded to our surveys, in order to hear whether their personal worldview aligns with the questions we have posed. While we are confident that these measures are both valid and reliable, we do not claim that they are beyond improvement. For now, they are a good start.

We aim to strike a balance between providing enough detail to be convincing and keeping the presentation intuitive. For those who want to know what the instrument looks like, the next section describes our measures and summarizes the statistical evidence that they measure something meaningful within the collective American psyche, but is light on the minutiae of our analysis. Those readers who want even more detail can consult the online appendix.[9]

We define personal secularism as the affirmative adoption of secular beliefs and identifications *irrespective of one's level of religiosity*. That is, to be personally secular is to partake of a secular worldview. By a secular worldview we simply mean that people are guided by their understanding of the observable, natural world (such as science and philosophy), in contrast to an unobservable, supernatural realm (such as scripture and revelation). Although many people who hold a secular worldview are not religious in any meaningful sense of the term, it is important to note that many religious traditions have space for beliefs that come from the natural realm, such as science and philosophy.[10] Therefore, as we define secularism, it is not zero-sum with religiosity. Just as someone can enjoy both baseball and soccer, someone who is religious can also partake of a secular worldview. Likewise, not all nonreligious people affirmatively embrace a secular perspective on the world. Obviously, to make a distinction between secularism and nonreligiosity requires measures that differentiate between them.

The first building blocks in the Personal Secularism Index are personal beliefs that embody secular ideas, values, and principles. In developing these measures constructing our scale of secular beliefs, we walk a fine line. On the one hand, we must ensure that secular beliefs are not reduced to the absence of religion.

---

[9] See secularsurge.com for the online appendix.
[10] See *Secular Faith: How Culture Has Trumped Religion in American Politics* (Smith 2015) for an extended discussion of how religions themselves change and evolve in response to secular society.

On the other hand, our measures should resonate with people who place secular values ahead of or alongside religion in their lives.

To create our Personal Secularism Index we have consulted the expansive body of writing espousing secular social and political thought, including the work of social theorists such as George Jacob Holyoake (1871), Immanuel Kant (1781 [1999]), and David Hume (1777 [2014]); the recent volumes by "new atheists" such as Richard Dawkins (2006), Sam Harris (2005), and Christopher Hitchens (2007); and the statements of belief found on the websites of secular organizations such as the American Humanist Association (AHA) and the International Humanist and Ethical Union (IHEU). Based on these sources, we have distilled three core principles common among Secularists.

One core principle is a commitment to *science and objective evidence* as the basis for understanding the world. For example, Kant contends that "everything in the world happens solely in accordance with laws of nature ... we have nothing but nature in which we must seek the connection and order of occurrences in the world" (1999, 485). In *Humanism and Its Aspirations*, published in 2003, the AHA contends that "knowledge of the world is derived by observation, experimentation, and rational analysis."[11]

A second core principle of secularism is the view that only *human experience and knowledge* provide the proper basis for comprehending reality and making ethical judgments – in other words, "humanism."[12] A humanist perspective is found in *Principles of Secularism Illustrated*, in which Holyoake contends that "Secularism relates to the present existence of man ... inculcating the practical sufficiency of natural morality" (1871, 11). Hitchens notes that "Einstein said that ethics is an exclusively human concern" (2007, 271). The IHEU's vision statement calls for "an ethics based on human and other natural values."[13] The Atheist Alliance speaks of "objective moral truths that can be discovered using reason (and science), and the process does not require belief in a god." Similarly, Harris writes that "we can easily think of objective sources of moral order that do not require the existence of a lawgiving God ... If there are psychological laws that govern human well-being, knowledge of these laws would provide an enduring basis for an objective morality" (2008, 23).

A third core principle of secularism is "freethought," the idea that human development and understanding should be based on *logic and reason*, rather than

---

[11] "Humanism and Its Aspirations: Humanist Manifesto III, a Successor to the Humanist Manifesto of 1933." American Humanist Association (website), n.d. https://americanhumanist .org/what-is-humanism/manifesto3/.

[12] It is worth noting that humanism is not incompatible with many forms of religion, hence the distinction between "religious" and "secular" humanism.

[13] "Humanists and IHEU on CNN." Humanists International (website), November 7, 2002. https://iheu.org/about/humanism/.

received authority, dogma, or tradition. Kant is often quoted as saying "the death of dogma is the birth of morality" (quoted in Taber 1897, 86), and Holyoake held that "secularism ... utterly disowns tradition as a ground of belief" (1871, 14). Secular organizations and authors typically speak of rejecting the Bible as the source of old traditions and beliefs. However, secular advocates do not limit their rejection of what is old to scripture, as the IHEU states that they "reject any reliance on blindly received authority."[14] Even more provocatively, well-known atheist Madalyn Murray O'Hair once argued that "these ancient ideas are silly and we no longer need to cling to them. Some of these beliefs are an insult to you and me. They are an insult to our intelligence, to our common sense, and to our own experience which we have gained from living" (1972, 38).

We measure secular beliefs with a series of questions that gauge support for these core secular principles: the degree to which a respondent's perspective is informed by sources other than the supernatural (a term we use non-pejoratively). The core of our secular beliefs scale consists of eight statements, to which our respondents indicated their level of agreement.[15]

To minimize response set bias, the questions were not all worded in the same direction. Five of the statements are worded to affirm secular perspectives:

- *Factual evidence from the natural world is the source of true beliefs*
- *The great works of philosophy and science are the best source of truth, wisdom, and ethics*
- *To understand the world, we must free our minds from old traditions and beliefs*
- *When I make important decisions in my life, I rely mostly on reason and evidence*
- *All of the greatest advances for humanity have come from science and technology*

The other three statements represent the rejection of secular values:

- *It is hard to live a good life based on reason and facts alone*
- *What we believe is right and wrong cannot be based only on human knowledge*
- *The world would be a better place if we relied less on science and technology to solve our problems*[16]

---

[14] Ibid.

[15] Specifically: strongly agree, agree, neither agree nor disagree, disagree, strongly disagree.

[16] The 2010–2012 SAS panel included only four of these statements – the first three worded in a secular direction and the first one worded in a nonsecular direction. For all of the analyses we undertake with the 2017 SAS, the results are very similar if we use just these four indicators rather than the full battery. In the online appendix, we present the exact question wording for our various measures of personal secularism and personal nonreligiosity and indicate which items we use for particular chapters or parts of our analysis. Also in the online appendix, we provide descriptive statistics for all indicators of secularism and nonreligiosity in the 2017 SAS, and, for those indicators included in the 2010–2012 SAS panel, their levels of stability across panel waves.

It has been our experience that because these measures of secular beliefs are new and thus unfamiliar, there are often questions about their validity.[17] In anticipation of such questions, we provide evidence that supports our claim that these statements do indeed reflect the way Secularists see the world. If we really are tapping into beliefs held by people with a secular orientation, we should expect that these questions reflect the attitudes of "known Secularists." To that end, we turn to a survey we conducted of the membership of the AHA, an organization that is explicitly secular. We included the secular beliefs on the survey of AHA members, which enables us to see whether these statements reflect the opinions of people who, by virtue of their membership, presumably have a secular worldview. We provide more information about the AHA and our survey of its membership in A Closer Look 2.1.

These secular beliefs do indeed find resonance among self-identified Secularists as, across the board, AHA members agreed with them. For each question, the AHA members have a lopsided distribution of responses, heavily skewed toward the most secular end of the scale. To provide a few examples, 95 percent of AHA members either agree (75 percent) or strongly agree (20 percent) that "factual evidence from the natural world is the source of true beliefs," while 79 percent agree (including 41 percent who strongly agree) that "the great books of philosophy and science are the best source of truth, wisdom, and ethics." Overall, these statements find considerable support among this group of card-carrying Secularists, which supports our claim that they serve as an effective instrument to detect who is actively secular among the general population.

We included these same secular belief questions on the 2017 SAS which, the reader may recall, includes interviews with a cross-section of all Americans. Counterposing the results from the two surveys enables a comparison between "known Secularists" and the population as a whole, as shown in Figure 2.1. As would be expected, the general population is less likely to endorse these beliefs. Nonetheless, we still find a nonnegligible share of Americans who, like the AHA members, hold these secular views.[18]

A second building block of secularism is to ask about individuals' self-identification with the various kinds of secular groups. This measure is a more overt indication of affirmatively holding a secular perspective than holding secular beliefs. Respondents to the SAS were asked which, if any, of a long list of terms described them. We have consistently found that four of these potential identities are closely related: humanist, secular, atheist, and

---

[17] In the spirit of full disclosure, these are not the only statements of secular beliefs that we developed. For example, we originally included the statements that "one must be skeptical of human reason in understanding the world" and "values are more important than factual evidence in making moral decisions." In our analysis, we found that neither was related strongly enough to the other items to be included in the index.

[18] Figure 2.1 combines those who agree/disagree and strongly agree/disagree (depending on the polarity of the question).

A Closer Look 2.1:
Members of the American Humanist Association

In this chapter, we employ 2018 survey data from the membership of the American Humanist Association (AHA) to help validate our measures of personal secularism and nonreligiosity; elsewhere we will employ these data to better understand secular activists. We are grateful to the AHA leadership, especially Executive Director Roy Speckhardt, for allowing us to survey random samples of AHA members in 2018, 2011, and 2002 (the results of which were shared with the AHA leadership).

The AHA membership is a good place to look for Secularists. The AHA describes itself as "advocating for progressive values and equality for humanists, atheists, and freethinkers" and is among the broadest, largest, and oldest Secularist organizations in the United States. Founded in 1941, it was inspired by the original Humanist Manifesto of 1933 (Wilson 1995). Commonly known as "Humanist Manifesto I," it was followed by "Humanist Manifesto II" in 1973 (Kurtz 1973) and "Humanist Manifesto III" in 2000 (Kurtz 2000). The symbol of AHA and other humanist organizations, such as the Humanists International, is the "happy human" icon.

As Figures 2.2a and 2.2b show, the AHA membership is characterized by very high levels of both personal secularism and nonreligiosity, fitting well into the core of our conceptual category of Secularists in Table 1.1. But as activists, the AHA members are more homogenous in beliefs, activities, and identifications than the group of Secularists we have identified in the general public, shown in Table 2.1.

The demographic characteristics of the AHA members show many of the same tendencies as the general public Secularists in Table 2.1, but also resemble the features of American political activists as a whole. The AHA members tend to be *white but more so* (98 vs. 77 percent of our 2017 SAS respondents), *well-educated but more so* (85 percent with bachelor's degrees or higher vs. 34 percent), *male but more so* (72 percent male vs. 57 percent), and *affluent but more so* (43 percent with annual income greater than $100,000 vs. 17 percent). AHA members are also *older* (80 percent more than 60 years old vs. 25 percent), and have dramatically *fewer young people* (1 percent 18–29 years old vs. 23 percent; average age 70 vs. 46 years).

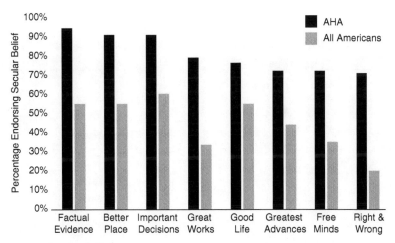

FIGURE 2.1 Secular beliefs
Source: 2017 Secular America Study; 2018 American Humanist Association Survey

agnostic.[19] Responses range from 6 percent who chose "secular," 6 percent who selected "atheist," to 7 percent who identified as "agnostic," and 11 percent who picked "humanist." All in all, 21 percent of the population says that at least one of these terms describes them.[20]

Not surprisingly, self-identification with secular labels was common among members of the AHA. As one would expect of a group of card-carrying humanists, an overwhelming majority (86 percent) say that "humanist" describes them. Sixty-four percent say that they are atheists, and 60 percent chose to describe themselves as "secular" (they could choose more than one label). Reflecting the firm views of this population, only 24 percent are agnostics (unsure about the existence of God), presumably because so many identify as atheists (do not believe in God).

A third building block of secularism is an explicit measure of receiving personal guidance from elements of a secular worldview. To do so, we created a question that parallels a long-used item about religious guidance. First, respondents are asked whether they "consider nonreligious beliefs, such as derived from science or philosophy," to be an important part of their lives or

[19] The other terms are ecumenical, mainline, charismatic/Pentecostal, nontraditional believer, fundamentalist, born again/evangelical, and spiritual but not religious. Exploratory factor analysis demonstrates that, among all these terms, the four secular identities "hang together" (i.e. they form a single factor).

[20] These figures are similar to those found in the work of other scholars (Edgell et al. 2016a; Edgell, Gerteis, and Hartmann 2007; Hunsberger and Altemeyer 2006; Smith 2011, 2013).

TABLE 2.1 *Comparing the demographics of the four secular-religious groups*

	Religionists (37%)	Secularists (28%)	Non-Religionists (18%)	Religious Secularists (16%)
Education				
% High school or less	45	32	52	40
% Bachelor's or higher	24	33	16	31
Income				
% > $100 K	9	17	8	15
Age				
18–29	18	23	19	25
60+	35	25	23	29
Average age	50	46	45	46
Gender				
% Male	44	58	48	44
Race/Ethnicity				
White	65	76	69	53
Black	15	7	11	15
Hispanic	13	10	14	23

Source: 2017 Secular America Study.
As discussed in the text, the four secular-religious groups are created by splitting the secularism and nonreligiosity indices at their means.

not. If they answer yes, they are then asked how much guidance those nonreligious beliefs provide in their day-to-day life: some, quite a bit, or a great deal. The result is a four-part scale that ranges from "no" guidance to a "great deal" of guidance. We leave it up to the individual to decide what constitutes nonreligious beliefs; these could be anything from science to spiritualism.[21]

In the general population, roughly 45 percent say that they receive at least some guidance from nonreligious sources, although only 8 percent say that such beliefs guide them a "great deal." The nearly even split between those who do and do not see nonreligious beliefs as a source of guidance means that it serves to discriminate within the population, the very *raison d'être* of any measurement instrument.

---

[21] Using such guidance is a form of secular activity, albeit largely a mental one. Our surveys also included measures of secular activity that mirror religious activity, such as Sunday Assembly, a secular counterpart to worship. These measures were neither as helpful nor valid in defining secularism, and furthermore, did not fit into an overall secularism scale. We discuss them in more detail in Chapter 4.

We again turn to the AHA membership for validation. Over 9 in 10 AHA members endorse nonreligious beliefs as a source of guidance in their lives. Furthermore, a plurality – 43 percent – say that such beliefs provide a great deal of guidance.[22] In sum, this question resonates with known Secularists, and is thus another method of detecting the secular among us.

QUALITATIVE VALIDATION OF SECULARISM

Given that these measures of secularism are novel, skeptical readers are right to ask whether our instrument has detected a signal and not merely noise. In order to find out whether respondents perceived our secularism questions in the way intended, a few months after the survey was fielded, our team conducted in-depth interviews with a number of respondents to the 2017 SAS. These interviews confirmed the guiding premise of the Personal Secularism Index, as we generally found that people who scored high on the index lead what any reasonable observer would call a secular life.

Consider James, a cabdriver from Montana, who was a high-scorer on personal secularism. When asked about his worldview he said this:

I am a cross between an atheist and an agnostic but I am really a non-theist ... Facts are science. Faith means anti-science. I find it amazing people are willing to take things for granted that come out of religion.

Similarly, Herschel is retired, living in Florida. He too scored high on the Personal Secularism Index and describes himself this way:

As an atheist I have a positive belief in the non-existence of God. As science progresses, it convinces me more than ever that there isn't a divine being. Atheists are just as ethical if not more so than some Christians. Humanism puts the emphasis on life, society, and people on earth and not something supernatural. I think the scientific method relies on developing and discovery through an empirical process based on evidence. It takes into account contradictory evidence. Science is not a god in itself, but a methodology. You need an open mind, not an ideology.

These two respondents are prototypical cases of people who have a secular worldview. Many others are better described as nonreligious but without such sharply defined set of secular beliefs or identity. Chris, who lives in Syracuse, New York, is an example. When asked how he identifies himself he simply said "I am humanist, not secular. I wasn't really sure what the word [secular] meant, maybe just living life based on fact and reason." Notice that in spite of Chris's uncertainty about secularism, he nonetheless endorsed the idea of basing life decisions on fact and reason, which figures prominently in the secular beliefs scale.

---

[22] Thirty percent say they receive quite a bit of guidance from a secular source, while 20 percent get some guidance.

Importantly, however, we found other examples of people who combine religious and secular aspects of their lives. One is Jorday, an undergraduate college student in Oregon. Contrary to the archetypal story of young people coming to college and losing the religious faith of their childhood, Jorday entered college without a religious background, but upon discovering that many of his chemistry professors were both scientists and religious believers, decided to reconsider religion. He now considers himself a Christian and attends church. Given this background, it is not surprising that his responses to the secular beliefs scale varied depending on the question. On the one hand, he was reluctant to disavow religious texts as a source of truth while also endorsing the idea that one can live a good life based on reason.

These qualitative interviews suggest that the personal secularism questions work as intended. As a scale, the Personal Secularism Index enables us to identify people who have a clearly-defined secular worldview, while also capturing the ambivalence regarding secularism and religion that many Americans experience.

QUANTITATIVE VALIDATION OF SECULARISM

While our measures of personal secularism appear to correspond to the understandings of real people, this pattern still leaves us with the question of whether our index actually adds anything new to our understanding of the secular population beyond a conventional measure of nonreligiosity. While our instrument can describe the degree of both nonreligiosity and personal secularism among Americans, for these concepts to be useful analytically they must meet two criteria. First, they must each form coherent elements of secularity. That is, the elements of personal secularism should fit together statistically (e.g. endorsing one secular belief should be related to endorsing another, and also to selecting one or more secular identity), as should the components of nonreligiosity. Second, personal secularism and nonreligiosity should be distinct from one another, such that being nonreligious does not necessarily mean that someone is personally secular, and vice versa. At the same time, we would expect a fair degree of correlation between the two. They should be related, but more like cousins than twins.

To see if this is true, we undertake a statistical method known as factor analysis, which allows us to search for the existence of consistent patterns and relationships within the many data points. We begin with an "exploratory" factor analysis, allowing the data to tell us what goes with what. We provide the details of all of our factor analyses in the online appendix, but the bottom line is that the nonreligiosity and personal secularism measures represent distinct orientations. Not surprisingly, the items measuring nonreligiosity – the absence of religious beliefs (including belief in God and scripture), religious affiliation, religious guidance, worship attendance, and prayer – are strongly connected to each other. This pattern is to be expected. A generation's worth of social science has demonstrated that measures of religiosity (and thus also their absence) can be grouped together (Smidt, Kellstedt, and Guth 2009). More importantly, we also find that our personal secularism indicators of beliefs, identifications and guidance fit together and are distinct from the nonreligiosity measures.

We then turn to a "confirmatory" factor analysis, which allows us to assess how well the data fits our theoretical expectation that secularism and nonreligiosity represent distinct, but related, orientations. It also allows us to account for measurement error in our indicators. There is an unavoidable messiness that occurs when people answer survey questions; this method is a way to cancel out the noise in order to focus on the signal. When we are able to purge the noise from our measures, we find even clearer evidence that our personal secularism indicators form a single, coherent orientation and that secularism and nonreligiosity are distinct orientations, not merely two ways to measure the same thing. However, the evidence is just as clear that they are related.

In our 2017 SAS data the correlation between personal nonreligiosity and personal secularism is .54.[23] Given that correlation coefficients range from 0 to 1, this is relatively high but far from a perfect relationship. When we purge the noise from the measures that correlation rises to .75. While obviously higher, this pattern is to be expected given that the signal is coming through loud and clear. The key point is that the two orientations are distinct and the correlation is still nowhere near complete.

Our hope is that other scholars will adopt these measures. For anyone who is interested in doing so, please consult A Closer Look 2.2 for advice.

HOW SECULAR ARE AMERICANS?

Having seen the evidence that nonreligiosity and secularism are indeed distinct from one another, one might wonder: how much secularism is there in the American population and how does it compare to Americans' nonreligiosity? As a benchmark, we can again compare the American population to a group of prototypical Secularists, the membership of the AHA. Figure 2.2a displays how personal secularism – measured with an index of all our secularism indicators – is distributed across the American population as a whole.[24] Notice that it is a nearly perfect "normal" (bell-curve) distribution. Most Americans are in the middle, with decreasing numbers as you move away from the middle. A careful look reveals, though, that the tail on the right-hand (pro-secular) side is slightly fatter, indicating that the population skews a little toward secularity. By

---

[23] This is the correlation between the secularism and nonreligiosity indices created by summing our observed indicators of either secularism or nonreligiosity, each weighted by its loading in our confirmatory factor analysis.

[24] For this figure, we use the additive index for personal secularism.

A Closer Look 2.2:
The Secularism and Nonreligiosity Indices

As we explain in our online appendix, confirmatory factor analysis allows us to account for and deal with both "random" measurement error, which arises from the usual messiness of conducting and taking surveys. It also allows us to deal with a form of "non-random" measurement error that arises from having some of our secular belief items worded in a secular direction and some worded in a non-secular direction. Green and Citrin (1994) propose a remedy for this "response set bias," and we employ and explain that remedy in the online appendix.

While the scales of nonreligiosity and personal secularism created using confirmatory factor analysis are the most methodologically sound, they correlate highly with simple additive indices (over .95). Therefore, in most cases we opt to use the additive indices, although in every case the results would be nearly identical with the scales created from confirmatory factor scores. The exception is in Chapter 5, where we examine how nonreligiosity, personal secularism, and a variety of political orientations are related to one another over time. For the models in that chapter, we employ the measurement error correction afforded by confirmatory factor analysis.

If other scholars use our measures of personal secularism – which we hope they will – an additive index will suffice for nearly all purposes.

---

comparison, AHA members are nearly all concentrated on the secular side, precisely as we would expect for a group of self-identified Secularists.[25]

---

[25] We are pleased that our personal secularism measure follows a normal distribution as that means it adheres to the assumptions of all of the statistical methods we employ and that our indicators are, on average, not biasing respondents' reactions in a secular or nonsecular direction. However, when respondents are clustered around the middle position on a scale, it may be an indication of the classic problem of "nonattitudes" in survey research (Converse 1964). In other words, many respondents may take positions near the middle on many of our secularism indicators not because they are truly torn between accepting and rejecting Secularist perspectives, but simply because they have no feeling whatsoever about the matter – they have a "nonattitude" – and the middle response (e.g. "neither agree nor disagree" on our secular belief statements) provides an easy way out.

One way to assess how much the normal distribution of personal secularism is due to nonattitudes is to compare its measurement properties across education groups. If respondents are unfamiliar with the ideas contained in our indicators or are having a hard time understanding the concepts, that should be most evident among less well-educated respondents. Accordingly, the clustering of responses around the middle position of survey scales and the instability of respondents' orientations toward secularism across panel waves – response instability in panel surveys is the classic indicator of nonattitudes – should be greatest among our least-educated respondents.

We compared three indicators of variation and clustering of personal secularism – the index's standard deviation, its interquartile range, and the percentage of respondents falling in the middle

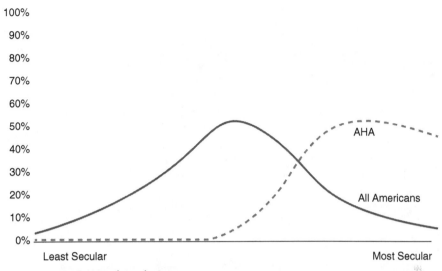

FIGURE 2.2A Personal secularism

Figure 2.2b does the same, but for nonreligiosity.[26] As expected, we see that the AHA members are nearly all on the nonreligious side of the scale, to an even greater extent than for secularism. Among the American population as a whole, we see a very different pattern – a nearly even distribution across the spectrum of nonreligiosity. There is a slight bump on the most religious side, reflecting that even in the midst of the secular surge, the United States is still a highly religious nation.

These figures are visual confirmation that secularism and nonreligiosity are not the same thing, as they are distributed differently across the general population. In particular, the pattern for personal secularism shows that we

---

range of the scale – across education levels. We also compared the correlation between respondents' levels of personal secularism in waves 2 and 4 of our panel study across education groups. And, we compared all of this to the same analyses for nonreligiosity and two political orientations (ideological identification, and attitude about levels of government services and spending). We show the results in our online appendix and there is no evidence of systematic variation across education groups in the variance, clustering, or stability of personal secularism. In fact, there is more education-related variation in these things for political orientations than for personal secularism. In short, we have no reason to believe that the distribution of personal secularism is due to nonattitudes, at least not to any greater degree than for other variables in survey data.

[26] Because the SAS and AHA surveys did not include all the same measures of religiosity, the nonreligiosity index used in Figure 2.2b only contains three items: belief in God, religious affiliation, and religious guidance. In the SAS, which includes all six of the nonreligiosity items we use in the full index, the correlation between the three-item and six-item version is .93, meaning they are nearly identical.

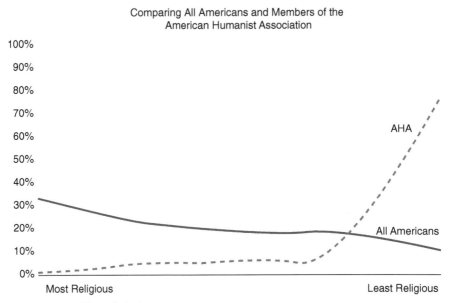

FIGURE 2.2B Nonreligiosity
Source: 2017 Secular America Study; 2018 American Humanist Association Survey

have "found" a greater degree of secularity among Americans than is typically assumed. Nonetheless, the comparison with the AHA membership also highlights that America is far from being a fully secularized nation.

SECULARISM IN THE WILD

We have shown that secularism and nonreligiosity are distinct from one another. But is this a distinction with a difference? To find out, we follow the credo of political scientists everywhere that anything worth studying can be presented as a two-by-two table. Recall that in Chapter 1, we suggested that the population can be divided into four secular-religious groups based on whether they are low or high in nonreligiosity and secularism. Here we look to see if these four groups actually exist "in the wild" by splitting both the indices of nonreligiosity and secularism at their means. Why the mean? As shown in Figure 2.2a, the Personal Secularism Index has a bell-shaped distribution, suggesting that splitting it at the mean neatly divides the population into two mirror images (just as splitting it at the median value would). It also suggests that most Americans are not highly secular or highly nonsecular; most are somewhere in the middle with a *tendency* toward either secularism or nonsecularism. Thus, dividing the scale at the mean captures these tendencies better than would choosing some more clearly secular or non-secular cut point. And, even though the distribution of nonreligiosity has a very different shape (Figure 2.2b), most Americans fall somewhere between the most religious and nonreligious extremes. Using the midpoint captures Americans' tendency toward religiosity or nonreligiosity rather than identifying the most and least pious citizens.

If secularism and nonreligiosity are simply two sides of the same coin, we would not find anyone high in one and low in the other. But we do find a sizable number of these "off diagonal" people, confirming that secularism and religiosity do sometimes overlap. The relative size and demographic characteristics of these four secular-religious groups are presented in Table 2.1.

Throughout this book we will at times refer to these four secular-religious groups. In doing so, the reader should keep in mind that these groups are not necessarily discrete categories, as we have created them by drawing lines on continuous scales that do not have any sharp breaks. By analogy, consider the spectrum of colors. The spectrum is continuous, but lines are drawn to distinguish between different colors: blue vs. green, for example. We measure nonreligiosity and secularism similarly, by drawing lines to distinguish between one group and another, with some fuzziness where one group starts and the next one begins, just as it is a little fuzzy to say where blue ends and green begins. Thus, think of people within one group versus another as displaying a tendency toward, say, greater secularism or greater nonreligiosity.[27]

About one in five (18 percent) members of the population are *Non-Religionists*. They are high in personal nonreligiosity (thus are low in conventional measures of religiosity), but also have a low degree of personal secularism. They do not have much religion in their lives, but neither do they have a secular worldview. They are truly defined by what they are not.

Secularists, on the other hand, are high in both nonreligiosity and secularism. That is, they have little to no religious involvement and possess secular orientations. In addition to holding secular beliefs this can even extend to having a secular identity, including the self-description as an atheist. Secularists comprise a little over one in four Americans (28 percent).

Reflecting the high levels of religiosity among Americans, we find that a plurality – roughly 37 percent – are *Religionists*: low in nonreligiosity (that

---

[27] In the chapters to follow, when we present data from the four secular-religious groups, they are always defined by dividing the secularism and nonreligiosity scales at their means. As a robustness check, we have also operationalized the four groups by drawing lines at the 25th and 75th percentiles (i.e. the interquartile range). For instance, using this method the Secularists are defined as being at the 75th percentile of the Personal Secularism Index and the 75th percentile of the nonreligiosity index, while the Religious Secularists are also at the 75th percentile of the Personal Secularism Index, but only the 25th percentile of the nonreligiosity index (which, recall, means that they are highly religious). When we use this alternative method of creating the four secular-religious groups, we find nearly identical relationships between the four categories and political orientations as when the cut points are at the mean of each index. At other points in the book, instead of displaying the four secular-religious groups, we instead use the full indices in statistical models. As in this chapter, we do this to see trends in the overall level of secularism and nonreligiosity or, in subsequent chapters, to examine an empirical relationship between secularism and/or nonreligiosity and other attitudes or behaviors.

is, above average in religiosity) and low in secularism. Finally, another 16 percent are *Religious Secularists*, who are low in nonreligiosity but high in secularism. The people in this category combine both religious belief and a secular worldview.

To make these abstract categories more concrete, we can provide some examples of typical people who would fall into each of them using a few illustrative items of the nonreligiosity and secularism indices.

Non-Religionists do not receive guidance from nonreligious sources (or, for that matter, from religious sources either), nor do they see true beliefs as coming from the natural world. They are also very unlikely to attend religious services, but neither do they self-identify with a secular label. On Sundays, a typical Non-Religionist is likely to be found at home, watching football on TV.

Secularists are like the typical member of the AHA: someone who receives guidance from nonreligious sources, believes that factual evidence is the source of true beliefs, chooses a secular self-identification, and never attends religious services. Secularists' Sundays are likely to be spent at a coffee shop discussing a story in the latest *New Yorker* or perhaps attending a lecture at the local natural history museum.

Religionists are not guided by nonreligious sources, but instead by religious beliefs. They are not likely to say that true beliefs come from factual evidence; nor do they identify with a secular label. In fact, 30 percent of them choose "born again/evangelical" as an identification. As you would expect, they are more likely than not to attend religious services frequently. Their Sundays are spent at church – many at an evangelical Christian congregation.

Religious Secularists also endorse secular beliefs – both nonreligious guidance and the importance of factual evidence – but also attend religious services regularly and do not generally choose a secular label to describe themselves. Like the Religionists, they are likely to be found at church on Sunday, but more likely at an Episcopalian congregation or, on Friday evening, at a Reform synagogue.

To further illustrate that personal religiosity and secularism are not necessarily at odds, and that some people are able to combine both in their lives, we can examine the overlap between personal secularism and the major religious traditions. Not surprisingly, there are few Secularists among evangelical Protestants (6 percent), Black Protestants (5 percent), and Mormons (1 percent). However, 29 percent of Jews, 16 percent of mainline Protestants, and 10 percent of Catholics are all classified as Secularists. We also find a sizable number of Jews (21 percent), mainline Protestants (23 percent), and Catholics (23 percent) who are Religious Secularists – that is, they blend a secular perspective with religious commitments.

Taken as a whole, one half of American Jews, two fifths of mainline Protestants, and a third of Catholics score above average on the Personal Secularism Index. Thus, a sizable number of Americans who identify with these three of the nation's major religious traditions also embrace a secular worldview. Conversely, we also find that to be a None does not necessarily mean having a secular worldview: only 43 percent of Nones are Secularists, while 45 percent are Non-Religionists – and interestingly, 8 percent of Nones are Religionists.

Table 2.1 displays the full demographic details of these four secular-religious categories. We draw your attention to the sharp differences in education between Secularists and Non-Religionists. Over half of the Non-Religionists have no more than a high school education, compared to just 32 percent of Secularists. Similarly, when compared to Non-Religionists, more than twice as many Secularists have a college degree (16 and 33 percent, respectively). Zuckerman et al. summarize the extant literature by noting that "one of the most consistent findings in the social science literature is that secular men and women are disproportionately well-educated" (2016, 110). We can now add that it is those who have an explicitly secular worldview who have the highest levels of education. Religionists also are less educated than Secularists, but more educated than Non-Religionists. However, the Religious Secularists and Secularists have comparable levels of education. These patterns lend support to the hypothesis that secularization in America is associated with higher education and its link to the authority of secular professionals, as noted in Chapter 1.

Separating personal nonreligiosity from secularism unravels the ambiguity regarding the relationship between education and religion. As noted, many observers argue that education and religion are in tension; more of the former means less of the latter (Norris and Inglehart 2011). On the other hand, others have argued that religion is that rare area of American society where we do not see sharp divides by class, and thus education (Verba, Schlozman, and Brady 1995). Both are right. Or, more accurately, each is right depending on how (non-)religiosity and secularism are defined. The share of Religionists with a college degree is only slightly below that for the population as a whole: 24 percent vs. 26 percent. However, Secularists are, on average, more highly educated. With more education often comes a greater embrace of secular beliefs, self-identification, and guidance.

We also see dramatic income differences between the Non-Religionists and Secularists, which of course are also related to their differing education levels. While only 9 percent of Non-Religionists earn over $100,000 per year, 17 percent of Secularists have that level of income – the highest of all the groups. There is, in other words, a gaping class divide between those people whose orientations toward religion and secularism are defined only by *what they are not* and those who also are defined *by what they are*. These patterns offer mixed results for the hypothesis (discussed in Chapter 1) that secularization in America is associated with higher economic status and thus less risk of economic insecurity.

In terms of age, more Secularists than Non-Religionists are between 18 and 29 (23 and 19 percent, respectively). But the group with the largest share of under-30s is Religious Secularists (25 percent). Consistent with the literature, Religionists have more older people (over 60 years) at about one third (Hout and Fischer 2014). But roughly one quarter of the three other categories are older as well, and the average ages of all four groups are comparable. These patterns raise some doubt about the hypothesis that secularization in America is driven mainly by generational change, as discussed in Chapter 1.

The fact that Secularists are more likely to be men is not unexpected given that women generally have higher levels of religiosity (Baker and Whitehead 2016; Edgell, Frost, and Stewart 2017; Schnabel 2015). Furthermore, secular activism has been characterized as a male-heavy domain (Schnabel et al. 2016). Likewise, it comes as no surprise that minorities, Blacks and Hispanics especially, are underrepresented among the Secularists, as these are communities with higher-than-average levels of religiosity (Baker and Smith 2015). It is, however, notable that both Blacks and Hispanics have a sizable representation among the Religious Secularists. This pattern suggests that a considerable share of these two minority populations have secular inclinations even while maintaining a degree of religious commitment.

NONRELIGIOSITY AND SECULARISM OVER TIME

In light of the rise in personal nonreligiosity, one might wonder whether personal secularism is experiencing the same sort of growth. Because we

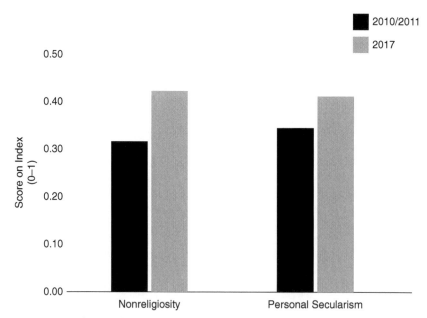

FIGURE 2.3 Both nonreligiosity and personal secularism are rising
Note: In the panel study, nonreligiosity measures are from the first (2010) wave; personal secularism is from the second wave (2011).
Source: 2017 Secular America Study; Secular America Panel Study

created these measures, they are not available in long-running surveys like the GSS, making it impossible to trace long-term trends as we can with measures of nonreligiosity. It is possible, though, to make comparisons between the first and second SAS. Figure 2.3 displays the overall level of personal secularism in the 2011 and 2017 versions of the SAS. For the sake of comparison, it also includes the levels of nonreligiosity in the two years.[28] Everything has been coded to be on a common scale so that we are only making apples-to-apples comparisons. Interestingly, there is not only a rise in both, but the increase is of nearly identical magnitude.

CONCLUSION

We are witnessing a critical juncture in American secularity. We have seen that the United States is more secular than suggested by the common narrative of Americans as a highly religious people. There is no question that the United States is indeed a religious nation, especially when compared to other advanced industrial democracies. But with the right instrument, we can detect a greater degree of secularism within the American population than is generally acknowledged. Furthermore, we can clearly differentiate between personal nonreligiosity and personal secularism.

To return to the types of secularity described by Charles Taylor (see Chapter 1), the rise in nonreligiosity that we have documented reinforces evidence from other scholars that there has been an increase in Secularity 2: a turn away from conventional religious practices. Our measurement of personal secularism also makes clear the United States is in the throes of Secularity 3, the idea that belief in religion is one among competing worldviews. Recall that about one in four Americans is a Secularist, meaning that they have an affirmatively secular worldview and also little to no religious influence in their lives. However, secularism often complements as well as replaces religiosity, as seen with the Religious Secularists.

In addition, it is important to note that to be a Secularist does not necessarily mean being hostile to religion. Only 37 percent of Secularists say that individuals are better off without religion in their lives. But 67 percent say that religion has too much influence in society – more than question its suitability as an individual's choice, but still far from unanimity. Interestingly, the difference in attitudes toward private versus public religion suggests that many Secularists are less concerned about whether individuals choose to be

---

[28] Results for nonreligiosity are for 2010, the first wave of the SAS panel study. Recall that the secular belief items were first included in 2011, and so that is the baseline used for the Personal Secularism Index. In this figure, the Personal Secularism Index only includes the four secular beliefs asked about in the 2011 survey: specifically, "factual evidence," "great works of philosophy," "free our minds," and "hard to live a good life." Both indices have been coded on a 0–1 scale.

religious than the public role that religion plays, which is a theme we explore further in the next chapter.

All of this work is a prelude to the question motivating this whole book: do personal nonreligiosity and personal secularism have political relevance? While the sheer size of the secular population suggests that it is ripening as a potential political constituency, there are many ways of slicing and dicing the population into groups large and small. Most, though, have no political salience, such as being a dog owner or a fan of *Dancing with the Stars*. Is being a Secularist politically meaningful, like being a gun owner or, perhaps most aptly, an evangelical Christian? And how might this differ from the Non-Religionists? If you are interested in the answer, keep reading. Chapter 3 starts the examination of personal secularism's political relevance by focusing on the area of policy where we should most expect it to matter: attitudes toward public secularism.

3

Public Secularism

The previous chapter made the case that Americans are more secular than is often realized, based on our new measures of personal secularism. Now we turn to the question of whether these new measures add anything to our understanding of American politics. Specifically, does personal secularism shape public opinion beyond existing measures of nonreligiosity, or anything else for that matter? Is this anything new?

To answer that question, we start with the area of public opinion where personal secularism should matter most: public secularism, or views about religion's proper role in American society. Found both in law and custom, this area of public opinion has received less attention than it deserves.[1] As we learned in Chapter 1, disputes over the public role of religion are a prime motivation for secular political activism, while Chapter 2 showed that personal secularism is closely associated with the view that religion has too much influence in society.

This chapter focuses on Americans' views on the always-fraught subject of the line between church and state,[2] or what in some circles is called religious liberty. It then looks beyond constitutional questions to Americans' views on civil religion, the customary quasi-religious endorsement of the American secular state, such as President Obama's first inaugural address. In brief, personal secularism does shape attitudes on public secularism in both law and

---

[1] For earlier analyses of public opinion toward church and state, see Jelen and Wilcox (1995); Jelen (2010); Castle (2015; 2017). We are particularly indebted to Clyde Wilcox and the late Ted Jelen for their pioneering work.

[2] We acknowledge that the phrase "church and state" is a misnomer, as these issues often involve religions whose members do not worship in churches but rather synagogues, mosques, and temples, or perhaps not in a dedicated sacred space at all. For the sake of brevity, however, we will use the short-hand term "church and state" to refer to issues involving any and all faiths, regardless of their particular place of worship.

custom, sometimes in surprising ways. A first step is to put such attitudes in political context.

RELIGIOUS RIGHTS AND SECULAR SCHISMS

In the not so distant past, "religious liberty" was right next to motherhood and apple pie in America, noncontroversial and bipartisan. Politicians' speeches on the freedom of religion were typically paeans to religious diversity. Norman Rockwell even featured "freedom to worship" in his iconic paintings of the four freedoms. But during the secular surge, it has become a highly charged issue. Consider the words of former US Attorney General Jeff Sessions at a White House summit on religious liberty:

[I]n recent years, the cultural climate in this country – and in the West more generally – has become less hospitable to people of faith. Many Americans have felt that their freedom to practice their faith has been under attack. (2018)

Notice that Sessions refers to "people of faith," grouping believers of many stripes together, in spite of past or present interreligious antagonisms. Furthermore, he invokes the imagery of their "freedom to practice their faith" being "under attack," underscoring that religious liberty has become a lightning rod for controversy. Sessions then went on to provide a list of what he describes as examples of such attacks, including "nuns ordered to buy contraceptives," nominees to federal office being asked about their religious "dogma," and, referencing the plaintiff in a recent US Supreme Court case, "the ordeal faced so bravely by Jack Phillips."

The reference to Phillips throws the meaning of religious liberty in sharp relief, as the US Supreme Court case in which he was a plaintiff highlights the contested meaning of the Constitution's protection of religious free exercise. Phillips is a baker who refused to make a custom wedding cake for a same-sex couple, as he believed that doing so would violate his religious convictions. Does religious liberty mean that Phillips has the right to block certain parts of his business from customers based on their sexual orientation? How far does the free exercise of religion go?

The High Court decided that Phillips was entitled to withhold his services from same-sex weddings (*Masterpiece Cakeshop, Ltd. et al.* v. *Colorado Civil Rights Commission et al.* 2018). Interestingly, in his decision Justice Neil Gorsuch repeatedly refers to the "secular values" of those who support same-sex marriage, in contrast with the religious values of opponents. He portrays the case as pitting secularism against religion – although many Americans would disagree with his description, given that a large and growing share of religious believers in the United States support same-sex marriage (Vandermaas-Peer et al. 2018). Writing for the majority, Justice Anthony Kennedy went even further to portray the case as secularity versus religiosity. His decision claims there was animus toward Phillips's religious beliefs from the Colorado Human

Rights Commission, the body that originally adjudicated the case. A case that was ostensibly about the limits of religious free exercise instead centered on whether a state commission had expressed hostility toward the plaintiff's religion, and whether that was grounds to decide the case in his favor.

The *Masterpiece Cakeshop* case was framed by those who supported the right of Jack Phillips to refuse to make a custom cake for same-sex weddings as a matter of religious exercise, thus invoking the Free Exercise Clause of the First Amendment. Equally contentious are cases that deal with the other religion-related statement in that same amendment, the Establishment Clause, which prohibits government from "establishing" religion. This phrasing has led to lots of litigation over just what it means for religion to be established. Can student-led prayers be said before public high school football games? Should the Pledge of Allegiance contain the words "one nation *under God*"? Often, cases involving the Establishment Clause expose the tensions of addressing vestigial forms of public religion that in an earlier era caused little or no controversy, such as Christian crosses and Ten Commandments monuments on public land.

A quintessential example is *Town of Greece* v. *Galloway*, a US Supreme Court case that took up the question of whether a town board in Greece, New York could have clergy pray before its monthly public meetings. Interestingly, this practice only began in 1999, and thus is not a long-held practice. From 1999 to 2007, all of the prayers were given by Christian clergy, often using sectarian language such as "We acknowledge the saving sacrifice of Jesus Christ on the cross" or closing the prayer in the name of Christ.[3] Two local residents, Susan Galloway and Linda Stephens, objected to these prayers, arguing that they violated the Establishment Clause.

In a 5–4 decision, the US Supreme Court disagreed, with Justice Kennedy again writing for the majority. He compared the prayers at this town's board meeting to other legislative prayers, such as in the US Congress and state legislatures. "Legislative prayer has become part of our heritage and tradition, part of our expressive idiom, similar to the Pledge of Allegiance, inaugural prayer, or the recitation of 'God save the United States and this honorable Court' at the opening of this Court's sessions" (*Town of Greece, New York* v. *Galloway et al.* 2014). Writing in dissent, Justice Stephen Breyer concluded that the prayers did not reflect the religious diversity of the town's population, including those who, like Linda Stephens, are atheists. Quoting *Lemon* v. *Kurtzman*, a well-known Supreme Court case on religious establishment, Breyer's concern was that the practice exacerbated "political divisions along religious lines."

It is no coincidence that these kinds of controversies have arisen as the secular population in the United States grows in size and salience, because opinion on the public role for religion is often divided among religious and secular

---

[3] After Galloway and Stephens objected to the Christian-only prayers at a town board meeting, non-Christian prayers were subsequently offered: one Jewish, one Ba'hai, and one Wiccan.

Americans. Many of the organizations supporting the plaintiffs in these cases are advocates for greater secularism, such as the American Humanist Association, the Freedom From Religion Foundation, and Americans United for Separation of Church and State. However, as much as the debates over religious liberty, nonestablishment, and nondiscrimination are rooted in tension between religious and secular values, as with so much else in the contemporary United States, it is also the case that opinion often breaks cleanly along partisan lines. Jeff Sessions is an archconservative Republican, while religion cases before the Supreme Court routinely pit justices appointed by Republican presidents against colleagues appointed by Democratic presidents. Given that religion and secularism are tightly intertwined with partisanship, one wonders whether disputes over religion's public role are as much a matter of partisanship as principle.

PUBLIC OPINION ON PUBLIC SECULARISM

To this point, we have defined personal secularism by studiously avoiding the inclusion of attitudes toward religion's place in society. Some readers may be puzzled by this omission, as it may seem natural to assume that to be secular is to believe that religion and government should not mix. Recall that Charles Taylor (2007) describes one type of secularism as the withdrawal of religion from the public sphere (Secularity 1). Similarly, in defining multiple concepts of the secular, Daniel Philpott refers to "a differentiation between religion and other spheres of society" (2009, 185). Indeed, virtually all definitions of secularism distinguish between the public and private spheres. In the words of Jonathan Fox, a scholar of religion and secularism worldwide, "It is possible for an individual to be personally religious but still believe that a government should stay out of religion" (2015, 31). In short, public and personal secularism – while often correlated – are not the same. We agree with José Casanova that "social scientists need to recognize that, despite all the structural forces, the legitimate pressures, and the many valid reasons pushing religion in the modern secular world into the private sphere, religion continues to have and will likely continue to have a public dimension" (1994, 66).

Further complicating our understanding of public secularism, the United States is an unusual case when compared to other nations. Constitutionally, it has a secular government, as there is a prohibition on an established state religion – unlike nations such as Britain, Germany, and Sweden (Fox 2015). Yet, culturally, the United States is also highly religious, due at least in part to the constitutional protection of religion's free exercise. The contrast with France, another country born of revolution and with a secular constitution, is especially sharp (Bowen 2008; Kuru 2009). The French concept of *laïcité* means prohibitions on religious expression that many – but, as we will show, not all – Americans find unacceptable.

Public secularism is complex, both as a matter of law and custom. Broadly speaking, there are two schools of thought, reflecting the two religion clauses in the First Amendment to the US Constitution. On one side there are *separationists*, who prioritize a high level of nonestablishment, typically described as "a wall of separation between church and state." The separationist doctrine is primarily concerned with protecting religious minorities from the dominant religious communities. On the other side are the *accommodationists*, who "believe government may both recognize and extend benefits to religion in a non-discriminatory manner" (Wald and Calhoun-Brown 2018, 76). Importantly, the accommodationist doctrine is primarily concerned with reflecting the views of the historical majority of Americans with roots in the Judeo-Christian traditions.

Public opinion is split between the two perspectives, which we can see in two ways of asking about them. One is to contrast a "high wall of separation between church and state" with the alternative that "the government should take special steps to protect America's religious heritage," language meant to distill a common accommodationist position. When, in the Secular America Study (SAS), we asked Americans to choose between the two we found a close split, although more Americans favor the accommodationist view that the government should protect the nation's religious heritage (58 percent).[4]

Another point of debate between the two perspectives is over the meaning of the Establishment Clause. Accommodationists often argue that the constitutional prohibition on the establishment of religion only refers to government favoritism toward a particular religion, and that government endorsement of religion *in general* is permitted. Separationists, on the other hand, interpret the clause to mean that government should not favor religion at all. To differentiate between the two perspectives, we asked respondents to choose the statement that comes closest to their view: "the government should not provide any support to any religion" or "the government should support all religions equally." On this question, the public is more evenly divided: 53 percent for the accommodationists' position vs. 47 percent for the separationists' perspective.

Given the high state of partisan polarization – including on religious matters – it should come as no surprise that Republicans and Democrats often differ on these matters. In general, Republicans are more likely to favor the accommodationist position, while Democrats are more likely to be separationists. For example, 74 percent of Republicans believe the government should protect the nation's religious heritage over ensuring a high wall of separation between church and state, compared to 45 percent of Democrats who have the same view. Note that Democrats' opinions are more divided than Republicans' – a hint of a theme that will recur throughout this book, namely that the Democrats' coalition is more religiously diverse than the Republicans'.

---

[4] Both of these questions were asked in the second wave of the SAS panel survey, in 2012.

Yet, as suggested by the internal division among Democrats, public secularism cannot simply be reduced to partisan differences. For example, Republicans and Independents are split 50/50 on the question of whether the government should support religion in general. Perhaps surprisingly, Democrats slightly favor the accommodationist position that government should support all religions equally, by a margin of 56 percent to 44 percent. The Democrats' differences of opinion suggest that public secularism is not merely a proxy for partisanship. As we will see, these attitudes are also shaped by an individual's worldview, whether it is religious or secular.

Not all questions regarding the role of religion in the public square center on the Constitution, as custom often matters more than law. In a famous essay, Robert Bellah (1988) introduced the concept of civil religion, arguing that public expressions of religion imbued with governmental authority is a binding force in American culture. Like the fish that does not know it is swimming in water, the way that religion permeates many civic rituals is often invisible to Americans themselves. It is America's civil religion that helps account for the frequent religious references in American politics compared to most other liberal democracies.

The discussion to follow has two objectives. First, it will describe what rank-and-file Americans think about a range of issues regarding religion's place in public life. For comparison, the chapter also includes data from the membership of the American Humanist Association (AHA), as exemplars of ardent secularism. How do these "known Secularists" differ from the general population and how are they similar? To foreshadow the discussion to come, the data reveal that Americans are divided on many constitutional questions regarding church and state. At the same time, most Americans are comfortable with civil religion – specifically, the cultural expression of religiosity by their president.

The second objective is examining how attitudes toward religion and public life are related to personal secularism. If personal secularism is really a heretofore undiscovered political fault line, at a minimum it should influence church–state attitudes above and beyond both nonreligiosity (the absence of religiosity) and partisanship – and further, it should equal or rival the impact of both. It is not just that personal secularism is something new. How much does it matter? The results show that personal secularism generally has more impact on church–state views than either nonreligiosity or party identification. Nonetheless, there is nuance in Secularists' views. While they are staunchly opposed to anything that suggests the establishment of religion, their attitude on free exercise depends on the particular situation in question, and they are relatively accepting of civil religion.

CONSTITUTIONAL QUESTIONS

We asked both our sample of Americans in general and the membership of the AHA a series of questions about controversies involving public secularism, all of which are drawn from real-life controversies in recent years. We divided the questions into two categories: cases involving nonestablishment and those about free exercise. In each category, we chose some issues that we expected to be highly contested and others where we anticipated near consensus. Some are "ripped from the headlines," while others are issues that seemingly could arise in the future. While one survey could not cover every possible controversy, we are confident that we have addressed a wide range of issues within this domain. We asked respondents "whether [they] agree[d] or disagree[d] that each of the following should be permitted under the US Constitution."[5] We then presented them with each issue, one at a time, in a random order.[6]

We start with the questions regarding the practical application of the Establishment Clause. All of these scenarios deal with the fundamental issue of whether government is inappropriately endorsing, and thus "establishing" religion.

Public School Children Say the Pledge of Allegiance, Which Refers to "One Nation Under God"

In the 1940s, the Supreme Court decided that, if it violated their religious beliefs, children could not be compelled to recite the Pledge, which in those days did not include the phrase "under God," as it was only added in the 1950s (Ellis 2005). More recently, Michael Newdow sued the school district of Elk Grove, California, arguing that exempting children from saying the Pledge is not enough, as the religious language itself is unconstitutional. After working its way through the lower courts, the Supreme Court took the case but then decided not to decide, instead determining that Newdow did not have standing to sue (*Elk Grove Unified School District* v. *Newdow* 2004). It seems likely that this issue will return to the national public agenda, as lower courts continue to hear cases about objections to the religious language of the Pledge (Moore and Kramnick 2018).

A Copy of the Ten Commandments Is Displayed in a County Courthouse

The Supreme Court has ruled on the question of displaying the Ten Commandments in government settings, but the decisions can charitably be called complex – some would say incoherent. In two cases decided on the same day, the Supreme Court ruled that it is constitutional to have a Ten

---

[5] Response options ranged from Strongly Disagree to Strongly Agree, with a neutral midpoint. We show the exact question wording for our indicators of public secularism and of all of the key political orientations throughout the book in the online appendix (see secularsurge.com for the online appendix).

[6] By randomizing the order, we eliminate any concern over question-ordering effects; that is, that the answer to one question systematically affects the answers to another.

Commandments monument on the grounds of a state capitol, but unconstitutional if the commandments are posted inside a county courthouse. Their constitutionality depends on how long the Ten Commandments have been on display and whether they have caused controversy (*McCreary County* v. *ACLU* 2005; *Van Orden* v. *Perry* 2005). This question foreshadows Chapter 6, where we take up the case of Roy Moore. When Moore was the chief justice of the Alabama state Supreme Court, he refused a federal court order to remove a Ten Commandments monument he had installed in the courthouse rotunda. The monument became his version of the bloody shirt, as he took it on tour around the country while decrying the removal of God from the courts (Green 2005). Moore's use of the commandments as a rallying cry illustrates how this issue goes to the heart of religion's place in America's government institutions.

A State Legislature Declares Christianity to Be the Official Religion of the Government

In spite of the First Amendment's prohibition on an established religion, in 2013 a bill was proposed in the North Carolina state legislature declaring Christianity to be the state's official religion. Its proponents argued that because the federal Constitution says that "*Congress* shall make no law respecting the establishment of religion," it leaves open the possibility that a state government may do so (Graham 2013). The bill failed, as it was more a symbolic statement than a serious attempt at making law. Admittedly, this matter is a fringe issue, but that is precisely why we have posed it. How much support is there for something that seems far from mainstream thought, even in accommodationist circles? Perhaps it is not so marginal among the American public, especially given the common refrain that the United States is and has been a "Christian nation" (Cox and Piacenza 2015; Pew Research Center 2007).

Figure 3.1 displays the attitudes of both the general population and the members of the AHA on these three scenarios. Each bar represents the percentage who disagree with the proposal in question or, in other words, favor the nonestablishment of religion. First, note that relatively few Americans outright oppose the inclusion of "under God" in the Pledge of Allegiance or the display of the Ten Commandments in a county courthouse. This seeming consensus, though, is more nuanced than it might appear at first, as 22 and 26 percent of the population, respectively, express ambivalence by choosing the neutral option. Roughly 50 percent of the population oppose the declaration of Christianity as a state's official religion; 30 percent are ambivalent. Among the membership of the AHA, there is nearly universal opposition to each scenario.

Generalizing across the full set of Establishment Clause questions, we see that many Americans take the accommodationist side of the debate over public secularism, believing that religion should receive the state's seal of approval. A smaller number take the separationist side, wary of mingling

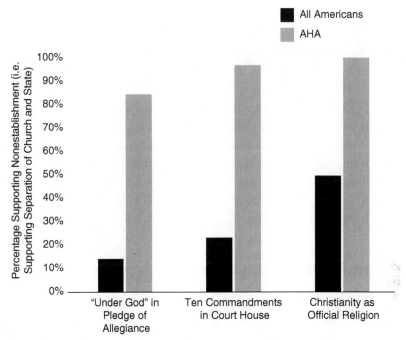

FIGURE 3.1 Few Americans support the separation of church and state; most AHA members do
Note: Results combine "Strongly Disagree" and "Disagree."
Source: 2017 Secular America Study; 2018 American Humanist Association Survey

church (or mosque or synagogue) and state. In contrast, among the highly secular population of AHA members, there is clear opposition to any hint of an established religion. These self-identified Secularists are staunch separationists.

While nonestablishment cases deal with what the government can and cannot do, free exercise involves government protection of the religious actions of individuals. On these issues, it is often not clear how Religionists and Secularists will respond. In the abstract, one would expect religious believers to favor the free exercise of religion, but in practice it often depends on the particular religion making the free exercise claim. Naively, one might think that Secularists would be unsympathetic to religious expression, but that is not necessarily the case. They may see a connection between the freedom to exercise religion and protecting the freedom of nonbelievers, especially given the high degree of animus toward atheists (see Chapter 10).

Each of the following free-exercise cases asks about a different type of religious expression.

A Public High School Prohibits Students from Wearing Religious Symbols, Such as a Christian Cross, a Jewish Skullcap, or a Muslim Headscarf

This question gauges Americans' opinions on an issue that has received a lot of attention in Europe and, more recently, Quebec. Laws vary, but in general they have sought to prevent women from covering their faces in public or when receiving public services. The specific wording of this question most closely reflects a law in France: the French prohibit "ostentatious" religious symbols in schools. While the law applies to symbols from all faiths, it arose because of public concern over female Muslims' attire, including the hijab, niqab, and burka (Bowen 2008). To our knowledge, no American school has actually attempted to enact such a policy, but given the issue's salience elsewhere in the world, we thought it would be interesting to see what Americans think. Because it has not been a matter of debate in the United States, at least not yet, we can examine opinions in a partisan "vacuum."

While Headgear Is Generally Not Allowed in Driver's License Photos, a Devout Muslim Is Permitted to Wear a Headscarf in Her Photo

While the question about a high school's ban on religious symbols is largely hypothetical in the United States, this issue is not. There have been cases in multiple states over whether Muslim women can be required to remove their headwear for identification photos or in other public settings (Warikoo 2015). In general, state departments of motor vehicles do allow this religious accommodation, although exact policies differ. Given that this question centers on Muslims – a group viewed with suspicion by many Americans – we expect it to be divisive.

Houses of Worship Lose Their Tax-Exempt Status If They Publicly Endorse Political Candidates

Currently, because of what is commonly known as the Johnson Amendment, federal law prohibits tax-exempt charitable organizations, including religious congregations, from endorsing political candidates. While the IRS rarely enforces this law, it technically means that religious leaders who explicitly endorse a candidate for office could cause their congregation to lose its tax-exempt status – a huge financial hit that many houses of worship could not sustain. In recent years, many Religious Right leaders have chafed at this restriction, with some even challenging the IRS to investigate them for their political activity. In the 2016 presidential election campaign, Donald Trump took up this cause, promising evangelical leaders that he would eliminate this restriction on their political advocacy (Bailey 2017). Politics over the pulpit, however, is not limited to congregations on the right, as many left-leaning houses of worship – particularly black churches – often address political subjects and invite candidates to speak (McDaniel 2008).

For Religious Reasons, a Florist Refuses to Provide Flowers for Same-Sex Weddings

Recall from the above discussion that whether religious free exercise extends to commerce has become a touchstone for the Religious Right. At issue is whether business owners can "conscientiously object" to providing certain services to LGBTQ clients, on the grounds that they have a moral objection to same-sex marriage. On the other side, the argument is simply that this behavior is discrimination akin to the racial restrictions of the Jim Crow era. Just as businesses do not have the right to refuse service on the basis of race, neither can they refuse to do business on the basis of sexual orientation or gender identity. Like the question about political endorsements by houses of worship, this matter too has been highly partisan (Lipka 2017).

At the time of our survey in the fall of 2017, the debate over same-sex weddings may well have been on our respondents' minds. Oral arguments in the *Masterpiece Cakeshop* case were heard in December of 2017 and there was a lot of news coverage and public discussion of whether religious free exercise enables business owners to deny commercial services to members of the LGBTQ community. The *Masterpiece* case was about a baker while our question was about a florist, but otherwise the issue is identical.

Figure 3.2 displays the opinions of both the general population and AHA members on these free-exercise issues. The height of each bar is the percentage of the population who take a pro-free-exercise position. Across these examples of contested claims about the boundaries of religious exercise we see a wide diversity of opinion. On some, the general population and AHA diverge but on others they look pretty much the same.

There are two issues where the general population and AHA membership do not differ: whether high school students should be able to wear religious symbols at school and whether Muslims' driver's license photos can include headscarves. Sixty percent of all Americans, as well as the AHA, favor students displaying religious symbols. Roughly 40 percent of both groups approve of the headscarf photo. In comparing these issues, note that approval of the photo is 20 percentage points lower than religious symbols at school. It is telling that the form of free exercise with less support refers to Muslims only, while the item about religious symbols at school mentions Christians and Jews as well. We return to this point below.

On the other two free-exercise questions – denying service to LGBTQ customers and political endorsements by religious organizations – there is more distance between the general public and the AHA. Only one quarter of Americans agree that houses of worship should be able to remain tax-exempt if they engage in politicking, while nearly 40 percent agree that a florist should be

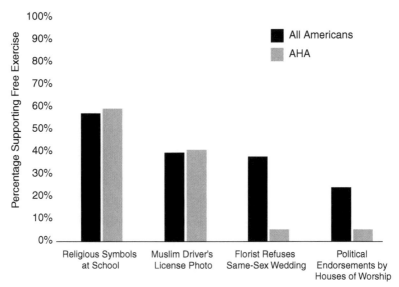

FIGURE 3.2 Attitudes on free exercise of religion vary by issue
Note: Results combine "Strongly Agree" and "Agree." Polarity has been reversed for Religious Symbols and Political Endorsements.
Source: 2017 Secular America Study; 2018 American Humanist Association Survey

able to refuse to do business with a same-sex couple. In both cases, very few (5 percent) AHA members agree.

To summarize our findings on both nonestablishment and free exercise to this point, attitudes on Establishment Clause issues are fairly consistent – in public opinion parlance they are "constrained" (or consistent). In contrast, the questions about free exercise are much less constrained – which means that knowing someone's opinion on one item does not significantly improve your chance of guessing their opinion on another.[7] This pattern makes sense in light of the fact that the free-exercise questions include a range of faiths and types of expression. All in all, these results demonstrate that, when it comes to attitudes toward free exercise, it depends on what is being exercised and by whom. And this result is as true for "known Secularists" as it is for the population as a whole.

Importantly, two of these issues – service to LGBTQ customers and political endorsements by clergy – have also been promoted by the Religious Right, suggesting that people's opinions are shaped by partisan predispositions. This fact would also help explain why these are the two issues on which the AHA members, who are overwhelmingly liberals and Democrats, support a restriction on religious expression. It also leaves open the question of

---

[7] The Cronbach's alpha is .80 for the nonestablishment items but only .43 for the free-exercise items.

whether personal secularism and/or nonreligiosity have any independent impact on these views, or whether they are driven solely by political partisanship.

PUTTING PERSONAL SECULARISM TO THE TEST

Having described what Americans in general think on constitutional issues, we turn next to examining what shapes their thinking. Specifically, we are interested in knowing whether attitudes are driven primarily by personal secularism, nonreligiosity, or partisanship. Of course, cross-sectional statistical models such as these cannot tell us what is *causing* what. Accordingly, when we use words like "impact," "influence," or "shape" to describe the relationship between variables, we do not mean to imply causation. We are simply referring to the fact that these things move together (i.e. they co-vary). Later on, in Chapter 5, we will show that there are reciprocal relationships between secular and political orientations – meaning that they influence each other – so sorting out the causal order is complex. Our purpose here is not to determine which comes first, but only to see whether each of the measures has any relationship to public opinion while simultaneously accounting for the others. In particular, we are looking to see whether personal secularism offers any explanatory leverage above and beyond nonreligiosity and partisanship.

Figure 3.3 displays the relative impact of party identification, nonreligiosity, and personal secularism on attitudes toward the nonestablishment of religion, while controlling for a host of demographic characteristics. Because attitudes on all three nonestablishment questions are similar, they are combined into a single index. Party identification is coded so that higher values mean a stronger orientation toward the Democrats. A bar in the positive direction means that Democrats score higher than Republicans, and a negative-pointing bar means the opposite. For those interested in more details about the statistical models used to generate this figure, as well as Figures 3.4a–d and Figure 3.6, please see A Closer Look 3.1.

Note that all three variables are positive and statistically significant, meaning that each one is related to support for nonestablishment of religion. The fact that personal secularism is statistically significant means that it is not just a proxy for either nonreligiosity or partisanship. Furthermore, its impact is actually the largest of the three. In sum, personal secularism has a previously unrecognized, and sizable, connection to attitudes on the nonestablishment domain of attitudes on church and state.

Opinion on free exercise is more complex to describe, since attitudes depend on the specific way in which religion is being exercised. Therefore, instead of combining the free exercise items into a single index, they are presented separately in Figures 3.4a–d. The results for the questions about the florist denying service to LGBTQ couples and political endorsements by houses of worship are similar. In

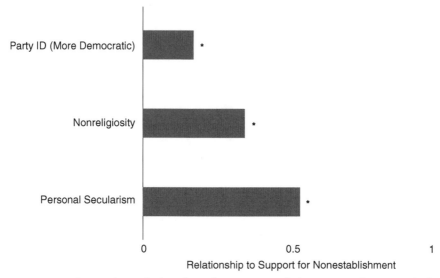

FIGURE 3.3 Personal secularism has the strongest link to attitudes toward the nonestablishment of religion
* = *Statistically significant at p < .05*
Note: *Bars represent the relationship, measured as the size of an OLS regression coefficient, of each variable on support for the nonestablishment of religion. Both independent and dependent variables are coded to range from 0 to 1. Model estimated with demographic controls.*
Source: *2017 Secular America Study*

both cases, all three variables are highly significant and in the anti-free-exercise direction. This finding means that among the factors shaping opposition to both issues are Democratic partisanship, nonreligiosity, and personal secularism – but it is personal secularism that has the biggest impact.

To presage a theme that we will revisit later, the question about political endorsements by religious leaders is dependent on the respondents' race. When the model is limited to African American and Latino respondents only, there is a very different impact for party identification. Among minorities, Democrats are more likely to support political endorsements by clergy – the opposite of the result for white Democrats.[8] The reason is no doubt because religious congregations frequented by both African Americans and Latinos often feature political messages, but favoring Democrats over Republicans. This difference between white and minority Democrats speaks to a more in-depth discussion in Chapter 8 of the challenges that the rise of secularism holds for the Democratic Party.

---

[8] For no other question, either on free exercise or nonestablishment, do the results change for minorities.

(a)

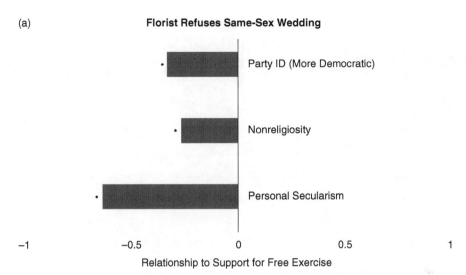

(b)

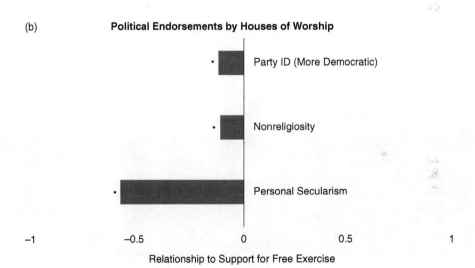

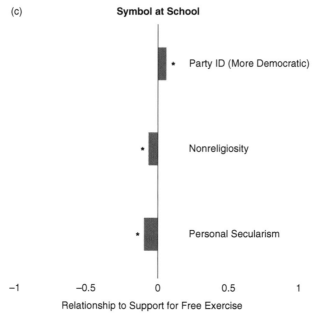

(c)   **Symbol at School**

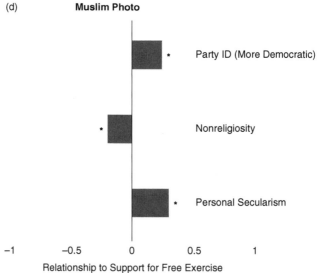

(d)   **Muslim Photo**

FIGURE 3.4 How personal secularism and religiosity link to attitudes toward free exercise of religion depends on the issue
* = *Statistically significant at p < .05*
Note: Bars represent the impact, measured as the size of an OLS regression coefficient, of each variable on support for the free exercise of religion. Both independent and dependent variables are coded to range from 0 to 1. Models estimated with demographic controls. Polarity has been reversed for Religious Symbols and Political Endorsements.
Source: 2017 Secular America Study

A Closer Look 3.1:
How We Did Our Public Secularism Analyses

To generate Figures 3.3, 3.4a–d, and 3.8, we employed statistical models that include personal secularism, nonreligiosity, and party identification as explanatory variables, while also controlling for other demographics that might be correlated with attitudes on public secularism. Control variables include age, gender, education, race (African American or Hispanic), and religious tradition (white evangelical Protestant, mainline Protestant, Catholic). We can thus compare the relative size of the relationship between each of these variables and the specific attitudes in question, over and above any potentially confounding demographic characteristics. Nonreligiosity and personal secularism are both coded as additive indices, as described in Chapter 2. Party ID is the standard 7-point scale, ranging from Strong Republican to Strong Democrat. All of the variables (including the dependent variables) are coded on a 0–1 scale in order to compare their magnitudes. Results are estimated using OLS regression. For attitudes on nonestablishment, the three items are combined in an additive index. Our results are substantively the same if they are combined using a factor score.

Turning next to the question about banning religious symbols, perhaps most notable is that the size of each relationship is small but statistically significant. These results mean that none of these three variables has much impact on this issue. To the extent that there are impacts, party identification points in a different direction than both nonreligiosity and personal secularism.[9] While Democrats are (modestly) *more* likely to think that a school should *not* ban religious symbols, the opposite is true for nonreligious and secular Americans. That is, people who score highly on nonreligiosity and those who score highly on personal secularism are both a bit more likely to agree with a ban on all religious symbols. Once again it is personal secularism that has the biggest – albeit still relatively small – impact.

Recall that the question about religious symbols at school references a Muslim headscarf, suggesting that perhaps a willingness to ban religious symbols is a reflection of anti-Islamic views (Bowen 2008). Because the question mentions other religious symbols too, it is also possible that the responses reflect a principled objection to all religious garb, or at least a willingness to grant high schools the discretion to impose a general ban on religious wear. Further insight into attitudes toward Muslims' free exercise can be had with the question that asks about a Muslim woman wearing a headscarf in a driver's license photo. As with

---

[9] For both the question about religious symbols at school and the Muslim driver's license photo, all three variables are significant at $p < .01$.

religious symbols at school, the impact of political party again indicates that Democrats are more likely to approve of free exercise. Note, though, that the nonreligious are less likely – meaning that *religious* Americans are more likely – to support the right of a Muslim woman to exercise her religion freely. For personal secularism, the results differ from those regarding symbols at school in one important way: people high in personal secularism are more likely to favor free exercise, just the opposite of their views on the high school ban on religious displays. While the size of the impact for personal secularism is very close to that of party ID, it is again the largest of the three.

While we have shown results from a statistical model that weighs the simultaneous impact of personal secularism and nonreligiosity, it is also informative to compare attitudes among members of our four secular-religious groups (created in Chapter 2) without any statistical controls, as in Figure 3.5. As we would expect, Secularists are the most likely to favor the nonestablishment of religion, while Religionists are the least likely. However, note the similarity between Non-Religionists (high in nonreligiosity but low in personal secularism) and Religious Secularists (low in nonreligiosity – that is, highly religious – and high in personal secularism). Both groups are cross-pressured and thus end up with similar attitudes.

Figure 3.6 provides the same comparison across the four secular-religious groups for attitudes on the free exercise of religion. To underscore that support

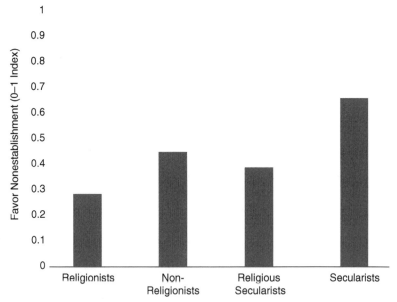

FIGURE 3.5 Secularists are most likely to favor nonestablishment of religion
Source: 2017 Secular America Study

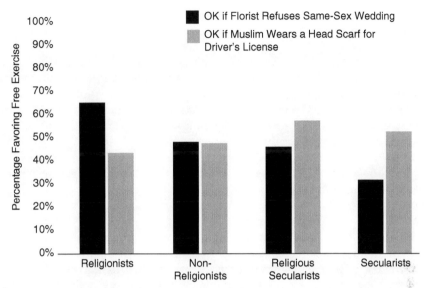

FIGURE 3.6 Religionists and Secularists have differing views of religious free exercise
Source: 2017 Secular America Study

for free exercise depends on who is doing the exercising, we display the attitudes for two issues: whether a florist can refuse to provide service to a same-sex wedding and whether a Muslim woman can wear a headscarf in a driver's license photo. Three points are worth noting. First, the views of Religionists and Secularists vary sharply. Religionists are more likely to support the florist; Secularists are more likely to support the Muslim headscarf. Second, as with religious nonestablishment, Non-Religionists and Religious Secularists hold similar attitudes on both issues. Third, attitudes on the Muslim headscarf do not vary much across the four groups, but the two groups most likely to favor the headscarf, Secularists and Religious Secularists, are both high in personal secularism.

The fact that Secularists are supportive of a headscarf photo indicates that their views on religious symbols at school are not driven by animus toward Muslims in particular. Instead, it suggests that they are willing to accept a ban on religious symbols in school – or at least a willingness to defer to schools on the question – if it is applied equally. In this one context at least, American Secularists appear to agree with the French version of secularism, or *laïcité*, in which public expression of religion is curtailed.

BEYOND THE CONSTITUTION: CIVIL RELIGION

One of your authors (Campbell) was reminded of the importance of civil religion when, a few years ago, he spoke in Germany about the role of religion in American politics – a "bread and butter" topic in the analysis of US elections. His presentation was met with incredulity, as many audience members expressed shock that US presidents speak so openly about their faith. In contrast, religion is *verboten* in German elections, not because of a formal stricture but because, culturally, it is considered either inappropriate or irrelevant. In contrast, the public face of the American presidency is steeped in civil religion – speeches that end with "God bless America," an oath of office punctuated with the extra-constitutional phrase "so help me God," and regular appearances of the president with religious leaders.

Our examination of public secularism continues by examining Americans' attitudes toward the president's use of religious symbolism. As public acts by the nation's leader they test what the public sees as the boundaries of the public imprimatur of religion, even if they generally do not raise constitutional questions per se (at least not yet).

We asked SAS respondents whether they approve of presidents talking about their own faith, endorsing religion in general, invoking God in the oath of office, and praying in public. These questions were asked using a 100-point scale, allowing respondents to provide a fine-grained response. The higher the number, the more the public approves of "presidential civil religion." As displayed in Figure 3.7, among the general public, all these forms of presidential civil religion meet with widespread approval, as each receives an average score over 50.[10] Americans are most supportive of presidents who pray in public (73) or speak about their own religion (71). There is slightly less approval for a president who invokes God in the oath of office (68) or endorses religion in general (60). This difference may be explained by the fact that the first two questions involve the president acting out of his or her personal beliefs, while the oath of office and a general endorsement of religion imply that the president is acting in an official capacity, embodying the nation as a whole.

For contrast, Figure 3.7 also includes results for the same four questions asked of members of the AHA.[11] Not surprisingly, these self-identified Secularists are much less likely to approve of each form of presidential civil religion, although their opinion depends on the specific form of religious expression. They are most likely to approve of a president talking about religion (36) – although that is still well below the midpoint of 50. Interestingly, they are modestly more likely to endorse a presidential public prayer (24) than either the expression "so help me God" in the oath of office (16) or a presidential endorsement of religion (14).

In light of the above discussion of free exercise and nonestablishment issues, these results for presidential civil religion naturally raise some further questions. To what extent are these views connected to either a secular or religious

---

[10] In order to ensure that these results are comparable to the AHA data, which come from a survey done in 2011, these were taken from 2012; the 2017 figures are very similar.

[11] These results are from the AHA survey conducted in 2011; see Brockway (2017) for details.

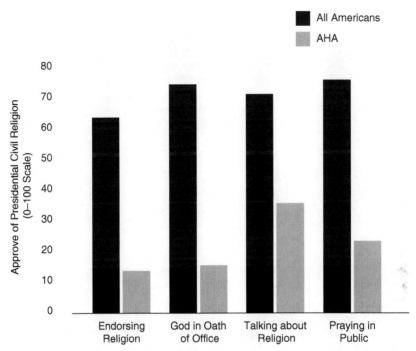

FIGURE 3.7 Most Americans are comfortable with presidential civil religion; AHA members are generally not
Source: 2012 Secular America Study; 2011 American Humanist Association Survey

worldview? Does partisanship matter? To find out, we have again used a statistical model to compare the importance of personal secularism, nonreligiosity, and party identification.[12] For simplicity, we have combined all of the presidential civil-religion questions into a single index. As seen in Figure 3.8, all three variables have a statistically significant, and negative, relationship to approval of presidential civil religion. Nonreligiosity and personal secularism are equal in impact, while party identification lags behind. Hence attitudes toward civil religion are less a matter of partisanship than either the absence of religiosity or a secular worldview.

Figure 3.9 displays the attitudes of the four secular-religious groups (again *sans* any statistical controls). We see that Religionists are the most likely to favor presidential civil religion, Secularists are the least likely, and the other two groups are in between. Just as importantly, however, we see that even among Secularists there is a fairly high degree of support for presidential civil religion.

[12] The presidential civil-religion index is an additive scale of the four items. Cronbach's alpha is .92. The model is identical to those used above, including the same control variables. The data come from the 2017 Secular America Study.

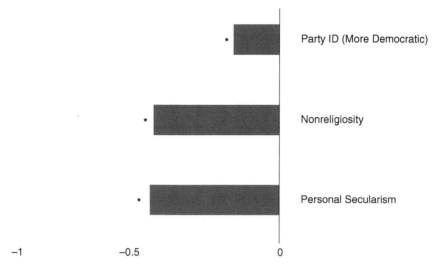

FIGURE 3.8 Personal secularism and nonreligiosity have equal connection to attitudes on presidential civil religion
* = Statistically significant at p < .05
Note: Bars represent the impact, measured as the size of an OLS regression coefficient, of each variable on support for presidential civil religion. Both independent and dependent variables are coded to range from 0 to 1. Model estimated with control variables described in the text.
Source: 2017 Secular America Study

    Notwithstanding the relatively limited role of partisanship, these results still raise the question of whether attitudes toward a president's deployment of religion depend on the president in office. While the survey items on civil religion were asked to gauge opinion about presidents in general, we might nonetheless think that respondents answer with the current president in mind, which in turn would shape their responses depending on what they think of that president. In other words, does having a Democratic or Republican president – Barack Obama or Donald Trump in particular – change people's views on presidential expressions of religion? In a word, the answer is no. When we contrast Americans' attitudes in 2012 (Obama) versus 2017 (Trump), we find very little difference.[13] Americans' views regarding civil religion do not seem to be driven by the identity of the current occupant of the White House.

    Why don't Secularists have the same degree of opposition to presidential civil religion as to the establishment of religion? One explanation may be that civil

---

[13] This statement is based on comparing the data from 2012 to 2017, using the same four-item additive index of presidential civil religion. Using an identical regression model in both years, the results are nearly the same. The coefficients are comparable, and the results generated from the model are nearly identical.

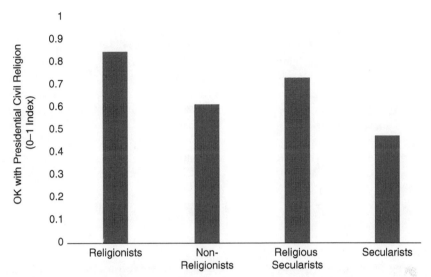

FIGURE 3.9 Religionists are most likely to favor presidential civil religion; Secularists are ambivalent
Source: 2017 Secular America Study

religion does not carry the same weight as law and so does not raise the same level of concern. Another possibility is that civil religion is more akin to views on free exercise than nonestablishment – after all, free exercise applies to individual presidents as well as other citizens. Still another explanation is that, as suggested by the differing reactions of American and German audiences to a discussion of how presidents employ religion, civil religion is so deeply embedded in American culture that it is largely taken for granted by Religionists and Secularists alike.

CONCLUSION

This chapter has accomplished two objectives. First, it has mapped the contours of public opinion on Americans' attitudes toward the separation of church and state, an issue for which a vacuum of data has been filled with heated rhetoric. We have seen that Americans have nuanced views on the question of religion's public role. In general, support for civil religion is high. Likewise, relatively few Americans object to "under God" in the Pledge of Allegiance or the placement of the Ten Commandments in government buildings. Yet fewer are willing to see Christianity declared an official religion.

On the free exercise of religion, Americans' opinions are even more complex. Most believe that high school students should be able to wear religious symbols at school, thus rejecting *laïcité,* the French type of secularism. However, few think that houses of worship should be able to maintain their tax-exempt status if they offer political endorsements. Opinion toward a Muslim exception to a law against headgear in driver's license photos and a business owner's refusal to provide service to LGBTQ customers is mixed. Overall, when it comes to the free exercise of religion, views vary according to who is exercising what.

The chapter's second objective has been to put our measure of personal secularism to the test. Does it add anything to our understanding of what shapes the contours of opinion on public secularism beyond personal nonreligiosity and/or partisanship? The answer is clear: personal secularism cannot simply be reduced to either one. Not only does our measure consistently have a statistically significant connection to public secularism, that connection is usually stronger than that of either nonreligiosity or party identification. It matters.

The growth of personal secularism suggests that the winds of change are blowing for public secularism, especially on issues regarding the nonestablishment of religion. As long as the secular surge continues, it means more Americans will likely hold separationist views like those of the "card-carrying Secularists" within the AHA. Since there is no reason to think that Religionists will abandon their advocacy for religious accommodation – particularly for Christianity – we should expect deeper disagreement on where the legal line should be drawn between church and state. It will be interesting to see if such divisions eventually extend to the custom of presidential civil religion.

Furthermore, it seems likely that public secularism will come to have even more partisan overtones, forming an increasingly salient division between Republicans and Democrats. Throughout this chapter, we have "explained" public secularism by pitting partisanship against both personal secularism and nonreligiosity. This test has served the objective of ensuring that personal secularism offers something new to the understanding of what shapes the public's attitudes on church and state. Such an analysis, though, skirts the possibility that secularism and partisanship influence one another, which we take up in Chapter 5.

Ultimately, however, whether church–state issues become more prominent in our politics depends, in part, on the degree to which Secularists and Religionists are active in the public sphere. A lot of research has shown that religiosity leads to greater civic engagement, including overtly political activity (Putnam and Campbell 2012; Smidt et al. 2008; Verba, Schlozman, and Brady 1995). Chapter 4 looks at whether the same holds true for people who are personally secular.

4

Secularism and Civic Engagement

A few years ago, one of your authors (Campbell) spoke at a conference on interfaith community service held on the campus of George Washington University. Walking into the student center where the conference sessions were held, I was greeted by a familiar scene: amidst the usual hustle and bustle of the student center were tables set up by various student organizations in conjunction with the conference, complete with the usual posters, buttons, T-shirts, and sign-up sheets. Most were religious groups advertising their presence, promoting their charitable service, and seeking new recruits. One table in particular caught my eye. It was far and away the most prominent, as the group seemed especially well organized and eager. Even though the conference was on inter*faith* service, the group at this table was the Secular Student Alliance (SSA), the primary secular organization for high school and college students. Since its founding in 2001 it has grown rapidly, with local chapters nationwide. This particular SSA chapter was determined to demonstrate that secular students are engaged in good works and willing to partner with religious groups to perform community service.

The SSA, however, does not only engage in community voluntarism, but also trains and organizes its members for political action. Its mission states that one objective of the SSA is to "set a course for lifelong activism." In an interview, the SSA's national president, Ken Bolling, described to us how the organization ran a voter registration drive in 2018 and is planning on doing more political activity in 2020.[1] These plans include holding their annual conference in Washington, DC, where attendees will be trained in political action by members of a sister organization, the Secular Coalition for America. They hope to have SSA members put that training to immediate use by lobbying their local representatives.

[1] Interview with Ken Bolling, May 6.

The activities of the SSA raise the question of the extent to which Secularists are engaged in civic activity, both of the political and nonpolitical varieties. Are Secularists civic slackers or doers? On the one hand, examples like the eager chapter of the SSA suggest that Secularists are primed to be highly engaged in civic life. On the other hand, religious folks are generally considered to be the civic stalwarts – the ones who belong to community groups, serve as volunteers, and engage in political activity (Pew Research Center 2019; Putnam and Campbell 2012; Smidt 2003; Smidt et al. 2008). To many observers, the fact that religious Americans are highly engaged implies that secular people – of all kinds – are not.

Once again, it is important to distinguish between nonreligiosity and secularism. Generally speaking, Non-Religionists are indeed civic slackers, while Secularists are actually civic doers. But the story is more complicated than that, as the degree of engagement of Secularists and Religionists depends on whether it is political or not. We find that while Secularists have a moderate level of *nonpolitical* engagement – lower than Religionists, but higher than Non-Religionists – their *political* activity matches that of Religionists.

CIVIC ENGAGEMENT: RELIGIOSITY VERSUS SECULARITY

Civic engagement is defined as public-spirited collective action, such as volunteering for a charitable organization or an election campaign. Note two important elements of this definition. First, "engagement" refers to behavior (what people do) and not attitudes (what people think or feel). Second, civic engagement includes behaviors that both are and are not *political* in nature. This feature requires linguistic specificity, as we need to distinguish between the genus – civic – and the two different but related species, namely activity that does and does not have an explicitly political character. Political activity is directed toward influencing public policy; nonpolitical action lacks a policy motivation (Campbell 2006; Verba, Schlozman, and Brady 1995; Zukin et al. 2006). As examples, volunteering in a homeless shelter is a nonpolitical activity; working for a political candidate who runs on a platform of ending homelessness is political. When we are referring to engagement in general, we describe it as civic; otherwise we distinguish between activity that is political and that which is nonpolitical.

The motivation to examine civic engagement, writ large, is both old and new. Most famously, it was Alexis de Tocqueville who described Americans' penchant for "forever forming associations" (Tocqueville 1995, 513). Such associations – Edmund Burke's "little platoons" – are mediating institutions between the state and the market, or what is often called civil society (Burke 2009). Voluntary associations enable people to come together in a common cause, to engage in collective action for the benefit of others. In an otherwise individualistic society, civil society enables people to learn the art of association

(Bellah et al. 2008). A vibrant civil society makes democracy work (Putnam 1994).

Given their understanding of civil society's significance for a healthy democracy, social scientists began to express concern over the erosion of American civil society in the 1990s (Putnam 2001). Virtually every indicator of civic involvement – both political or not – was in free fall. Today, American society is reeling from the consequences of this decline, as fraying civic bonds have exacerbated Americans' many divisions (Levin 2017).

Until recently, religious organizations had been the rare bulwark against this tide (Finke and Stark 2005; Norris and Inglehart 2011; Putnam 2001). Indeed, a great deal of evidence shows that religion is a source of all sorts of civic engagement. In summarizing many different ways that people can be engaged in public life, Robert Putnam and David Campbell show that "religious Americans are up to twice as civically active as secular Americans" (2012, 454). Importantly, however, their definition of secular refers only to the *absence* of religiosity.

In seeking to explain the strong empirical connection between religiosity and civic engagement, some scholars have emphasized the features of religious participation that foster community involvement. For example, Corwin Smidt and his colleagues write:

Corporate worship is a public occasion, and interaction with other believers occurs in a public space. Participation in these public events and spaces provides a wide variety of opportunities in which to develop an interest in and concern for public life, as well as provides numerous opportunities to learn important civic values and skills. (2008, 11)

It is easy to see how places of worship are incubators of nonpolitical forms of engagement, both inside the congregation and out – think mission trips, soup kitchens, summer camps, and the like. Congregations often foster political activity too. Although it would be inaccurate to describe most congregations as hotbeds of political activism, religious institutions often cultivate the capacity for people to become involved in politics. The skills learned doing the Lord's work are transferable to the work of Caesar.

In their seminal research, Sidney Verba, Kay Schlozman, and Henry Brady (1995) demonstrate that religious congregations are where many Americans learn to run meetings, give speeches, write letters, and mobilize others in a cause. Furthermore, religious institutions are uniquely able to mobilize large numbers of people. What other type of organization assembles so many people on a weekly basis, to hear moral instruction reinforced with powerful symbols and music, often accompanied by requests to give of their time and treasure to charitable causes, and occasionally by political appeals?

In contrast, most secular people do not have the same opportunities to share in the sort of common culture fostered by religion. This point is captured by comedian Steve Martin's satirical song "Atheists Don't Have No Songs." As the lyrics go, "Born agains sing He is risen, but no one ever wrote a tune for godless existentialism." And while "Lutherans have their Christmas trees," atheists "do have Sundays free."[2]

The literature on religion and civic engagement – not to mention Steve Martin – could easily leave the impression that all irreligious people are sitting on the civic sidelines. Yet, just because religious institutions do a lot to foster civic engagement, it does not necessarily mean that the secular population is uniformly disengaged. Not all civic activity is rooted in religion, as much civic engagement is motivated by secular causes. Secularists, recall, have a well-defined worldview and therefore might be engaged in organizations that advance causes that matter to them (just without the songs). As supporting evidence suggesting that personal secularism can foster engagement, Jacqui Frost and Penny Edgell (2018) find that people who define themselves by what they are – atheists, agnostic, spiritual but not religious – are more civically engaged than people who are simply not religious, for example the Nones. Put another way, personal secularism is an alternative to religion in kind and not just degree. In contrast, we would expect the nonreligious to be civic dropouts. They have little or no involvement with religion, and also do not have an alternate identity or worldview. It makes sense that they would not be invested in other civic institutions: their noninvolvement in religion is probably symptomatic of a broader disconnection with civil society.

SOCIAL CAPITAL

An important – arguably the most important – reason that religiosity leads to high levels of engagement is that religious organizations foster social networks that drive civic engagement, of both the political and nonpolitical varieties. While there are many precursors to an individual's civic engagement, social networks are especially important for understanding what it is about religious involvement specifically that spurs civic involvement. Civic engagement of all types is facilitated by interpersonal connections, also known as social capital, as such networks foster a sense of generalized reciprocity and trust in other people. As people form networks of reciprocity and trust they are able to overcome the dismal logic of collective action. Individuals only interested in weighing their personal costs and benefits would, rationally, never do anything for the collective good. But when embedded in a network of social relationships – that is, when social capital is high – people are more likely to act for the benefit of the commonweal (Coleman 1990; 1988; Halpern 2005; Putnam 1994).

Here we use the term social network in its original meaning of relationships between actual human beings, "in real life," and not merely the online version

---

[2] For video of Martin performing the song, accompanied by the Steep Canyon Rangers, see www .youtube.com/watch?v=xmwAD7nHqaY. Lyrics available at www.lyricsmode.com/lyrics/s/ste-ve_martin/atheists_dont_have_no_songs.html.

of networks formed through social media such as Facebook. Having a wider network – that is, knowing more people – means more opportunities for people to ask for participation in something (a food bank, blood drive, and so on). Networks are all the more impactful when their members share a collective identity or common worldview. In the language of the social capital literature, these are bonding relationships, in which birds of a feather flock together (Putnam 2001). They are in contrast to bridging social capital, which consists of relationships among people with different backgrounds. While bridging has many other salubrious effects (including fostering tolerance) it is more often bonding relationships that spur people to action (Mutz 2006), and that will therefore be our focus.

Among the ways in which people can bond, social networks among coreligionists are especially effective in fostering civic engagement of all types. This result is because (a) religious groups are often engaged in social causes, and therefore there are many requests to get involved and (b) those requests come from people with shared interests and a common moral vocabulary. In other words, people enmeshed in a religious community are often asked to do things by a lot of people to whom it is hard to say no. In fact, past research on the links between religion and civic engagement has found that the primary explanation for why religious people are so civically involved lies in the social networks formed through their religious community and not in the doctrinal beliefs espoused by their religion (Putnam and Campbell 2012). However, being embedded in a network of people who share a common worldview not only leads to volunteering for the choir or a food drive, but can spur overtly political activity as well. In the words of Diana Mutz, "like-minded social environments are ideal for purposes of encouraging political mobilization" (2006, 127).

The fact that civic engagement has its roots in social relationships opens up the possibility of a parallel between religiosity and secularity. If secular Americans are able to form social networks with people who share their worldview, it suggests that they may also have a relatively high level of civic engagement, even absent the trappings of religious involvement.

SECULAR AND RELIGIOUS AMERICANS' SOCIAL NETWORKS

We start our examination of civic engagement among religious and secular Americans by comparing their social networks, using the 2017 Secular America Study (SAS). Respondents were asked about their social networks, specifically whether they have friends who share either their religious or secular views. Those who, earlier in the survey, indicated that they have a religious affiliation were asked how many of their five closest friends share their religion, while those who identified themselves as atheists, agnostics, or religiously unaffiliated were asked how many of their five closest friends "have a secular view of the world." Asking about one's five closest friends is a good measure of close, but nonfamilial, relationships, broader than a single best friend but more circumscribed than one's entire set of friends or acquaintances.

Among Americans with a religious affiliation, on average three of their five closest friends share their religion; secular Americans have only 1.5 friends with a secularly oriented view of the world.[3] In comparison, members of the American Humanist Association (AHA) – who, recall, are self-identified Secularists – report that roughly half of their closest friends share their worldview. Speaking of "fractions of friends" is rather artificial, so a more intuitive way to think about these statistics is that religious Americans report that over half of their five closest friends share their religion, while secular Americans in the general population say that a majority of their friends do not share their secular outlook on life. Members of the AHA, a rough analog to church members, are in between – with fewer like-minded friends than religious Americans but more than Secularists in general.

We should not be surprised that secular people have fewer like-minded friends than do religious folks. It is likely more difficult for members of the secular population to find friends with their worldview, as there are simply more Americans who are religious versus secular. That is to say, the pool is smaller. Similarly, we would expect Harry Potter aficionados to find it easy to befriend fellow wizarding enthusiasts; fans of a less popular franchise will have a more difficult time finding friends who share their interest. Secularists' difficulty in finding like-minded compatriots is compounded by the social stigma still associated with secularism in some circles, which means that many people with a secular self-identity may not advertise that fact.

Further compounding the challenge of Secularists forming simpatico networks, it is not easy to find organized groups of secular people, especially when compared to the ubiquity of religious congregations. Over the years of our research, we have experimented with different ways to tap into such participation. Asking about "secular" organizations is not sufficient, since in common parlance that word can simply mean "not religious," and could thus include everything from the Kiwanis Club to a college alumni association. In the 2010 SAS, we asked respondents who chose at least one in a series of secular identities whether they also belong to "an organization for people who don't believe in religion."[4] Only 2.5 percent said they did. In the 2017 SAS, we asked a similar question about participation in a secular group, but first included a definition of secularism:

---

[3] This difference is statistically significant at p < .01.

[4] The identities are atheist, agnostic, secular, humanist, or deist. As we obviously created this survey before we knew the frequency with which Americans would select the various secular identities, we included "deist" as a screener for the question about belonging to a secular group. We found that vanishingly few Americans describe themselves as deists, and thus it is not included in our subsequent analyses of secular identities. Nonetheless, in 2010 two respondents identified as deists who belonged to a secular group.

People seek to understand the world and their lives in a variety of ways. Some people rely on secular perspectives (or secularism), meaning that they view the world in non-religious, humanist, or rational ways. How often do you do the following things?

We then asked about a series of potential secular activities, including "belonging to a group that promotes secularism." When asked this way, roughly 4 percent of the population say that they belong to an organization that promotes secularism, which could be anything from the AHA to the SSA.[5] Given that membership totals of such Secularist advocacy groups are nowhere near this size, it must be that our respondents took an expansive view of what constitutes a secularism-promoting organization – perhaps thinking of museums, schools, and scientific associations. Even with an expansive definition, though, this figure is still a far smaller share of the population than that of those who attend religious services.

It is also possible that asking about membership in a formal organization undercounts the level of secular social capital, as it could be that Secularists are more likely to gather informally in, say, coffee shops and bookstores. To capture the degree to which Americans are gathering in an unstructured environment in which they engage in secular talk, we also asked how often our respondents discuss secular perspectives as a way of understanding the world with their family and friends. While 38 percent of Americans say they do this occasionally, only 7 percent do so frequently. This figure means a majority, 55 percent, never engage in any conversation regarding a secular worldview. In contrast, an overwhelming majority of Americans – 90 percent – discuss religion with their family and friends at least occasionally, and 57 percent do so at least monthly.[6]

Among the general public, the results for both formal membership and informal gatherings align with the data on friendships – religious and secular Americans differ in their networks of bonding social capital, which in turn likely corresponds to their level of civic engagement. Importantly, however, other evidence from the AHA suggests that, while atheists may not have any songs, this does not necessarily mean that they are intrinsically incapable of being organized, either formally or informally. Roughly half of the AHA members, for example, report that they gather in groups of fellow Secularists at least occasionally (14 percent do so frequently), while 20 percent report at least some participation in AHA activities.[7] Even more common among the AHA

---

[5] We also asked whether they "gather with larger groups of people who share a secular perspective," in case there are gatherings that do not fall under the auspices of a formal organization. Four percent of the population also say that they do this "frequently," essentially identical to membership in secular organizations.

[6] Data from the Faith Matters survey (Putnam and Campbell 2012).

[7] One quarter of AHA members reported attending some sort of local group at least a few times a year, including a local humanist community, an Ethical Society, a Jewish humanist congregation, a Unitarian-Universalist Fellowship, a Sunday Assembly, a Quaker meeting, or the events of local atheist, freethought, and secular groups.

members are conversations with friends and family about secularism. Eighty percent report having these conversations at least occasionally, including 21 percent who have them frequently.

Keep in mind, though, that these data do not tell us anything about the nature of the interactions within these networks. Specifically, we do not know whether religious and secular Americans differ in the types of engagement they discuss among their like-minded friends. For example, given the myriad charitable endeavors sponsored by religious groups, it could be that Religionists are more likely to encourage one another to engage in charitable activity. Contrariwise, we might expect Secularists to be highly engaged in politics, given that secularism is a strong predictor of political attitudes (see Chapter 5).

In sum, while there are hints, these data leave unclear whether we should expect secular people to have a level of civic engagement to rival that of people who are religiously committed, and if it matters whether the activity is political in nature or not. These are empirical questions, to which we turn next.

VARIETIES OF ENGAGEMENT

As we have noted, past research has long shown that religious involvement leads to civic engagement of all types; accordingly, we find that being nonreligious – the absence of religiosity – means a low level of civic involvement. So, what's new? Our contribution is that secularism is *positively* related to civic engagement. The absence of religiosity means less civic engagement, while the presence of a secular worldview means more. In more technical terms, no matter how civic engagement is measured in a statistical model, our nonreligiosity scale has a negative relationship with civic engagement while our personal secularism scale has a positive relationship – and both scales have a large impact that is statistically significant.

Figure 4.1 has the details. Nonpolitical activity includes community volunteering and membership in civic groups, while political participation encompasses a wide range of activities from voting to working on a political campaign to posting political content on social media.[8] (For those who are interested, A Closer Look 4.1 provides more detail on how civic engagement has been measured.) The bars show the size of the statistical relationship that personal secularism and nonreligiosity have with civic engagement, both of the political and nonpolitical variety. For comparison, we also display the magnitude of two variables commonly referenced in the literature on civic engagement: education and age. Note that personal secularism has a positive impact on both political and nonpolitical engagement; in contrast, nonreligiosity has a negative

---

[8] These indices have been constructed to simplify the presentation of results, as the patterns reported here hold for each individual form of participation, although the frequency of different actions of course vary. For the purposes of Figures 4.1 and 4.2, the two indices have been coded on a 0–1 scale.

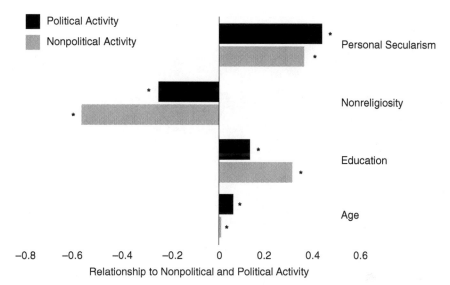

FIGURE 4.1 More secularism means more civic engagement – both political and nonpolitical

* = Statistically significant at p < .05

Note: Bars represent the impact, measured as the size of an OLS regression coefficient, of each variable on levels of civic engagement. Both independent and dependent variables are coded to range from 0 to 1.

Source: 2017 Secular America Study

impact (another way of saying, of course, that religiosity has a positive impact). We also draw your attention to the fact that personal secularism has a larger impact than age and, especially, education – the latter being the most consistent predictor of civic engagement (Nie, Junn, and Stehlik-Barry 1996).[9]

Because nonreligiosity and secularism work at cross-purposes for civic engagement, it is informative to compare people who are high and/or low on each by means of our four secular-religious groups (see Chapter 2 for details). Figure 4.2 displays how these four groups vary in their levels of civic engagement, political and nonpolitical.

Looking first at nonpolitical activity, we see that the Non-Religionists have the lowest level of engagement of the four groups. As we suspected, their disengagement from both religion and a secular worldview corresponds with

---

[9] Figure 4.1 is based on OLS regression models in which indices of nonpolitical and political activity are regressed on both nonreligiosity and personal secularism, with a suite of standard demographic controls (age, education, gender, African American, Hispanic, white evangelical Protestant, mainline Protestant, Catholic). All variables are coded on a 0–1 scale. Both the size and direction of the relationships that secularism and nonreligiosity have with both types of civic engagement are virtually unchanged with or without controls.

A Closer Look 4.1:
How We Measured Civic Engagement

We measure civic engagement with two additive indices for nonpolitical and political activity respectively. In other words, each index simply tallies the number of activities the respondent has performed. Each index is then recoded to be on a 0–1 scale.

Nonpolitical Activity

Volunteering

Some people volunteer, others don't. Did you happen to volunteer in the past 12 months? By volunteering, we mean any unpaid work you've done to help people besides your family and friends or people you work with. Yes/No

Group Membership

Respondents were asked about their membership in a variety of organizations; religious groups were not included. Thus, we are not stacking the deck in favor of finding a connection between religiosity and organizational membership. Specifically, the question asks:

> Have you been involved with any of the following types of groups or organizations in the past 12 months? Yes/No
> A hobby, sports, arts, music, or other leisure activity group
> A service, social welfare, or fraternal organization
> A youth, parent, or school-support organization
> A professional, trade, farm, or business association
> A neighborhood, ethnic or political association
> A support group or self-help program for people with specific illnesses, disabilities, problems, or addictions, or for their families

Political Activity

Voting

Thinking back to the 2016 election, in which Donald Trump and Hillary Clinton ran for President, do you remember for sure whether or not you voted in that election? (Check all that apply)

- I did not vote in this election.
- I thought about voting, but didn't.
- I usually vote, but didn't this time.
- I am not eligible to vote.
- I am sure that I voted.
- "I am sure that I voted" coded as 1, all others as 0.

Other Political Activity

In the past month, did you do any of the following things?
- Persuasion: Try to convince anyone that they should vote for or against a party or candidate
- Attend Rally: Go to political meetings, rallies, speeches, dinners, or things like that in support of a particular candidate or party
- Wear Button: Wear a campaign button, put a campaign sticker on your car, or place a sign in your window or in front of your house
- Work for a Campaign: Do any work for a party or candidate
- Give Money: Give money to a party or candidate
- Attend March: Take part in a protest, march, or demonstration
- Boycott or Buycott: Buy or boycott a certain product or service because of the social or political values of the company that provides it
- Social Media: Post anything on social media about a political candidate or party
- Contact Official: Contact or visit a public official – at any level of government – to express your opinion.

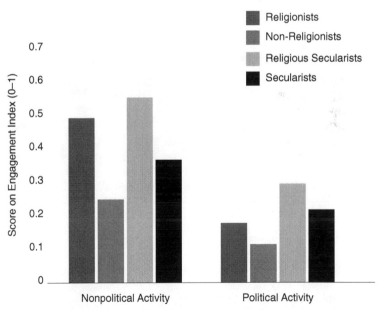

FIGURE 4.2 Comparing civic engagement across the secular-religious groups
Source: 2017 Secular America Study

a similar disengagement from civic life. Compared to the Non-Religionists, Secularists have a higher degree of nonpolitical activity, revealing that the presence of a secular worldview boosts civic engagement. Nonetheless, personal secularism pales in comparison to religiosity as an accelerant of the nonpolitical variety of civic engagement, as Religionists are much more engaged than Secularists. But note that the Religious Secularists, who combine both religiosity and secularism, are the most engaged in nonpolitical activity, suggesting that a mixture of religion and a secular worldview is civically combustible. Instead of the two ingredients canceling each other out, they spark an even greater reaction than either one alone.[10]

For political activity, we again see the highest degree of engagement for the Religious Secularists and the lowest for the Non-Religionists – mirroring the pattern for nonpolitical activity. Most notable, however, is where the nonpolitical and political results differ: instead of being far apart, Religionists and Secularists have nearly the same degree of political engagement, and Religious Secularists are again highest.

The high level of political activity among Secularists is confirmed by the membership of the AHA members. While, as members of an association, we would expect them to have a relatively high level of civic engagement, they nonetheless have a remarkable degree of political activism. For example, 30 percent of them report having worked on a presidential campaign in the past. Forty percent have contributed money to a presidential candidate just in the past year. Nearly half have attended a rally or protest at some point, while 34 percent have done so in the previous twelve months.

With the cross-sectional data we have, a definitive causal explanation for the connection between secularism and civic engagement remains elusive, although we suspect that it parallels the explanation for religiosity's connection to engagement, namely social networks of like-minded people.

One way to see the impact of social networks on civic engagement is to simulate what the levels of civic engagement would be if the social networks of religious and secular Americans were comparable. In other words, what would happen if secular Americans had as many secular friends as religious Americans have religious friends? When we use a statistical model to simulate a world in which both religious and secular Americans report that five of their closest friends share their worldview, we find that the degree of nonpolitical engagement is almost identical.[11] But for political engagement, Secularists are

---

[10] As a further test that nonreligiosity and personal secularism work in tandem, in an OLS model, an interaction term between the two scales is positive and statistically significant (p = .02) for nonpolitical engagement, and positive and nearly significant (p = .14) for political engagement.

[11] Results based on an OLS regression model including separate variables for number of co-Religionist and co-Secularist friends (coded 0 if it does not apply, e.g. Secularist friends for someone with a religious affiliation), as well as the indices for personal secularism and non-religiosity. Religionists with five co-Religionist friends have a slightly higher level of nonpolitical engagement (.504) than Secularists with five friends with a secular worldview (.479), but the

well ahead of Religionists. When religious folks are friends, it corresponds to a slight rise in political engagement; friendships among Secularists lead to a much greater increase. Obviously, such a simulation is purely hypothetical, since it assumes a world in which everything else remains constant, when other things would almost certainly change. This sort of simulation is nonetheless a useful exercise, as it underscores the link between social networks and civic engagement.

CONCLUSION

In light of the long-standing concern about America's civic health, these results indicate that one should not conclude that the secular surge necessarily means a major blow to the nation's dwindling stock of social capital. While we only have data from one point in time and thus must be cautious about projecting trends, we nonetheless engage in some speculation about what is to come. There is wisdom in the adage that prediction is hard, especially about the future.

If one only knew that nonreligiosity was rising, it would appear that civic engagement is destined to decline even further. But such an extrapolation is too naive. That growth in nonreligiosity is counterbalanced by an accompanying rise in secularism which, as we have seen, leads to greater civic engagement. Furthermore, these results also suggest that as the number of Secularist Americans grows – making it easier for Secularists to find and befriend one another – their political activity is likely to increase. As a consequence, it appears that a growth in secularism could change the mix between nonpolitical and political engagement, leading to more of the latter.

The finding that secular social networks correspond to greater political engagement is consistent with the other evidence we have presented that secularism and politics are intertwined. Religionists are highly engaged in politics too, of course, but their political engagement often exists alongside their nonpolitical engagement. While hardly civic deadbeats, Secularists are more likely to specialize in politics.

We are not alone in drawing a connection between secularism and high levels of political engagement. In discussing results from a recent study by the Public Religion Research Institute, Emma Green of *The Atlantic* describes the growing secular population as greatly politicized, even suggesting that, for them, politics has replaced other forms of identity such as ethnicity and even religion. In her words:

---

difference is not statistically significant. For political engagement, Religionists with five friends of the same religion score .215 on the index, compared to .247 for Secularists with a fully secular friendship network, a difference that is significant at $p < .10$. The variable for religious friends is not statistically significant, while the one for secular friends is ($p < .01$). That is to say, while adding more religious friends does not boost nonpolitical engagement for Religionists (once nonreligiosity is controlled), adding more secular friends does for Secularists.

Religiously unaffiliated voters, who may or may not be associated with other civic institutions, seem most excited about supporting or donating to causes, going to rallies, and expressing opinions online, among other activities. Political engagement may be providing these Americans with a new form of identity. (2018)

While Green is painting with a broad brush by referring to religiously unaffiliated voters, the politicization she observes is far more pronounced among Secularist Americans.

The heightened political engagement within Secularists' social networks leads to the question of how those relationships come to be. How, when, and why do secular Americans find one another, especially given that few belong to organizations that promote secularism, or gather in groups with other Secularists? In some cases, it may be that a common political cause has brought these people together. Perhaps they became friends because of a shared political affiliation. Instead of secular friendships leading to political activity, it could be that political activity led to the friendships. Or even if they formed friendships on other grounds, it could be that politics deepens their bond. It might even be that they became friends because of a shared political perspective, which in turn has led them to become more secular. Even if the precise causal mechanism linking secularism and civic engagement remains a question for future research, the existence of the connection is nonetheless noteworthy. The bottom line is that Secularists are as engaged in politics as religious Americans.

The uncanny equivalence in political participation among secular and religious Americans suggests two opposing groups squaring off in the public arena. But is that really the case? Where do Secularists direct their political energy? Chapter 5 takes up that question, examining how secularism shapes both partisan and policy preferences, but also how political views can shape secularism.

5

Secularism and Political Attitudes

In detailed interviews we conducted with several of our respondents to the 2017 Secular America Study (SAS), many people noted a clear link between secularism and American party politics – with the Republican Party being more religious and the Democratic Party more secular. Kelly, for example, notes that "My sister is a far-right Republican and is conservative religious. Those things seem like they go together. Religion is driving people to the right. Secular is linked to Democrat." Another interviewee, Brendon, agrees, noting that "In my opinion, my lack of faith translates into being more progressive. Most religious people are conservative." Likewise, Linda, who views herself as nonreligious, says "I think the Democratic Party is more attractive to people who aren't religious. The two things [politics and nonreligion] are tied together. Democrats attract people who aren't religious to them." Matt makes the connection most colorfully, saying that politics and religion "definitely go together, but maybe they shouldn't. I vote Democrat because Republicans shove religion down your throat."

This perceived connection between religious people and the GOP, on the one hand, and between secular people and the Democrats, on the other hand, extended to our full 2017 SAS sample. We asked respondents to tell us whether they thought of the members of various religious and secular social groups as "mainly Democrats, mainly Republicans, or a pretty even mix of both." In Figure 5.1, we show the responses to these questions for four groups: evangelical Christians, "religious people," "people who aren't religious," and atheists.

Given the American public's notorious inattention to politics, it is perhaps not surprising that the plurality choice for most groups was "a pretty even mix" of Democrats and Republicans. Evangelical Christians were the only group that a majority of respondents connected to a party, and a clear majority viewed evangelicals as "mainly Republicans." A partisan image is not quite as strong

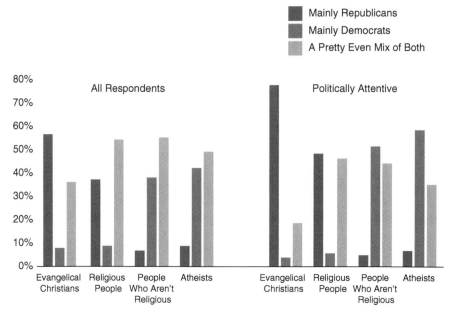

FIGURE 5.1 Americans associate religion with the Republicans, secularism with the Democrats
Source: 2017 Secular America Study

for the other groups, but far more people linked "religious people" to the Republicans than to the Democrats. Meanwhile, more respondents saw "people who aren't religious" and atheists as "mainly Democrats" than as "mainly Republicans."

The picture is even clearer if we look at politically attentive people – respondents who say they follow news and politics most of the time and talk with their friends and family about politics at least weekly. Over three fourths of this group says evangelicals are mainly Republicans. Nearly three fifths view atheists as mainly Democrats. A majority sees nonreligious people aligning with the Democratic Party. And half see religious people as mainly Republicans. In short, the American public – especially the attentive public – recognizes a connection between religious and secular people and the major political parties.

Interestingly, however, our respondents offer different accounts of the reason for this connection. Some identify religion and secularity as the catalysts, believing that religion is "driving people to the right" or that nonreligion "translates into being more progressive." Others seem to suggest that their political attachments and their perspectives on religion in politics drive their religious and secular orientations. John falls into that camp when he says that Donald Trump's presidency has caused him to "become stronger in [his] beliefs as an atheist." The reason, he says, is that "religious people who support Trump are hypocrites." William provides a similar perspective, but attributes his move away from religion more to political issues such as abortion and same-sex marriage. He notes that "in college social views turned me away from religion, pushed me away from religion on things like marriage equality and abortion."

Another group of people see influence in both directions. When we asked Linda, who recently has abandoned her attachment to the GOP and begun to vote for Democratic candidates, whether she has changed her political ties because of religion or her religious tendencies because of politics, she replied "I think both. I mean it is hard to ignore it when they [Republicans] flaunt it [religion] so much."

Whether or not our respondents' perceptions are correct points to the key question of this chapter: What are the implications of the secular surge for the political attitudes and behaviors of American citizens? Are secularism and nonreligiosity connected to political orientations such as party identification, ideology, attitudes on policy issues, and evaluations of political candidates? Is the connection due to people bringing their political attitudes into line with their secular and religious orientations or to these orientations changing in response to politics? Is secularism or nonreligiosity more strongly related to Americans' political attitudes?

The answers to these questions may have implications for not only secularism's political importance, but also the nature of American political polarization. If the divide between secular and religious people is linked to political attitudes, that may help explain ideological polarization – ordinary Republicans and Democrats moving farther apart ideologically and on policy issues. Because of their fundamentally different ways of understanding the world and humans' place in it, Secularists and Religionists should have sharply different views on policy issues and help to push their respective political camps farther apart on those issues.

A secular–religious divide in politics also may illuminate why, above and beyond their ideological differences, ordinary Democrats and Republicans increasingly dislike and distrust the leaders and members of the other political camp – what political scientists have labeled "affective polarization" (Iyengar and Westwood 2015; Martherus et al. 2019; Mason 2018). Their very different worldviews may spur Secularists and Religionists to view each other with suspicion and perhaps even hostility, thus encouraging animosity and distrust between their political teams.

Secularism's connection to politics also may shed light on a related debate about whether the political divide in the US public is characterized by "sorting" or "polarization." Some scholars argue that growing ideological distance between the Democratic and Republican coalitions is mainly people sorting themselves into the parties based on ideology – liberals growing more Democratic and conservatives more Republican (Fiorina, Abrams, and Pope

2011). Others see real increases in mass polarization (Abramowitz 2010), due in part to Democrats' policy views moving in a liberal direction and Republicans growing more conservative (Layman and Carsey 2002; Levendusky 2010).

Sorting and polarization also represent alternative explanations for the growing political divide between secular and religious people. As we noted in Chapter 1, part of the reason for America's secular surge may lie in politics – Democrats and liberals abandoning religion and growing more secular in response to the connection between traditional religiosity and the Republican Party (e.g. Hout and Fischer 2014). The flip side may be that Republican identifiers are growing even more religious (Patrikios 2008; Schnabel and Bock 2017, 2018). If this change is occurring, then we may be witnessing politically driven polarization: increases in the secular population coming disproportionately from Democratic and liberal citizens, while traditional religion increases primarily among Republicans and conservatives. But if secularism and religiosity independently influence citizens' political orientations, then political sorting is underway. In other words, Secularists are moving into the Democratic and liberal camps, while Religionists draft themselves onto the Republican and conservative teams.

Finally, whether nonreligiosity or secularism is more strongly associated with citizen politics also has implications for polarization. If nonreligiosity is most important, that may suggest that the long-standing political divide between more and less religious Americans continues to be deep, but might dissipate as the nonreligious population grows. However, if secularism is most important, a very different type of political divide – one based less on how religious people are and more on how much they embrace secular beliefs and identities – may be emerging. And, with secularism gaining ground in the American public, such a political cleavage may be with us for some time.

We examine secularism and American political attitudes with data from the 2017 SAS and the 2010–2012 SAS panel. We first use the 2017 data to examine the connections of secularism and nonreligiosity to Americans' political orientations. Our evidence confirms the connection between secularism and political behavior and shows that secularism is more closely connected than nonreligiosity to politics.

Next, we turn to our panel data to assess whether secularism and nonreligiosity are associated with changes in citizens' political tendencies or whether they simply change in response to political factors. We find that political orientations do encourage change in both secularism and nonreligiosity, but there is reciprocal movement as well: changes in citizen politics are related to secular orientations. However, only secularism is associated with political change. Nonreligiosity moves in response to political orientations, but does not encourage political movement itself.[1]

---

[1] A similar analysis of the 2010–2012 panel data appears in Campbell et al. (2018).

SECULARISM, NONRELIGIOSITY, AND POLITICAL ATTITUDES

A long-standing literature documents the "religion gap," the clear political divisions between religious and nonreligious Americans (Green 2007; Putnam and Campbell 2012). But is there a clear political divide between secular and nonsecular people? Is the "secular" gap in political orientations as large as, or larger than, the nonreligiosity gap? In Figure 5.2, we show the party loyalties and 2016 presidential voting decisions of people at the low (bottom quartile) and high (top quartile) ends of the secularism and nonreligiosity scales we developed in Chapter 2.

There are indeed large secularism and nonreligiosity gaps in American electoral politics. People high in secularism are much more likely than people low in secularism to identify with the Democratic Party and to have voted for Democratic candidate Hillary Clinton. And nonreligious people are markedly more likely than religious people to identify and vote Democratic.

However, the secularism gap between the parties in the electorate is somewhat larger than the nonreligiosity gap. For example, nearly 65 percent of the most secular citizens identify as Democrats while only 27 percent of the least secular are Democrats – a 38-point gap – while the difference in Democratic identification between the least religious and most religious Americans is only 18 percentage points (51 to 33 percent).[2]

The pattern for the 2016 presidential vote is similar. There is a 52-point gap between the most secular (82 percent for Clinton) and least secular citizens (30 percent for Clinton). That compares to a 38-point gap between support for Hillary Clinton among the least religious (72 percent) and most religious (34 percent) Americans. Thus, the nonreligiosity gap in American partisanship and voting behavior remains substantial. However, the secularism divide may be even larger, as Secularists seem to be even more attracted than nonreligious people to the Democratic Party and its candidates.

This pattern is not surprising. We would expect secularism to be important for citizens' political attitudes, attachments, and decisions, because it encompasses commitment to a set of distinctive beliefs and a sense of social identity. As we noted in Chapter 1, the worldview of Secularists provides a cognitive basis for consistent political perspectives. This political consistency should extend to liberal political values, progressive positions on a range of policy issues, and to Democratic identification and electoral support. Likewise, a Secularist identity also is politically important because social identity shapes policy attitudes (Brady and Sniderman 1985), underlies party

---

[2] Readers may find it surprising that such a high percentage of the most religious Americans identify with the Democratic Party. This pattern is largely due to racial minority groups being both more religious and more Democratic than whites. Over 34 percent of African Americans and over 30 percent of Latinos are in the most religious group as compared to 22 percent of whites. Meanwhile, 67 percent of blacks and 54 percent of Latinos identify as Democrats, while only 37 percent of whites are Democrats.

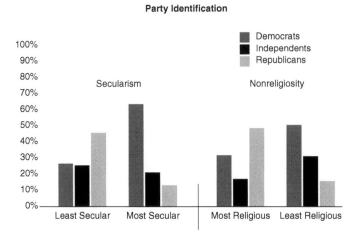

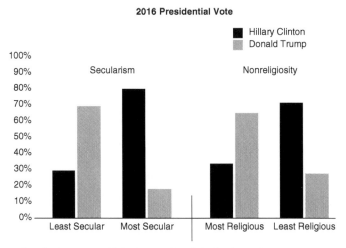

FIGURE 5.2 Secularism, nonreligiosity, and political orientations
Source: 2017 Secular America Study

attachment (Green, Palmquist, and Schickler 2002), and encourages a sense of group consciousness that motivates electoral behavior (Achen and Bartels 2016). In contrast, nonreligiosity is defined by an absence of belief and identity – forsaking religion, but not necessarily embracing a secular worldview. That may make nonreligious people less likely to display the distinctly Democratic and liberal tendencies exhibited by Secularists.

To further evaluate the secularism and nonreligiosity gaps, we take a page from the literature on American voting behavior and examine their connections to the long-term and short-term factors that structure citizens' electoral decisions (Campbell et al. 1960; Lewis-Beck 2008; Miller and Shanks 1996). We do this not because we want to assert a specific causal ordering to political orientations, but simply to help us identify where and when secularism and nonreligiosity are politically relevant.

Partisanship, Ideology, and Core Values

We turn first to long-term factors that persist over time and shape how citizens feel about particular issues and candidates. That means starting with the preeminent long-term factor in American electoral behavior: party identification (Campbell et al. 1960; Lewis-Beck 2008). Most research on the partisanship of secular people has focused on Non-Religionists and found them to be largely independent of the two major political parties (Green 2007; Layman 2001). As noted in Chapter 4, one explanation is that these citizens' detachment from religion may be a symptom of a general disconnection from societal institutions – particularly institutions like political parties that traditionally have based their coalitions within the major religious traditions (Layman and Green 2006). So, even though nonreligious voters typically support Democratic candidates, they may do so not because of an affinity for the Democratic Party, but because they are opposed to the Republican Party – the party most closely associated with traditional religion.

By contrast, the special beliefs and identities of Secularists may foster a positive attachment to the Democratic Party. Secularist identity may be particularly important for partisanship as some scholars see party identification itself as a social identity, grounded in the social groups associated with the parties (Green, Palmquist, and Schickler 2002; Greene 1999). Thus, people who identify themselves as Secularists may be especially likely to identify as Democrats. Strongly supporting this expectation is the partisanship of organized humanists – 93 percent of our American Humanist Association (AHA) respondents identify as Democrats and 58 percent call themselves strong Democrats.

Other long-term elements in Americans' political dossiers include ideological identification – attachment to liberal or conservative ideological labels (Kinder and Kalmoe 2017) – as well as "core" values. Such values include moral relativism – the belief that moral standards change with the circumstances of human existence (Layman 2001) – and its opposite, moral traditionalism. Other core values are humanitarianism, "the belief that people have responsibilities toward their fellow human beings and should come to the assistance of others in need" (Feldman and Steenbergen 2001, 659); egalitarianism, a commitment to the fundamental equality of all people (McClosky and Zaller 1987); and authoritarianism, a preference for conformity and obedience to authority over freedom and diversity (Hetherington and Weiler 2009).

Both secularism and nonreligiosity should be related to liberal ideological identification as well as moral relativism. Nonreligiosity's connection to both follows from religiosity's long-standing relationship with conservatism and moral traditionalism (Smidt, Kellstedt, and Guth 2009). Meanwhile, both proponents and detractors of secularism describe it as liberal or "progressive." David Niose (2014), past president of the AHA, notes that "it would be hard to find two words that better define 'humanist' than one who is secular ... and progressive." Conservatives warn of the dire threats posed by the "Secular Progressive Movement" (O'Reilly 2006). Here, too, these expectations are supported by the AHA members: 91 percent identify as liberal and 20 percent as extremely liberal.

Secularism also should strongly encourage moral relativism because of its humanist and rationalist view that moral principles derive from human experience and evidence rather than transcendent sources.[3] As the Atheist Alliance claims, "morality exists independently of God and, given enough time, humans could discover it through reasoning."[4]

We anticipate less similarity in how secularism and nonreligiosity are connected to other core values. Take, for example, humanitarianism. In *The Principles of Secularism*, George Holyoake declares that "Secularism is the study of promoting human welfare by material means; measuring human welfare by the utilitarian rule, and making the service of others a duty of life" (1871, 11). By contrast, without a devotion to humanist principles, nonreligious people should not be particularly humanitarian. In fact, because most religions emphasize charity and concern for the less fortunate, nonreligious citizens may put less priority on humanitarianism than religious people.

The story is similar for egalitarianism and authoritarianism. The human development goals of secular humanists may foster a commitment to equality. As Niose puts it, secular humanists' "egalitarianism comes not from any divine commandments or revelation, but from the naturalistic and pragmatic principles underlying humanism" (2015). Secularism also should discourage authoritarianism by emphasizing a "free-thinking" questioning of authority and disavowing homogeneity in belief and principles. As Holyoake contends, "Secularism accepts no authority but that of Nature. ... Secular principles involve for mankind a future, where there shall exist unity of condition with infinite diversity of intellect" (1871, 13–14). Meanwhile, some religions emphasize social and economic equality and others do not, and religiosity's connection to authoritarian views varies across faith traditions (Mockabee 2007). Thus, nonreligiosity's link to egalitarianism and authoritarianism is unclear.

---

[3] The AHA member surveys also reveal strong support for moral relativism, humanitarianism and egalitarianism, and strong opposition to authoritarianism.

[4] "Can Atheists Be Moral?" Atheist Alliance (website) (n.d.), www.atheistalliance.org/about-atheism/can-atheists-moral/.

Policy Issues

Turning to the shorter-term elements of electoral behavior and beginning with attitudes on policy issues, both secularism and nonreligiosity should be linked to views on cultural issues such as abortion and same-sex marriage. Religiosity is closely connected to cultural conservatism (Jelen 2009), so nonreligiosity should be associated with cultural liberalism. Secularism's conviction that morality is grounded in human experience, science, and reason also should tie it to liberal cultural views.

The relevance of nonreligiosity should be weaker and less consistent for other kinds of issues. Researchers show links between religiosity and issue attitudes in a variety of policy areas, including social welfare (Barker and Carman 2000), foreign policy (Barker, Hurwitz, and Nelson 2008), and the environment (Guth et al. 1995). However, those links vary considerably across religious traditions and political contexts (Guth 2009; Layman and Green 2006; Wilson 2009).

Secularism should promote liberalism on a wider variety of issues. Because devotion to science and evidence is at the heart of secularism, Secularists should strongly support funding for scientific research as well as positions on issues like environmental protection, climate change, and vaccinating children, on which the scientific community has reached consensus. Secularism also may encourage liberal perspectives on social welfare, immigration, and foreign policy. Concern for human agency and fulfillment may prompt secular Americans to support social programs for the needy, to prioritize the human rights of immigrants over border enforcement, and to back US engagement with other countries and international organizations to address human needs.

In fact, Secularist organizations say some of these very things in their policy statements. For example, the Council for Secular Humanism notes on its website that "We believe in support for the disadvantaged and the handicapped so that they will be able to help themselves."[5] On immigration, the AHA argues that "our values require us to stand up for human rights and the vulnerable" and "to assist those who came to this country looking for a fresh start."[6] The AHA also affirms "global standards for human rights" and "adherence to international institutions such as the International Criminal Court."[7] Indeed, our survey shows that the AHA members hold strongly liberal views on a wide range of cultural, economic, domestic, and foreign-policy questions.

---

[5] "Affirmations of Humanism," *Free Inquiry* (website) (n.d.) http://secularhumanism.org/index.php/12.

[6] Matthew Bulger, "Immigration Reform: A Humanist (and President's) Concern," *The Humanist*, February 21, 2013. https://thehumanist.com/commentary/immigration-reform-a-humanist-and-presidents-concern.

[7] "AHA Issues Summary," American Humanist Association (website) (n.d.), https://americanhumanist.org/key-issues/statements-and-resolutions/issuessummary/.

Electoral Choice

The final step in our exploration is the association of nonreligiosity and secularism with electoral choice – how citizens evaluate the parties' presidential candidates and, of course, how they vote. Because secularism should be connected to Democratic and liberal ideology, values, and policy stands, it should encourage strong support for Democratic Party candidates. Nonreligiosity's weaker and less consistent links to political factors likely make it a weaker basis for Democratic electoral support. The AHA members support these expectations as well: 97 percent reported voting for Hillary Clinton in the 2016 presidential election, 96 percent for Barack Obama in 2016, and 95 percent for a Democratic congressional candidate in the 2014 midterm election.

ASSESSING THE EVIDENCE

To determine how secularism and nonreligion are related to political attitudes in the American public, we conducted linear regression analyses in which various political orientations are the dependent variables – that is, these statistical models test whether nonreligiosity and secularism predict a variety of political attitudes.[8] In Figure 5.3, we present the most relevant results. For both secularism and nonreligiosity, the figure includes a bar representing the size and direction of its standardized regression coefficient – our estimate of each orientation's connection to political tendencies, independent of sociodemographic factors and each other.[9] For those readers unfamiliar with statistics, keep in mind that the size of the bar indicates the strength of the connection; a longer bar means a stronger link.

---

[8] To account for the nonrandom measurement error present in our secular belief indicators, we estimate these regression models as structural equation models in Mplus, treating secularism, nonreligiosity, and all dependent variables with multiple observed indicators (e.g. policy attitudes) as latent variables estimated through confirmatory factor analysis. However, the results can be interpreted simply as estimates from a linear regression model. In fact, we estimated all of the models shown here with simple ordinary least squares (OLS) regression – measuring nonreligiosity, secularism, and any multi-indicator dependent variables through additive scales – and the results are very similar to those shown here.

[9] Our models allow secularism and nonreligiosity to be endogenous to the sociodemographic control variables. The models for all political variables other than partisanship also include party identification as an independent variable and allow it to be endogenous to the sociodemographic controls. The control variables are education, income, gender, age, race (dummy variable for whites), region (dummy variables for Southerners, Northeasterners, and Westerners, with Midwesterners as the comparison group), a dummy variable for married people, and dummy variables for members of the three largest religious traditions: evangelical Protestants, mainline Protestants, and Catholics (with Protestant denominations classified as in Layman and Green 2006). To illustrate the estimation of our structural equation models, we show the full set of estimates for party identification in the online appendix (see secularsurge.com).

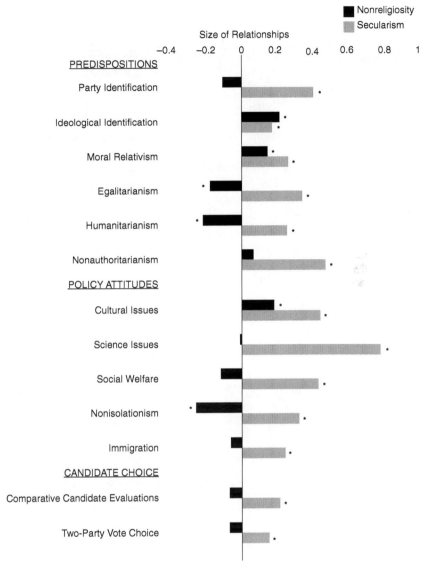

FIGURE 5.3 Political orientations: Secularism has a consistent connection, nonreligiosity does not

* = *Statistically significant at p < .05*

Note: Bars represent the impact, measured as the standardized maximum likelihood coefficient, of nonreligiosity and secularism on political orientations. All models include controls for sociodemographic variables and (except for the party identification model) party identification.

Source: 2017 Secular America Study

Starting with partisanship, nonreligiosity has no noticeable connection to party identification when we account for a positive commitment to secularism. In contrast, secularism is strongly and significantly related to Democratic identification. In other words, if we focus, as the religion and politics literature traditionally has, only on nonreligious people, we get the conventional result: nonreligious people do not have a distinct partisan profile. However, when defined as secular beliefs and identities, secularism clearly leads to identification with the Democratic Party.

The results for ideological identification and core values further highlight the political relevance of secularism.[10] Secularism is strongly and significantly related to liberal ideology, moral relativism, egalitarianism, humanitarianism, and nonauthoritarian values. Secularists are not just Democratic identifiers, but also hold a consistent set of core values that provide a strong foundation for policy liberalism and Democratic candidate choice.

The connections of nonreligious people to ideology and values are more varied. Nonreligiosity is significantly associated with liberal ideology, and interestingly, the connection is even slightly stronger than that of secularism. Nonreligion also has a significant relationship with moral relativism. As we suspected, religiosity's long-standing connection to conservatism and moral traditionalism means that nonreligiosity stands alongside the ideological and moral opposites of such values. However, nonreligiosity has no relationship with authoritarianism and its connections to egalitarianism and humanitarianism are significant, but negative. Holding secularism constant, nonreligious people are less egalitarian and less humanitarian than their religious counterparts.

We turn next to policy attitudes,[11] and the results highlight secularism's consistent connection with liberalism across policy domains – and, by the

---

[10] Ideological identification is a scale ranging from 0 for extremely liberal to 100 for extremely conservative. We measure the first three core values through respondent self-placement on scales between two statements, one running counter to the value and one representing it. The moral relativism scale ranges from "What is morally right and what is morally wrong will never change regardless of how much the world around us changes" to "The world is always changing and we should adjust our view of moral behavior to those changes." For egalitarianism, the scale ranges from "This country would be better off if we worried less about how equal people are" to "If people were treated more equally in this country, we would have many fewer problems." The humanitarianism scale ranges from "A person should always be concerned about the well-being of others" to "People tend to pay more attention to the well-being of others than they should." We capture nonauthoritarian values through two items on important child qualities that are commonly used to measure authoritarianism (Hetherington and Weiler 2009). Our items ask respondents to choose between "independence" and "respect for elders," and between "considerate" and "well behaved."

[11] Our indicators of cultural issue preferences are same-sex-marriage attitudes, views on abstinence-only sex education, and feeling-thermometer ratings of gay men and lesbians as the observed indicators. The science policy issues are government prioritization of science and technology programs, environmental regulations, evolution, global warming, and vaccines. Social welfare issues are level of government social services and spending, government-

same token, the consistently conservative leanings of people without secular perspectives. Secularism is very strongly related to liberal cultural attitudes and support for "science issues" – environmental protection, government efforts to promote science and technology, and scientific approaches to other societal issues. It also has a positive and statistically significant connection to social welfare liberalism, internationalism in foreign policy, and citizenship opportunities for undocumented immigrants. Secularists, it seems, provide a key constituency for contemporary policy liberalism.

The same is not true for nonreligious Americans. Nonreligiosity is positively associated with cultural liberalism, but the relationship is far weaker than that of secularism. It is statistically unrelated to attitudes on science issues, social welfare, and immigration. Nonreligiosity is connected to foreign-policy attitudes, but the connection is a negative one, with nonreligious people more likely than Religionists to embrace isolationism. Taking secularism into account, the absence of religion does not have a consistent connection to liberalism in US public policy.

Our final political inclination is candidate preference in the 2016 presidential election. We examine this in two ways. First, we look at how people rated Republican Donald Trump and Democrat Hillary Clinton on "feeling thermometers" that range from 0 for the "coldest" (most negative) feelings to 100 for the "warmest" (most positive) feelings, focusing on the difference between Clinton ratings and Trump ratings. Second, we evaluate how people actually voted with a variable coded one for Clinton voters and zero for Trump voters.[12]

The results continue a familiar theme – secularism is more relevant than nonreligion for contemporary citizen politics. Secularism is positively and significantly related to support for Clinton over Trump, both in thermometer ratings and vote choice. Because we control for party identification, this result means that Secularists' support for Clinton over Trump went above and beyond their attachment to the Democratic Party. In contrast, nonreligiosity has no connection to candidate preference in 2016 – measured by either candidate evaluations or the vote. Thus, secularism is strongly connected to electoral choice in a way that the absence of religion is not.

To summarize our results, the secularism gap appears to be at least as important as the nonreligiosity gap for contemporary political behavior. There continue to be important political differences between religious and nonreligious citizens. However, the differences between people who actively

---

provided health insurance, and the role of government vs. the free market in handling economic problems. Our other policy issues are the United States taking an active role in world affairs (labeled "nonisolationism") and a path to citizenship for undocumented immigrants.

[12] To maintain comparability with the other dependent variables in this chapter, the estimates for the presidential vote are from linear regression models. However, we also estimated the presidential vote model with Mplus's binary probit estimator. The probit results are very similar to those shown here.

embrace secularism and those who do not is larger. Secularists are significantly more likely than nonsecularists to identify with the Democratic Party and political liberalism, to hold left-leaning core values and policy attitudes, and to support Democratic candidates at the ballot box.

But before we proclaim that, in the face of secularism's importance for US citizen politics, the long-standing religiosity gap is a thing of the past, it is important to remember that we discovered nonreligiosity's relatively weak and inconsistent connections to political behavior when we controlled for secularism. There may still be big political differences between more-religious and less-religious Americans, but those differences may be accounted for by the differences in secularism between these groups.

In fact, when we undertake the analyses in Figure 5.3 with only nonreligiosity (leaving out secularism), the religiosity gap reemerges in impressive fashion (data not shown). Nonreligiosity has strong and statistically significant connections to Democratic identification, liberal ideology, moral relativism, nonauthoritarianism, cultural liberalism, support for "science issues," social welfare liberalism, support for the rights of immigrants, and favoring Hillary Clinton over Donald Trump. The connections of nonreligiosity to these political tendencies are generally weaker than those we show for secularism – and nonreligiosity still is not significantly related to humanitarianism or foreign-policy isolationism.[13] Overall, however, the evidence suggests that there remains a clear religiosity gap in citizen politics.

From that perspective, the most appropriate description of the political cleavage we have uncovered may be not simply a secular divide, but a secular–religious divide, rooted in the differences between Secularists and Religionists. In fact, an examination of the party loyalties of our four secular-religious groups (described in Chapter 2) reveals the importance of both secularism and nonreligiosity to the contemporary partisan divide.

As Figure 5.4 shows, the sharpest divide is between Secularists and Religionists. Secularists identify strongly with the Democratic Party, while Religionists are clearly the most Republican group. However, a closer inspection reveals a slightly different and subtler pattern for Democratic and Republican identification. For Democratic Party attachment, what appears to matter is secularism. There is a substantial gap in Democratic loyalty between our two groups that are high in personal secularism – Secularists and Religious Secularists – and our two groups low in secularism – Religionists and Non-Religionists. But there is very little difference in Democratic attachment when we compare Secularists and Religious Secularists with each other or, similarly, when Religionists and Non-Religionists are viewed side by side. Religionists are just as likely as Non-Religionists to identify as Democrats, and Religious Secularists are not much less Democratic than Secularists. Secularism, and not

---

[13] In these analyses, nonreligiosity is related to egalitarianism and the presidential vote, but the relationships just miss standard levels of statistical significance.

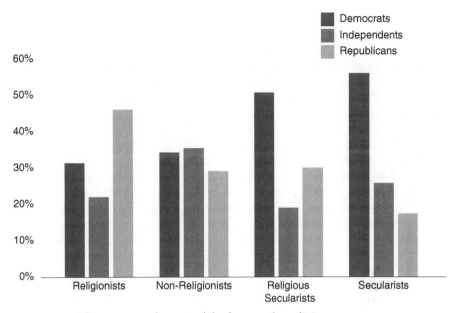

FIGURE 5.4 The party attachments of the four secular-religious groups
Source: 2017 Secular America Study

an absence of religion, seems to be the glue that binds these Americans to the Democratic Party.

In contrast, Republican identification is associated with both religiosity and secularism. Religious Secularists are noticeably more Republican than Secularists, and Religionists are markedly more attached to the GOP than are Non-Religionists. At the same time, Religionists are a good bit more Republican than Religious Secularists, and Non-Religionists are more Republican than Secularists. For Non-Religionists and Religious Secularists, their contrasting levels of religiosity and secularism seem to cancel each other out, and they are equally as tied to the GOP.[14]

SECULAR INFLUENCE ON POLITICS OR POLITICAL INFLUENCE ON SECULARISM?

The connections we have seen between secularism, nonreligiosity, and political orientations point to an important question: Do the connections result from

---

[14] Like party identification, the presidential vote in 2016 was associated with both secularism and nonreligiosity. Support for Hillary Clinton grows steadily from 33 percent among Religionists, to 42 percent for Non-Religionists, to 60 percent for Religious Secularists, and to 75 percent among Secularists.

secularism and nonreligiosity influencing political orientations or from political orientations affecting nonreligious and secular tendencies?

Traditionally, political scientists have assumed that these relationships arise from citizens' religiosity and secularity – people bringing their political views and identities into line with their religious and secular worldviews (Berelson, Lazarsfeld, and McPhee 1954; Layman 2001). This assumption has seemed reasonable because research showed that politics is not central to most people's lives. It was something about which they cared little and knew even less (Delli Carpini and Keeter 1996). So, if seemingly stable and deep-seated orientations like religious or secular worldviews were associated with political tendencies, then it made sense that these worldviews influenced politics rather than the other way around.

Recently, however, this traditional view has come into question. As the parties' coalitions have grown more ideologically and affectively polarized (Mason 2018), scholars have shown that party identification influences social proclivities as well as political perspectives. Indeed, partisanship shapes choices on things that are as seemingly nonpolitical as where people want to live, the sorts of products they purchase, and even who they find physically attractive and who they want their children to marry (Alford et al. 2011; Bishop and Cushing 2009; Iyengar and Westwood 2015; Nicholson et al. 2016).

Importantly, religious and secular identities are among the nonpolitical orientations that partisanship and ideology seem to affect. As we note in Chapter 1, one of the leading explanations for the rapidly increasing presence of Nones in the United States is politics – namely Democrats and liberals abandoning religion as it becomes more closely associated with conservatism and the Republican Party. The origins of this explanation lie with Michael Hout and Claude Fischer (2002). Armed with evidence – gathered through cohort analyses of General Social Survey (GSS) data – Hout and Fischer sought to explain both why the growth started when it did (late 1980s) and why it is confined to political liberals and moderates. As in an Agatha Christie story, they investigated every suspect and, by the process of elimination, concluded that the Religious Right did it. In their words, "Organized religion linked itself to a conservative social agenda in the 1990s, and that led some political moderates and liberals who had previously identified with the religion of their youth or their spouse's religion to declare that they have no religion" (188).

Other scholars have taken up Hout and Fischer's mantle and examined the possibility of political perspectives influencing religious orientations, using a variety of data and methods. Patrikios (2008) employs panel data from the American National Election Studies to show that while religion's growing connection to conservatism and the GOP might turn Democrats and liberals off religion, it spurs Republicans and conservatives to grow even more religious. Putnam and Campbell (2012) employ a large national panel study to show movement in both directions – Democrats growing less religious and Republicans becoming more religious. Hout and Fischer (2014) themselves return to their "politicized religion" argument with new data and more rigorous methods, employing GSS panel data to confirm that political ideology significantly shapes how likely people are to become Nones. Taking a slightly different perspective on the question of political influence on religion, Djupe, Neiheisel, and Sokhey (2018) focus on decisions to leave a particular congregation and find that views about the Christian Right only affect such decisions when support for the Christian Right movement is central to congregation life. Finally, in the most wide-ranging assessment to date of the impact of citizens' politics on their religious proclivities, Margolis (2018a) marshals an impressive array of data and methods – cross-sectional surveys, long-term panel surveys of parents and children, congregation-level surveys, and survey experiments – to show that deep-seated political identities formed in childhood structure religious identities, convictions, and behaviors well into adulthood.

In short, there is growing and convincing evidence that political identity shapes religious orientations. So, it is very likely that the patterns we have shown so far are partly a result of politics – people bringing their nonreligious and secular tendencies into line with their partisanship, ideology, and political attitudes.

Even so, there remains the possibility of secular and nonreligious influence – in other words, people bringing their political attitudes into line with their secularity or nonreligiosity. However, we believe secularism is more likely than nonreligiosity to be a source of political change. We expect this not only because secularism's connections to political identities and values are stronger and more consistent than those of nonreligiosity, but also because secular beliefs and identities should structure political attitudes more than the absence of religion. Green, Palmquist, and Schickler (2002) show that significant change in individual party identification occurs only when citizens' social identities become connected to their changing perceptions of the social group composition of the two parties. From this perspective, Democrats becoming known increasingly as the "secular party" and Republicans as the "religious party" means that secular social identity and commitment to secular beliefs should encourage stronger attachments to the Democratic Party and to political liberalism.

With these expectations in mind, we assess whether (a) secularism and nonreligiosity influence political orientations, encouraging people to become more liberal and Democratic over time, or (b) political factors influence nonreligiosity and secularism, affecting the degree to which people grow more or less religious or more or less secular over time, or (c) both kinds of influence take shape. To do so, we use the 2010–2012 SAS Panel, which allows us to follow the same respondents at different points in time.[15]

---

[15] We use the data from waves 2 to 4 of the SAS panel (because our active secularism measures did not appear in the first wave) to examine the reciprocal relationships across time.

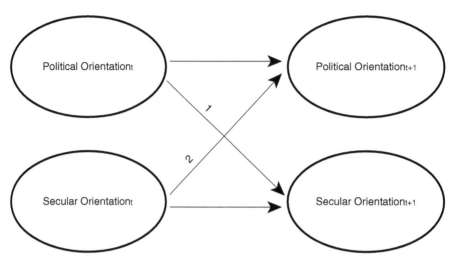

FIGURE 5.5 Model of "cross-lagged" relationships between political and secular orientations

Specifically, we use our panel data to estimate models of "cross-lagged" relationships between secularism and politics. We illustrate the simple structure of this model in Figure 5.5, with both variables being shaped by their own past values and the past value of the other variable. The arrows linking both political and secular tendencies to their own past values capture the expected stability of these factors for individual citizens.

Then, because we have controlled for the influence of past values on current values of secularism and political orientations, the cross-lagged arrows from each variable to the other capture the degree to which past values of each variable are associated with change over time in the other variable. Arrow 1 represents the degree to which previously held political tendencies are associated with change in secular tendencies from one panel wave to the next (Finkel 1995). Arrow 2 captures the extent to which prior secular orientation is related to change in political dispositions.[16]

Put differently, arrow 1 indicates whether people who are more liberal or Democratic in our first wave are more likely than people who are more conservative or Republican to grow more secular over time. Arrow 2 indicates whether being more secular in our first panel wave is associated with becoming more liberal or Democratic over time. For readers interested in knowing more

[16] The model for each political attitude or identification includes cross-lagged relationships between the political variable and both secularism and nonreligiosity, as well as cross-lagged influences of secularism and nonreligiosity on each other. To illustrate the estimation of our cross-lagged models, we show the full set of estimates for party identification and its cross-lagged relationships with secularism and nonreligiosity in the online appendix.

about what these statistical models can, and cannot, tell us about causal relationships, please consult A Closer Look 5.1.

Each of waves two through four of the SAS panel data include all of our indicators of nonreligiosity as well as nonreligious guidance, the secular identity count, and four secular belief statements (factual evidence, great works, hard to live a good life, and free our minds).[17] These three waves also include party identification, ideological identification, and attitude toward same-sex marriage.[18] We also turn to views on three policy issues included in both the third and fourth panel waves – government providing health insurance, environmental regulations, and the trade-off between fighting terrorism and protecting civil liberties.[19]

We show the cross-lagged effects between secularism and political orientations and between nonreligiosity and political orientations in Figure 5.6, with the bars indicating the size of the lagged effect of one variable on another and asterisks indicating whether or not the relationships are statistically significant.[20] Looking first at the models that use three waves of panel data (those for party identification, ideology, and same-sex marriage), we find clear evidence of political orientations affecting secularism and nonreligiosity.

Stronger identification with the Democratic Party is associated with increases in both secularism and nonreligiosity. Liberal ideological proclivities and same-sex-marriage attitudes also are associated with significant increases in secularism levels. The sizes of these lagged coefficients are relatively small: standardized effects of .10 or less (as compared to stability coefficients that are as large as .84). However, we would not expect the politics-based changes in secular orientations to be large, with a period of less than one year between each panel wave (and with corrections for measurement error). Cumulatively, these results could represent substantial change, with Democrats and liberals growing markedly less religious and more secular than Republicans and conservatives

---

[17] Our measurement models for the panel analyses, like those in the cross-sectional analyses, include corrections for nonrandom measurement error in secular beliefs and random measurement error in all of the other indicators of secularism.

[18] Having three waves of panel data enables a correction for measurement error in these observed indicators even though we only have one for each variable (Bollen 1989; Wiley and Wiley 1970). These corrections mean that any lagged relationship between political and secular orientations represents the connection between one variable and actual change in the other variable, not change due to measurement error. Our models also include sociodemographic control variables measured in the second panel wave and having effects on latent secular and political orientations in waves 3 and 4. These are education, income, age, race (dummy for whites), religious tradition (evangelicals, mainline Protestants, and Catholics), region (dummies for Southerners, Northeasterners, and Westerners), a dummy for married people, and a dummy for people with children living at home.

[19] With only two waves of data and a single indicator of each issue, we are not able to correct for measurement error in these attitudes.

[20] Secularism, nonreligiosity, and political orientations are all quite stable across panel waves, with stability coefficients that are strong and quite statistically significant.

over time. Thus, politics seems to provide part of the explanation for the secular surge: Democrats and liberals may have taken notice of the connection between religion and politics and, to a greater extent than conservatives and Republicans, moved in a more secular direction.

What about the reverse relationship? Are nonreligion and secularism related to increases in Democratic identification, liberal ideology, and support for same-sex marriage? For nonreligiosity, the answer is no. It does not have a significant connection to change in any of the political variables. The absence of religion does not encourage greater liberalism or Democratic loyalty. In contrast, secularism has a statistically significant lagged influence

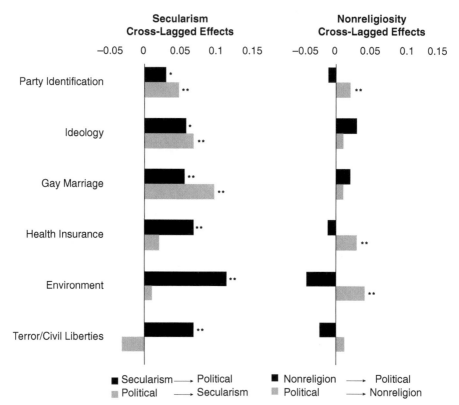

FIGURE 5.6 Politics affects secularism and nonreligiosity; only secularism affects politics

* = *Statistically significant at p < .10*

** = *Statistically significant at p < .05*

Note: *Bars represent the impact, measured as the standardized maximum likelihood coefficient, of lagged nonreligiosity and secularism on political orientations. All models include controls for sociodemographic variables.*

Source: *2010–2012 Secular America Study*

on partisanship, ideology, and same-sex-marriage attitudes. In other words, Secularists are more likely than nonsecularists to become more attached to the Democratic Party, grow more liberal, and become more supportive of same-sex marriage over time.

The last three rows of Figure 5.6 show the estimates for the models for which we have only two waves of data – those for attitudes on government providing health insurance, environmental regulations, and the trade-off between fighting terrorism and protecting civil liberties. The cross-lagged relationships there provide further evidence of secularism being more politically important than nonreligiosity. Nonreligion is not associated with changes in views on a government insurance plan, environmental regulations, or protecting civil liberties during the war on terror. Meanwhile, attitudes on both government-provided health insurance and environmental regulation have significant lagged connections to nonreligiosity, as liberal policy attitudes are associated with decreases in religiosity. In short, nonreligiosity does not seem to drive political attitudes. It is shaped by political orientations, but does not encourage change in them.

In contrast, secularism is positively and significantly related to change in all three policy attitudes. Secularists are more likely than nonsecularists to become more supportive of a government health insurance plan, more sympathetic toward environmental regulations, and more concerned about preserving civil liberties in the midst of the war on terror. None of these policy attitudes had any relationship to change in secularism levels.

A Closer Look 5.1:
Are These Relationships Causal?

It is important to note that our cross-lagged models cannot establish causality – that secularism causes change in political orientations or that politics cause change in secular tendencies. Cross-lagged models capture what quantitative methodologists call "between-person effects." They tell us the extent to which change in one variable can be predicted from existing differences between individuals on another variable (Hamaker, Kuiper, and Grasman 2015). For example, our analysis tells us that people who are more secular at one time point are more likely than people who are less secular to grow more Democratic between that and future time points. However, because there may be "unmeasured variables" (variables not in our data or not accounted for in our models) that are related to levels of secularism at the first time point and to change across time in party identification, we are unable to say for sure that those other factors did not cause the change in Democratic loyalty. So, we cannot be certain that secularism causes change in partisanship.

We believe our cross-lagged models still provide vital insight into how and why secularism is connected to politics. For one thing, they allow us to rule out the possibility that secularism's relationship to political orientations is due entirely to politics causing change in secularism (e.g. to Democrats being more likely than Republicans to gravitate toward secularism).[21] For another thing, because our cross-lagged models control for sociodemographic characteristics such as age, education, and race, we are confident that the relationship between secularism and changes in political orientations – or between political orientations and changes in secularism – is not due to the variables' mutual relationships with these social background factors.[22]

We also utilized other methods for analyzing panel data that come closer to establishing causal relationships by isolating "within-person effects" – the degree to which differences or changes in one variable for a particular person are associated with differences or changes in another variable for that same person. We estimated both "first difference" models (e.g. Allison 2009) and "random intercepts cross-lagged panel models" (Hamaker, Kuiper, and Grasman 2015). The results from those models, presented in our online appendix, were not as strong or consistent as the results shown here. However, especially for ideology and policy attitudes, they largely confirm the results from our cross-lagged models.

We should be clear: these results do not give us certainty that secularism causes change in political attitudes and identities or that politics causes change in secularism and nonreligiosity. However, they are strongly suggestive of reciprocal relationships between secularism and political orientations, and also of a one-way connection between politics and nonreligiosity. In summary, we find:

• *Politics Has Contributed to the Secular Surge*

It appears that politics is indeed one of the culprits for America's secular surge, as partisanship influenced change in both secularism and nonreligiosity; liberal ideology and support for same-sex marriage were associated with increases in secularism; and policy liberalism was related to a decline in religiosity. This provides further support for the backlash to politicized religion reported in Chapter 6. What we find there with controlled experiments, we discover here with "real-world" data. However, this also shows a more generalized effect of political orientations not just on religious affiliation, but on nonreligious and secular orientations broadly.

[21] If the relationship between secularism and party identification was due entirely to partisanship causing change in secularism, then we would see a lagged influence of party identification on secularism, but not the reverse. Because our analysis shows both a lagged influence of partisanship on secularism and a lagged influence of secularism on partisanship, it is possible that the relationship is reciprocal and also takes shape because secularists are more likely than nonsecularists to become Democrats.

[22] Of course, it is possible that other factors not included in our models or even in our data may account for both differences in secularism and changes in politics.

• *But Secularism Affects Political Attitudes Too*

The results also suggest that secularism gives as good as it gets in the political arena. Higher levels of secularism were associated with increases in Democratic Party loyalty, growth in liberal identification, and increased liberalism on a range of policy issues. This finding highlights the importance of understanding secularism for understanding contemporary politics.

• *Unlike Secularism, Nonreligiosity Does Not Drive Political Attitudes*

Nonreligion, by contrast, is not a political mover. Its relationship with political orientations seems to result entirely from politics affecting religiosity and not the reverse. Thus, to the extent that nonreligion and secularism shape citizen politics, secularism appears the more likely culprit. This is further evidence for why lumping together all nonreligious and secular people is misleading. Secularism is not only distinct from nonreligiosity, but also has distinct, arguably more important, political effects.

CONCLUSION

The people who participated in our in-depth interviews in 2017 perceived a connection between secularism and nonreligiosity on the one hand and political preferences on the other hand. The respondents were certainly correct about the political relevance of secularism. Secularism is strongly related to Democratic Party identification; liberal ideological identification; left-leaning core values; progressive positions on public policy issues; and a strong preference for Democratic presidential candidates over Republicans. And, while these relationships are due in part to citizens' political orientations shaping their levels of secularism, secularism also structures political change. Secularists are more likely than nonsecularists to move in Democratic and liberal political directions.

The respondents' perceptions about nonreligiosity were less accurate. Nonreligion is connected to some political orientations, but in weaker and less consistent ways than secularism. And its relationship to political orientations is principally as a follower, not a leader. Changes in nonreligiosity are influenced by political tendencies, but nonreligion does not appear to shape changes in those tendencies.

At the beginning of this chapter, we argued that the political relevance of secularism and nonreligiosity may have implications for contemporary political polarization. Our evidence sheds light on what those implications are.

First and foremost, there clearly are secular and religious elements to the contemporary partisan and ideological divides. That the Democratic and liberal bases consist disproportionately of Secularists while Republicans and conservatives are principally Religionists helps to explain the starkly different policy preferences of the partisan and ideological coalitions, as well as the growth of affective polarization between them. It is no wonder that political camps that have fundamentally different views of the world and understandings of human life tend to dislike and distrust each other. As the secular divide between these coalitions grows, affective polarization may grow along with it.

Second, the process through which secularism has been connected to partisanship and other political orientations appears to be one of both sorting and attitude change. The fact that secularism is related to political change, with Secularists being more likely than nonsecularists to move in a liberal and Democratic direction suggests that these groups are sorting themselves into the appropriate party and ideological coalitions. At the same time, there is evidence of polarizing attitude change. The fact that political orientations influence change in nonreligiosity and secularism ultimately may be related to greater societal polarization, as people in the Democratic and liberal political camps grow more secular and less religious, while members of the Republican and conservative political teams grow more religious and less secular.[23]

Finally, what does our evidence suggest about the duration of the "great divide" between the Democratic and Republican mass coalitions? Is it likely to quickly fade away or be an enduring feature of our politics? To answer that question requires attention to trends in both religiosity and secularity. If we only looked at religiosity, one might argue that the sharp rise of the Nones and the more gradual decline of strong religiosity would reduce the size and intensity of the nonreligiosity gap in American politics. However, it appears that the nonreligion divide has been joined and perhaps bolstered by a clear secularism gap. The partisan fault line between a Secularist Democratic Party and Religionist Republican Party may be both deep and durable.

We return to the implications of the secular surge for partisan politics in Chapters 7–9. First, however, we seek a firmer grip on whether political identity really does cause Americans to leave religion and, perhaps, grow more secular. Our panel analyses are suggestive of political influences on religion and secularism. In Chapter 6, we employ original survey experiments to seek a more definitive test of one form of political influence – whether the growth of nonreligion represents a backlash to religion's association with conservative Republican politics.

---

[23] Although it is not a focus of this analysis, our findings are consistent with evidence that religious intensity has not declined over time and may even have increased in relative importance (Lipka 2019).

6

Nonreligiosity and Backlash Politics

In the previous chapter, we saw evidence – consistent with a small but growing body of research – that politics can shape both personal nonreligiosity and secularism. That is, the secular surge is due, at least in part, to the political environment. While our use of panel data hints that the relationship is causal, it is not definitive. In this chapter, we employ a set of experiments, the "gold standard" to determine whether a causal relationship truly exists. Specifically, we use experiments to see whether one form of nonreligiosity, disaffiliation from a religious identity (i.e. the rise of the Nones), is caused by a backlash to politicized religion, especially the Religious Right. To set the stage for our experiments, we begin with an example "ripped from the headlines" that illustrates the how and why of the backlash effect – the curious case of Roy Moore.

In the fall of 2017, the eyes of the nation were on the special election for the US Senate in Alabama, formerly held by US Attorney General Jeff Sessions. This deep-red state race was a nail-biter that under normal circumstances would have been a shoo-in for the Republican candidate. But this election was anything but normal. Roy Moore, the GOP nominee, was highly controversial. Twice popularly elected as chief justice of the Alabama state Supreme Court, he was twice removed from office for defying a federal court: the first time for ignoring a court order to remove a two-ton granite monument of the Ten Commandments he had installed in the state judicial building (Green 2005), and the second time for defying the US Supreme Court's decision legalizing same-sex marriage.[1] These activities made him a cause célèbre among Religious Right activists.

An observant Southern Baptist, Moore capitalized on his reputation as a culture warrior, routinely employing incendiary rhetoric on the campaign

---

[1] Technically, he was suspended by a special Supreme Court and then resigned.

trail. Moore declared that homosexual conduct should be illegal, First Amendment rights should only apply to Christians, and that Representative Keith Ellison, a Muslim American, should not be allowed to take the congressional oath of office. If you called central casting and asked for the stereotypical Christian theocrat, they would send Roy Moore.

These controversies provoked strong reactions, even in Alabama (Blumberg 2017). But the most devastating criticism was the accusation that Moore had sexually assaulted teenage girls when he was an assistant district attorney in his thirties. While he denied the charges, Moore still became nationally known as an accused sexual predator (McCrummen, Reinhard, and Crites 2017). Such accusations would be damning for any candidate, but doubly so for someone who put traditional moral values at the forefront of his candidacy. On character, he would seem to be anathema to people who agreed with his policies. This disjunction created strong cross-pressures on traditionally religious voters, especially evangelical Christians.

For many evangelical leaders, policy trumped character (Tillett 2017). Over fifty pastors signed a public letter supporting Moore, describing him as "an immoveable rock in the culture wars." The letter ends with an endorsement of Moore, "We urge you to join us at the polls to cast your vote for Roy Moore" (Gore 2017).[2] Franklin Graham, son of Billy Graham, also took to Twitter to defend Moore: "so many denouncing Roy Moore when they are guilty of doing much worse than what he has been accused of supposedly doing. Shame on those hypocrites" (Smith 2017). As controversy swirled around Roy Moore, he was often linked to Donald Trump, as they shared both heavy evangelical support and the moral taint of sexual misconduct.[3]

Moore lost the election by a very small margin to Democrat Doug Jones, despite strong support from white evangelicals – 80 percent according to exit polls.[4] For our purposes, the significance of Roy Moore is not the results at the polls but the backlash his candidacy caused within some religious circles and, especially, the evangelical community. This backlash was perhaps best articulated in an op-ed piece penned by Peter Wehner, a well-known evangelical who has served in multiple Republican administrations, titled "Why I Can No Longer Call Myself an Evangelical Republican." In it,

---

[2] There is controversy over how many of these pastors affirmatively agreed to have their names affixed to this letter, which appears to have been recycled from the primary campaign and thus to have been written prior to the sexual assault allegations. At least four said that they had not agreed to sign the letter.

[3] Trump did not endorse Moore in the Republican primary but did in the general election.

[4] For full exit poll results, see "Decision 2017: Alabama Results," *NBC News*, January 30, 2018, www.nbcnews.com/politics/2017-election/AL. Interestingly, white evangelicals were also a slightly smaller share of the electorate than in previous elections (44 percent vs. 47 percent), suggesting that some evangelicals may have been troubled enough by Moore that they stayed home on election day.

Wehner describes pastors and organizations who have dropped the term "evangelical" because it has been tarnished by its association with Moore, Trump, and other politicians with questionable morals. He writes of one pastor who told him that evangelical has "become not a religious identification so much as a political one" (Wehner 2017). These words perfectly reflect the trigger for the backlash to the Religious Right – the politicization of evangelicalism and, by extension, religion more broadly.

While it is unlikely that these evangelical leaders left religion completely, there are contemporary public reports of evangelicals and others doing so (Dias 2018). For example, in the comments section on the *New York Times* website, a contributor named Stephanie wrote:[5]

I left the church in the last year because of what "evangelicalism" has come to stand for in America. Now I think of myself as someone who tries to live by the teachings of Jesus. Love your neighbor . . . I think Falwell and his ilk are wolves in sheep's clothing and that their hypocrisy and lack of genuine love for others is hastening the decline of the church in America.

Another commenter, Bobbie, went even farther and adopted a secular identification:

When I talk to Christians who say "God hates homosexuality, or abortion" and I do not believe their god exists . . . [t]he same Christians seem ready to completely ignore other parts of their Bible . . . where it says to Love your neighbor as yourself and care for the poor and disadvantaged. It isn't that I don't understand their religion, I went to an evangelical church for three or four years . . . I was on the fence about religion when I started that process and now I am an Atheist!

For our purposes, perhaps the most telling of these comments comes from Christie's comments on the same website, as she describes the cognitive dissonance she has faced between her faith and her politics.

When Trump was elected with an overwhelming support from evangelicals, I stopped going to church. I stopped reading my Bible. I could not handle the cognitive dissonance of a people who profess to follow Jesus on one hand but then overwhelmingly support the candidate whose actions scream hate. If being a Christian meant voting for Trump, then maybe I wasn't a Christian anymore.

The case of Roy Moore is obviously extreme and highly public, but the rest of this chapter demonstrates that the reaction to his candidacy is not unique. Many Americans turn away from a religious affiliation precisely because of cognitive dissonance between their religion and their politics.

---

[5] The quotes in this section come from comments posted on the *New York Times* website in response to a 2018 article on young evangelical Christians: Dias (2018), www.nytimes.com /2018/11/01/us/young-evangelicals-politics-midterms.html.

THE BACKLASH HYPOTHESIS

The overarching theme for our discussion of the backlash effect is that politics follows a variation of Newton's third law of motion: every action is met by an opposite reaction. The reaction may not be equal in force nor happen immediately, but it is a reaction nonetheless. In perhaps the best-known example in recent political history, the Democratic Party's embrace of civil rights in the 1960s led the Republican Party to move from being the party of racial liberalism to racial conservatism (Carmines and Stimson 1990). Today, there is a yawning gap between Democratic and Republican voters' racial attitudes. Similarly, today the Republican Party is home to white evangelical Protestants, a reaction to the growing divide between the parties on cultural issues such as abortion and LGBTQ rights (Layman 2001; Putnam and Campbell 2012).

The Newtonian reaction to the close association between religion and partisan politics can be found in declining religious affiliation. This intertwining of religion and politics means that many Americans are faced with dissonance between their religious and political identities. When the two do not line up, individuals can resolve the dissonance in one of two ways, by either changing their religion or their political affiliation. Given that religion is often described as something that rarely changes, many observers would predict that people are more likely to change their politics (Campbell et al. 1960; Green, Palmquist, and Schickler 2002). However, there is increasing evidence that at least some people react by holding onto their politics and dropping their religion.[6] The reasoning is as follows. Religiously affiliated Democrats who perceive the Republican Party as the party associated with religion, whether a specific tradition like evangelicalism or just "religion" more broadly, face cognitive dissonance. They look at the world and perceive that religious folks are more likely to be found in Republican, not Democratic, ranks. But they are Democrats. They respond by shifting from identifying, even if just nominally, with a religion to disclaiming a religious affiliation altogether. In other words, they shift from being a "something" to being a None.

A necessary precondition for the Newtonian reaction is that the Republican and Democratic parties are perceived by voters as split along religious lines: rightly or wrongly, the Republicans are known as the party of the religious, leaving the Democrats to be perceived as the party of the nonreligious (Campbell, Green, and Layman 2011). While policy positions taken by the parties are not perfectly aligned with a religious or secular worldview – for example, there are religious believers who support abortion rights and Secularists who do not – what matters is that, in general, these issues divide

---

[6] Other reactions might be to stick to religion but abandon politics, and still another is to find an attitudinal or practical middle ground. For examples of this happening among evangelicals in 2016 see Green (2018).

religious and nonreligious voters. In particular, as voters have come of voting age, they have divided themselves between the parties based on their religious or secular orientations (Margolis 2018b).

CONDITIONS FOR BACKLASH

The timing of the initial rise of the Nones fits perfectly for the backlash hypothesis. The rate of religious nonaffiliation began to rise just as the Religious Right was becoming a deeply entrenched movement within American politics, a highly visible component of the Republican Party's core supporters. But is there evidence that conditions are ripe for a backlash both *descriptively* (how citizens see the linkage) and *prescriptively* (how citizens evaluate the linkage)? In the 2017 Secular America Study (SAS), we asked both a descriptive and a prescriptive question about the amount that political leaders employ religious rhetoric.

Descriptively, we asked whether political leaders talk about "religious faith and prayer" often, sometimes, or never. Four out of five Americans perceive that political leaders talk about religion at least some of the time.

Prescriptively, we followed that question by asking whether the amount of religious talk is too much, not enough, or the right amount. In the population as a whole, there is a three-way split on the propriety of religious talk: of those who said that there is any talk of religion among politicians, 32 percent say there is too much, 33 percent think there is not enough, and 35 percent indicate that there is the right amount. However, that even split disguises a huge partisan divide on this question. Only 10 percent of Republicans say that there is too much religious talk, while 48 percent believe there should be more. Among Democrats, a far greater number, 51 percent, say there is too much, while only 23 percent favor a greater amount.

We also asked about the degree to which religious leaders are involved in politics. Slightly more Americans see religious leaders as wrapped up in politics than those who see politicians draped in religion – 88 percent say that clergy are at least sometimes involved in politics. Americans in general are also more likely to have a problem with clergy's involvement with politics than with politicians' involvement with religion. Forty-three percent say that clergy do too much politicking, compared to only 25 percent who believe there is the right amount. There is also a partisan divide on this question, although it is not quite as stark as on politicians talking about religion. Just over half (53 percent) of Democrats think clergy are too politically involved, while 28 percent of Republicans say the same. Republicans' concern about clergy political activism is relatively low, but recall that this figure is 18 points higher than the percentage of GOP-identifiers who say that politicians talk too much about religion.

Clearly, a vast majority of Americans perceive that religion and politics are often mixed together. Many object to this – especially to clergy's political involvement – and Democrats more so than Republicans.

It is one thing to note that Republicans and Democrats agree on the description of the intertwining of religion and politics, but disagree on whether this is a good or bad thing. It is quite another to show that these perceptions affect individuals' reported religious identities. In our 2010 SAS, we simply asked respondents without a religious affiliation whether they had ever identified with a religion and, if so, why they no longer did. We provided a list of possible reasons and, recognizing that there are often multiple motivations for human behavior, allowed them to indicate whether each one was an important reason for leaving.

Forty-three percent indicated that an important reason for leaving their faith was that it was "too mixed up in politics" – evidence that a distaste for the mixture of religion and politics can indeed drive people away from religion. On the one hand, this response fell behind "lost confidence in the religion's leaders" (56 percent) and "no longer shared the religion's beliefs" (65 percent), although it is worth noting that both of these responses could also be tied to a parting of the political ways. One might lose confidence in leaders who endorse opposing political views; likewise, the beliefs that one no longer shares with religious leaders could be tied to politically salient issues such as abortion or LGBTQ rights. On the other hand, the politics response was slightly more than the percentage who said that they had stopped believing in God (41 percent) and that their religion had placed too many constraints on their life (34 percent).

The 2017 SAS replicated this question and again found that a sizable share of people without a religious affiliation said that they had left their religion because they saw it as mixed up in politics – roughly 30 percent. It is not clear why the two surveys differ, but either way, a nonnegligible percentage of the non-affiliated point to politics as a reason for their estrangement from religion.[7]

A number of scholars have examined the backlash hypothesis using different data, and found consistent support for it (Patrikios 2008; Putnam and Campbell 2012). As further evidence, one study has found that religious nonaffiliation grew fastest in states where there is greater Religious Right activism (Djupe, Neiheisel, and Conger 2018). Still, definitive evidence is lacking and not everyone is convinced (Claassen 2015). We thus turn to the methodology best suited to investigating causality, a controlled experiment. Does the backlash hypothesis hold up under the rigor of an experiment?

---

[7] While we are unable to say definitely why there has been a decline in the percentage of people saying they have left religion because of politics, we can speculate on the reasons. It could be that the perception of the linkage between religion and politics has weakened, or at least changed. In the intervening years, the Republicans nominated a Mormon in 2012 and a decidedly nondevout candidate in 2016, while the Democratic president in office from 2009 to 2017 often employed religious rhetoric. It could also be that more people have become accustomed to the link between religion and politics, lessening its impact.

EXPERIMENTAL EVIDENCE

The three experiments described here follow a simple pre-post design. Subjects completed a short survey at time 1, which includes questions about their religious and secular orientations.[8] Roughly a week later, those same subjects were randomly assigned to read a realistic-looking news story, some versions of which describe a mixture of religion and politics of varying sorts, and one of which is a control story that includes no mention of religion and politics. Following the story, the subjects were again asked the same questions as at time 1. Since they were randomly assigned to the story they read, any differences between the groups is solely because of their exposure to the content of that article.[9] As both mild subterfuge and as a prompt to ensure that the subjects pay attention to the story, we included questions on the post-test about their reaction to the article, for example, "would you vote for this candidate?" All of our experiments were conducted online using reputable survey firms.[10]

In the first experiment, political candidates associate themselves with religion (the Clerical Campaign Experiment). In the second, clergy are involved with politics (the Political Pastor Experiment). Each presents a different mixture of religion and politics. Note that these two experiments were conducted in different years: the Clerical Campaign Experiment was conducted in 2012 and the Political Pastor Experiment in 2017. It is therefore possible that any difference in results between them is because the political environment had changed in the intervening years. However, the duration of time between them only strengthens our confidence in any findings they have in common.

Recall that the vast majority of Americans perceive that the mixture of religion and politics is common, which arguably works against our experiments. When we expose our subjects to news stories describing religious politicians and political clergy, we are not describing anything new or novel. They will have seen this sort of thing before. Most respondents are being primed to think about their previous experience with the intertwining of religion and politics. Any change in their attitudes or identification that we observe, therefore, is over and above whatever effects the real world has already had. In the language of the stock market, their response to the infusion of religion into politics has already been "priced in" to their attitudes. Note also that our experiments are fairly weak examples of religion and politics being mixed together. For example, the case of Roy Moore at the beginning of this

---

[8] Some of the results from the Clerical Campaign Experiment are reported in Campbell et al. (2018).

[9] The randomization was successful in all three experiments, as Tukey's Honestly Significant Difference tests show that the various treatment conditions did not vary by gender, race, education, income, or age.

[10] The Clerical Campaign Experiment was conducted by GfK (formerly Knowledge Networks). The Political Pastor Experiment and the Transactional Religion Experiment were conducted by YouGov.

chapter is far more extreme than anything described in the experiments. Since respondents will already be aware of the mixture between religion and politics, and have witnessed more intense examples of religious rhetoric in real life, these experiments are biased against uncovering any effects of politics on religion.

A third experiment differs from the previous two, and comes closest to reflecting the concerns raised by the online commenters quoted above. Specifically, the Transactional Religion Experiment assesses if the backlash effect depends on whether a candidate's connection to religion appears to be sincere or merely politics as usual. Would voters, Democrats especially, have a stronger backlash when religion is reduced to being treated like any other special interest? Or is the backlash limited to candidates who profess to be religious themselves?

CLERICAL CAMPAIGN EXPERIMENT

The Clerical Campaign Experiment gauges the reaction to politicians who invoke religion. For this experiment, a news story describes a race for an open congressional seat in "Summerville," a fictional community. The article introduces the Republican and Democratic candidates, complete with photos and biographical information. Other than their party label, we designed their descriptions to be as consistent as possible. Both are middle-aged white men, married with two children, with extremely common names and innocuous occupations. The Republican, Mark Brown, owns some local lawn and garden stores while the Democrat, Paul Davis, is a local public school administrator. They are both active in civic affairs. Brown belongs to the Rotary Club while Davis is a member of the Kiwanis. The key source of variation across our experimental treatments is the degree to which the Republican, the Democrat, or both candidates wrap themselves in religion. For each candidate, we had three different descriptions: one with no mention of religion at all, one with a "light" dose of religiosity, and one with a "heavy" dose of religiosity. The three different descriptions for each of the two candidates meant nine possible versions of the story. We randomly assigned our respondents to receive one of those nine versions.

While the experiments do not specify the religious denomination of the candidates or the churches they attend, the implication is that they are evangelically oriented Protestants. This choice is to resemble contemporary politics, as outward expressions of religion are most common among candidates with an evangelical tinge. At the same time, the way these candidates present their faith would not be terribly unusual for Catholic or mainline Protestant candidates. Figure 6.1 is an example of a news story our respondents were given to read. In this story, the Republican has a heavy dose of religiosity while the Democrat does not have any at all. A Closer Look 6.1 provides the details of how the stories varied, both textually and visually.

Sign In • Sign Up   Archives • RSS Feed • Advertise • Deals • Contact US

Summerville *Gazette*

Wednesday, February 1, 2012

HOME • NEWS • SPORTS • BUSINESS • ENTERTAINMENT • OBITUARIES • JOBS • CARS • CLASSIFIEDS

Candidates Vie for 3rd District Seat

Printable Version Email This   Share 15   Tweet 4   +1 0

By: Jake Smith
Summerville Reporter
6:34 p.m. EDT, January 31, 2012

SUMMERVILLE - Two strong candidates are running for the U.S. House seat of Representative Bill Miller, who is retiring after thirty years representing the 3rd district. "I'll miss public service," said Miller, "but it is time for new leadership. The people of the 3rd district will have good choices in the fall."

The choices are Republican Mark Brown, owner of a local lawn and garden chain, and Democrat Paul Davis, a public school administrator. It is the first run for elected office for both men.

Democratic candidate Paul Davis

Republican candidate Mark Brown

Both candidates are lifelong residents of the area. "My seventeen years as a local small businessman will bring some real world experience to government. My deep roots in the area and my commitment to Christ will help me represent the values of this community," says Brown. Davis argues that "Over fifteen years managing the local schools have given me an understanding of how government works. Being a lifelong resident of Martin County will help me to do right by the people of this district."

The two men have been active in numerous community organizations: Brown is a member of the Rotary Club and a regular worship leader at Oak Street Christian Fellowship. Davis belongs to the Kiwanis Club

Davis talks to reporters

3rd District Congressional Candidates		
	Mark Brown	Paul Davis
Political Party	Republican	Democratic
Age	44	42
Spouse & Children	Married for 19 years (Anne) 3 children (Trevor, Katie & Max)	Married for 14 years (Julie) 3 children (Anna, Grace & Connor)
Memberships	• Oak Street Christian Fellowship • Brothers at the Cross Christian Community • Summerville Rotary Club • United Way	• Summerville Education Foundation • Summerville Kiwanis Club • March of Dimes • Central State Achievement Society

For Brown, the key issue is reducing the size of government, "God has made Americans a free people. Government must stop over-spending and threatening that freedom." In contrast, Davis supports public programs: "Government must continue to provide crucial help for the disadvantaged. We should always help those in need."

Davis and Brown also disagree on environmental protection, foreign policy, and gay marriage. Davis supports gay marriage, arguing that "We need to stop discriminating against gay and lesbian Americans and give them the right to marry the person they love." Brown opposes gay marriage. In a speech he said that "God says marriage is between one man and one woman. To change that definition puts the institution of marriage at risk."

Early endorsements of Davis include the Central State Teachers Association and the Summerville Firefighters Association; Brown's endorsements include Christians for the Traditional Family and the Summerville Independent Business Association.

Brown at his church

One point of agreement between the candidates is praise for their predecessor, Congressman Miller. Brown notes "Bill Miller has been a model for public leadership," and Davis said, "Bill will be a tough act to follow."

Endorsements	
Mark Brown	Paul Davis
Christians for the Traditional Family	Central State Teachers Association
Martin County Chamber of Commerce	Summerville Firefighters Association
Summerville Independent Business Association	Martin County Sanitation Workers
Christian Freedom Council	Martin County Hope Foundation

FIGURE 6.1 Sample news story from the Clerical Campaign Experiment

A Closer Look 6.1 Content of the Clerical Campaign Experiment

	Republican	
No Religion	Light Religion	Heavy Religion
Candidate Quotes My deep roots in the area will help me represent the values of this community. Americans are a free people. Government must stop overspending and threatening that freedom. Society has historically said that marriage is between one man and one woman. To change that definition puts the institution of marriage at risk. **Community organizations** • Rotary Club **Endorsements** • Martin County Chamber of Commerce • Summerville Independent Business Association • **Central State Taxpayers Association** • Martin County Realtors Association	**Candidate Quotes** My deep roots in the area **and my religious faith** will help me represent the values of this community. Americans are a free people. Government must stop overspending and threatening that freedom. Society has historically said that marriage is between one man and one woman. To change that definition puts the institution of marriage at risk. **Community organizations** • Rotary Club **Endorsements** • Martin County Chamber of Commerce • Summerville Independent Business Association • **Christians for the Traditional Family** • Martin County Realtors Association	**Candidate Quotes** My deep roots in the area **and my commitment to Christ** will help me represent the values of this community. **God has made** Americans a free people. Government must stop overspending and threatening that freedom. **God says** marriage is between one man and one woman. To change that definition puts the institution of marriage at risk. **Community organizations** • Rotary Club • **Regular worship leader at Oak Street Christian Fellowship** **Endorsements** • **Christian Freedom Council**

- Summerville Independent Business Association
- **Christians for the Traditional Family**
- Martin County Realtors Association

No Religion	Light Religion	Heavy Religion
<u>Candidate Quotes</u>	<u>Candidate Quotes</u>	<u>Candidate Quotes</u>
Being a lifelong resident of Martin County will help me to do right by the people of this district.	Being a lifelong resident of Martin County **and a man of religious faith** will help me to do right by the people of this district.	Being a lifelong resident of Martin County **and a devoted Christian** will help me to do right by the people of this district.
Government must continue to provide crucial help for the disadvantaged. We should always help those in need.	Government must continue to provide crucial help for the disadvantaged. We should always help those in need.	Government must continue to provide crucial help for the disadvantaged. **The Bible says that we should always help those in need.**
We need to stop discriminating against gay and lesbian Americans and give them the right to marry the person they love.	We need to stop discriminating against gay and lesbian Americans and give them the right to marry the person they love.	**We are all God's children.** We need to stop discriminating against gay and lesbian Americans and give them the right to marry the person they love.
<u>Community organizations</u>	<u>Community organizations</u>	<u>Community organizations</u>
• Kiwanis Club	• Kiwanis Club	• Kiwanis Club
<u>Endorsements</u>	<u>Endorsements</u>	• **Teaches the weekly adult Sunday School class at East Side Christian Church**
• Central State Teachers Association	• Central State Teachers Association	
• Summerville Firefighters Association	• Summerville Firefighters Association	
• Martin County Sanitation Workers	• **Christians for the Common Good**	
• Martin County Hope Foundation	• Martin County Hope Foundation	

Endorsements

- **Faith Alliance for Equality**
- Summerville Firefighters Association
- **Christians for the Common Good**
- Martin County Hope Foundation

In sum, the light-religiosity treatments portray candidates who circumspectly reference religion. The heavy-religion stories show the candidates as overtly associated with religion.

The hypothesis, recall, is that the link between religion and the Republican Party triggers a backlash away from religion among the respondents. In the Clerical Campaign Experiment, Democrats are expected to experience cognitive dissonance when exposed to a Republican candidate who invokes religion. We hypothesize that the effect will be greater with a story featuring heavy religiosity, but were curious to see whether a light-religiosity treatment would be enough to trip the wire. Although the strongest expectation is for self-identified Democrats, there is still the possibility that Republicans will negatively react to partisan religion from the Democratic candidate. The design of the experiment also tests whether backlash depends on the relative balance in the use of religion between the two parties. Specifically, the analysis examines what happens when both the Republican and the Democratic candidates employ religious rhetoric. Do they cancel each other out or does the double-dose amplify the backlash?[11]

Does exposure to this linkage between religion and partisan politics trigger religious disaffiliation? The answer is yes, precisely in the manner that the backlash hypothesis would lead us to expect. In the Clerical Campaign Experiment, Democrats[12] become more likely to drop their religious affiliation after they read about the heavy use of religion by the Republican without a Democratic counterbalance. Democrats also grow more likely to become Nones when the Republican's heavy use is counterbalanced by a light-religiosity Democrat, but to a slightly lesser degree.[13] Meanwhile, Republicans are unmoved, regardless of whether one or both candidates are invoking religion.

[11] Since the randomization for each experiment ensured that there are no demographic or political differences between the treatment groups, our analysis does not require any control variables. We regress the post-test measurement of the dependent variable of interest – that is, the attitude or identity we are seeking to explain – on a set of dummy variables, one for each treatment (excluding the control as a baseline). We also include the pre-test version of the dependent variable as a control. The results are thus interpreted as the effect of exposure to each treatment on the outcome, controlling for the baseline. Here, a positive coefficient means that the treatment led to an increase in religious non-affiliation; a negative coefficient means a decrease. Put another way, does reading one of these news stories make someone more likely to report not having a religious identity?

[12] In all of the results we report, Republicans and Democrats include people who identify as strong, weak, and independent-leaning identifiers with their party.

[13] The effect for the heavy-religion Republican/light-religion Democrat treatment falls just short of statistical significance ($p = .14$), but its substantive effect is still relatively large, as seen in Figure 6.2.

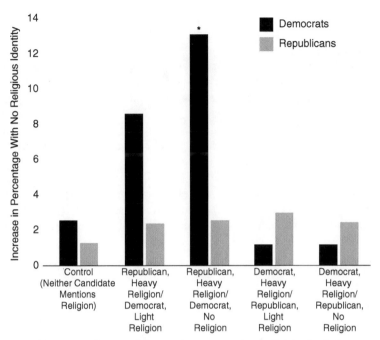

FIGURE 6.2 Democrats become Nones when exposed to politicized religion
* = Effect of experimental treatment statistically significant at p < .05
Source: Clerical Campaign Experiment

As seen in Figure 6.2, the effect is substantial, especially in light of the relatively weak "dosage" of the experiment.[14] When the Republican offers a heavy amount of religion and the Democrat offers no religion, religious nonaffiliation among Democrats rises by thirteen percentage points from the respondents' pre-experiment reports. As expected, the cognitive dissonance between religion and party only affects religious belonging, not religious beliefs or behavior. Exposure to politicized religion in the contrived setting of an experiment does not lead people to report a weaker belief in God. Nor does it lead to reports of less frequent attendance at religious services or less frequent prayer, which would be implausible given that we ask about

---

[14] Readers will note that we only show the effects for five of our nine experimental treatment groups in Figure 6.2. The reason is that the effect of the other four treatments (heavy-religion Republican and heavy-religion Democrat, light-religion Republican and light-religion Democrat, light-religion Republican and no-religion Democrat, and no-religion Republican and light-religion Democrat) on the likelihood of becoming unaffiliated from religion is neither statistically nor substantively significant. The logic behind showing the five groups seen in the figure is that we show the control group, the two heavy-religion-Republican treatments that had statistically and/or substantively significant effects on the likelihood of becoming a None, and the two analogous heavy-religion-Democrat treatments for the sake of comparison.

respondents' behavior immediately after they have read the story. Similarly, we do not find an effect for personal secularism, which suggests that it is a deep-seated orientation, not subject to change based on a single news story.

Granted, it might seem audacious to think that merely reading one news story about a congressional race could cause people to drop their religion. Note, though, the fluidity of religious identity, as mentioned in Chapter 1. Many people without a religious identity are actually "liminals," or existing between two states (Hout 2017; Lim, MacGregor, and Putnam 2010). Think of them as being "on the line" between identifying and not identifying with a religion. This experiment has induced some of those liminals to shift from affiliation at time 1 to nonaffiliation at time 2. The shift from having a religious identification, even if nominally, to a self-description as someone without a religion constitutes the cleanest test of cognitive dissonance. When the two identities of party and religion clash, party wins out – at least for Democrats.

POLITICAL PASTOR EXPERIMENT

While the Clerical Campaign Experiment tested how voters react when candidates drape themselves in religion, how do people respond when clergy wrap themselves in politics? The Political Pastor Experiment tests reactions to a member of the clergy who wears his politics on his sleeve. There is once again a realistic-looking news article, this time from the fictional *Maple City Herald*. The story describes a pastor speaking effusively about a local congressional candidate, Mark Cooper, during a recent rally. Since congregations' tax-exempt status is theoretically at risk if clergy overtly endorse candidates for office, the pastor stops short of formally endorsing the candidate. Instead he is quoted as saying, "I urge all voters to prayerfully consider their choice. Mark Cooper is the only candidate who stands for Biblical values. I know which way I am voting."

In all the versions, the pastor says that "America needs a moral reawakening. We must return to our Biblical roots." But just what those roots entail varies. In one variation, the pastor is supporting a Republican candidate and speaks about conservative issues. In another article, the pastor speaks in favor of a Democratic candidate and thus refers to issues on the political left. To leave no doubt that the pastor is highly supportive of the candidate, both the Republican and Democratic versions of the story end with a description of the candidate and pastor standing together with arms upraised. The pastor says that "I am in this for the long haul. I will do everything I can to see that we elect God-fearing leaders – like Mark Cooper – to restore morality in America."

Having versions of the story where a pastor supports either a Republican or a Democrat enables us to compare reactions to the intermingling of religion with the political right and left. In addition, we are also interested in whether any reaction is triggered by the overt mixture of religion with a campaign or if it is enough for the pastor to speak about politics, without the near-endorsement of a candidate for office. Is the backlash to a pastor plus politician, or just a pastor plus politics? To find out, the experiment also included two more stories. Each keeps the conservative or progressive language from the pastor but does not include the Republican or Democratic candidate.

Finally, there is a control group. These respondents also received a news story, but it includes no mention of religion and politics. Instead, it describes a "rally for reading," at which a local elementary school principal spoke about fostering a love of reading among children. This story was written to be as innocuous and non-partisan as possible, as even in our polarized times conservatives and liberals presumably can agree that encouraging reading among children is a worthy goal. In every other respect, though, the control story resembles the treatments – the newspaper and community are the same. The principal even has the same name as the pastor (Stephen Brown). And while we use a different photo for the pastor and the principal, they are both middle-aged white men with graying hair. A Closer Look 6.2 describes each experimental condition in detail, while Figure 6.3 displays one version of the story, in this case where a conservative pastor speaks in support of a Republican candidate.

A Closer Look 6.2:
Content of the Political Pastor Experiment

Conservative Pastor Only	Conservative Pastor and Republican Candidate
<u>Headline</u>	<u>Headline</u>
Local Pastor Speaks at Rally	Local Pastor Supports Republican Candidate
<u>Name of Rally</u>	<u>Name of Rally</u>
Rally for Traditional Values	Rally for Traditional Values
<u>Pastor Quotes</u>	<u>Pastor Quotes</u>
Voters in this upcoming congressional race must realize that America needs a moral reawakening. We must return to our Biblical roots.	Voters in this upcoming congressional race must realize that America needs a moral reawakening. We must return to our Biblical roots.
People of faith must work to end abortion, prevent the so-called transgender movement from destroying traditional roles for men and women, and to stop government harassment of businesses who exercise their right not to serve homosexual couples.	People of faith must work to end abortion, prevent the so-called transgender movement from destroying traditional roles for men and women, and to stop government harassment of businesses who exercise their right not to serve homosexual couples. In this race, I urge all voters to prayerfully consider their choice. Mark Cooper is the only candidate who stands for
I will do everything I can to restore morality in America.	

(*continued*)

(*continued*)

Conservative Pastor Only	Conservative Pastor and Republican Candidate
	Biblical values. I know which way I am voting. I will do everything I can to see that we elect God-fearing leaders – like Mark Cooper – to restore morality in America.

Liberal Pastor Only	Liberal Pastor and Democratic Candidate
Headline	Headline
Local Pastor Speaks at Rally	Local Pastor Supports Democratic Candidate
Name of Rally	Name of Rally
Rally for Progressive Values	Rally for Progressive Values
Pastor Quotes	Pastor Quotes
America needs a moral reawakening. We must return to our Biblical roots.	Voters in this upcoming congressional race must realize that America needs a moral reawakening. We must return to our Biblical roots.
People of faith must work to end the destruction of our environment, prevent tax cuts for the wealthiest 1 percent, and to stop government harassment of hard working immigrants.	People of faith must work to end the destruction of our environment, prevent tax cuts for the wealthiest 1 percent, and to stop government harassment of hard working immigrants. In this race, I urge all voters to prayerfully consider their choice. Mark Cooper is the only candidate who stands for Biblical values. I know which way I am voting.
I will do everything I can to restore morality in America.	I will do everything I can to see that we elect God-fearing leaders – like Mark Cooper – to restore morality in America.

Control

Headline
Local Principal Speaks at Rally
Name of Rally
Rally for Reading
Principal Quote
Reading is the keystone to a good education. We need to do everything we can to ensure that our children not only learn to read, but that they learn to love reading.
I will do everything I can to see that our kids become lifelong readers.

Since dropping a religious affiliation is a discrete change, making it a high hurdle to overcome, the Political Pastor Experiment added a variation from the first experiment, a continuous measure of self-described religiosity. Subjects indicated how they would describe themselves between the two poles of "I am very religious" and "I am not religious at all." This is a more sensitive gauge of one's attachment to religion than whether one has a religious identity; it is analogous to the difference between a weather report that tells you whether it is hot or cold and one that gives the temperature. It ranges from 0 (very religious) to 100 (not religious at all).

Among Republicans, none of the scenarios – conservative or progressive, support for a candidate or not – trigger a response in whether respondents describe themselves as religious. For Democrats, it is a different story, as they react in the same way to both stories that entail a pastor "endorsing" a candidate – that is, whether the candidate is a Republican or a Democrat. Each one leads them to say that they are less religious. The finding that Democrats are wary of political pastors suggests that their personal religiosity is especially sensitive to the mixture of religion and partisan politics. But, of course, movement on a 100-point scale is not the same as the "phase change" from holding a religious identity to dropping it. The backlash hypothesis, recall, predicts a change in identity – specifically, whether exposure to the fusion of religion and politics triggers an increase in religious nonaffiliation.

As displayed in Figure 6.4, the results for religious disaffiliation from the Political Pastor Experiment are consistent with those from the Clerical Campaign Experiment. Just as a Republican politician invoking religion pushed Democrats away from a religious identity, Democrats disaffiliate from religion when they read about a conservative pastor speaking in favor of a Republican candidate. The increase in religious nonaffiliation among Democrats is a sizable 8 percentage points when compared to their religious identification before they read the news story.

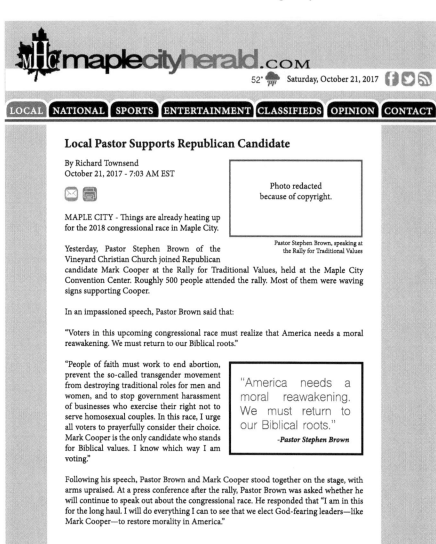

maplecityherald.com

52° Saturday, October 21, 2017

LOCAL NATIONAL SPORTS ENTERTAINMENT CLASSIFIEDS OPINION CONTACT

Local Pastor Supports Republican Candidate

By Richard Townsend
October 21, 2017 - 7:03 AM EST

Photo redacted
because of copyright.

MAPLE CITY - Things are already heating up
for the 2018 congressional race in Maple City.

Yesterday, Pastor Stephen Brown of the
Vineyard Christian Church joined Republican

*Pastor Stephen Brown, speaking at
the Rally for Traditional Values*

candidate Mark Cooper at the Rally for Traditional Values, held at the Maple City
Convention Center. Roughly 500 people attended the rally. Most of them were waving
signs supporting Cooper.

In an impassioned speech, Pastor Brown said that:

"Voters in this upcoming congressional race must realize that America needs a moral
reawakening. We must return to our Biblical roots."

"People of faith must work to end abortion,
prevent the so-called transgender movement
from destroying traditional roles for men and
women, and to stop government harassment
of businesses who exercise their right not to
serve homosexual couples. In this race, I urge
all voters to prayerfully consider their choice.
Mark Cooper is the only candidate who stands
for Biblical values. I know which way I am
voting."

"America needs a
moral reawakening.
We must return to
our Biblical roots."

-Pastor Stephen Brown

Following his speech, Pastor Brown and Mark Cooper stood together on the stage, with
arms upraised. At a press conference after the rally, Pastor Brown was asked whether he
will continue to speak out about the congressional race. He responded that "I am in this
for the long haul. I will do everything I can to see that we elect God-fearing leaders—like
Mark Cooper—to restore morality in America."

© 2017 *The Maple City Herald and MapleCityHerald.com*

FIGURE 6.3 Sample news story from the Political Pastor Experiment

Interestingly, the backlash in religious identity only occurs when
a conservative pastor appears with a politician. When the pastor is solo –
without the politician – there is no effect. And, once again dovetailing with
the first experiment, Republicans are unaffected, regardless of the pastor's

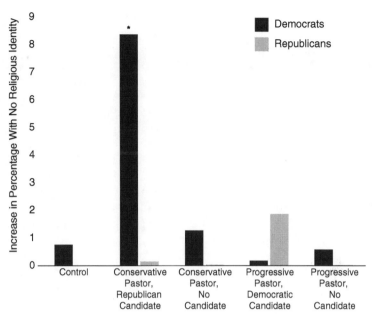

FIGURE 6.4 Democrats become Nones when exposed to political pastors
* = *Effect of experimental treatment statistically significant at* $p < .05$
Source: Political Pastor Experiment

politics or the presence of a politician. Also in keeping with the previous experiment, there are no effects on religious behavior or personal secularism – for either Republicans or Democrats.

It might initially seem puzzling that in the Political Pastor Experiment, Democrats become less likely to describe themselves as religious when exposed to politicized religion on both the left and right, while only the Republican-supporting pastor triggers disaffiliation from religion. Really, though, this pattern is not puzzling at all. It simply suggests that Democrats have a general aversion to the intermingling of religion and *any* partisan politics, even when religion is used to advance a political agenda with which they agree. When they hear religion mixed with politics, their connection to religion weakens. Since this pattern is observed for both a conservative *and* a progressive pastor, it is not dissonance between their own politics and their religion, but rather a distaste for the mixture of any religion with any politics. The dissonance only comes when it is a conservative pastor supporting a Republican candidate, and it is only when this dissonance occurs that Democrats are moved to disaffiliate from religion altogether.

To recap, some respondents drop their religious affiliation when simply exposed to a linkage between religion and politics. Remember, though, that religious nonaffiliation is often a liminal state, and so we would not expect our experiment to have pushed anyone out of religion permanently. Instead, we nudged people who were already walking a thin line over to one side. These are short-term effects. Yet if religious disaffiliation can occur in the admittedly artificial setting of a survey experiment, it suggests that repeated exposure to the mixture of religion and partisan politics in the real world over many years, often with even more heated religious rhetoric, would cause a large-scale turn away from religious affiliation – leading even more-committed members of a faith to abandon their religious identity.

Note that while these experiments provide evidence for the backlash hypothesis, they still leave many questions unanswered. Specifically, although each one employs a relatively large number of respondents, once divided into each "cell" (variation of the experiment), we are left with too few respondents to determine whether the effects we observe are stronger among particular demographic groups. In particular, since the rise in religious nonaffiliation has been most pronounced among young people, these experiments leave open the question of whether it is the young who have an especially strong allergic reaction to the mixture of religion and conservative politics. Fortunately, the third of our experiments doubled the sample sizes of the first two (from 1,000 to 2,000), thus enabling a focus on young people, and young Democrats in particular.

TRANSACTIONAL RELIGION EXPERIMENT

Both the Clerical Campaign and Political Pastor experiments were designed as straightforward tests of the backlash hypothesis, and demonstrate that religious nonaffiliation can be triggered by the mixture of religion and partisan politics. However, the results leave ambiguous the trigger for dissonance. Is it simply the mixture of religion and partisanship, specifically among Republican politicians? Or is it a concern over perceived hypocrisy, as in the case of Roy Moore? Furthermore, does people's reaction to the mixture of religion and politics depend on the perceived sincerity of the candidates involved? What if a candidate is not known to be personally religious but seeks the support of clergy and their coreligionists in purely transactional terms? This pattern, of course, is more than a hypothetical question. Many political observers contend that it describes many candidates who court the Religious Right, including none other than Donald Trump.

Unlike other Republican candidates who regularly cite scripture and reference hymns, Trump is better known for being profane than pious,[15]

---

[15] Trump has displayed an unfamiliarity with orthodox Christian doctrine and practices – saying that he does not feel he needs to ask for God's forgiveness, casually calling a communion wafer "the little cracker," referring to "Two Corinthians" instead of Second Corinthians in a speech at Liberty University (Moyer and Starrs 2016), and attempting to put money in a communion plate (Bailey 2016).

including the infamous tape in which he bragged about casually committing sexual assault, and revelations of an affair with a porn star. In the words of Michael Gerson, a former speechwriter for George W. Bush and a prominent evangelical Christian, "Trump's background and beliefs could hardly be more incompatible with traditional Christian models of life and leadership" (2018).

Putting aside his personal character, Trump's past policy positions would presumably not have garnered much support among religious conservatives. Prior to his 2016 presidential run, Trump had never advocated for the issues advocated by social conservatives, as he had been pro-choice on abortion and in favor of expanded LGBTQ rights. While he changed his position on abortion, Trump continued to endorse LGBTQ rights during the 2016 campaign, even mentioning them in his acceptance speech at the Republican National Convention (Keneally 2017). In that same speech, Trump acknowledged his gratitude to the "evangelical and religious community" for their support, while also acknowledging that "I'm not totally sure I deserve it."

Despite all of these reasons to vote against him, religious conservatives, particularly white evangelical Christians, voted heavily for Trump. And they did so in historic numbers, giving him 81 percent of their votes – a percentage slightly higher than even that won by fellow evangelical George W. Bush in either of his two presidential victories. A large part of why Trump was able to win evangelicals over were surgically precise promises that addressed their immediate policy concerns. For example, he committed to appointing judges opposed to abortion rights, including a pro-life justice to replace Antonin Scalia on the Supreme Court. Similarly, he vowed to repeal the Johnson Amendment, the provision in federal law that strips non-profit organizations, including churches, of their tax-exempt status if they make explicit political endorsements.

By making these promises, Trump was engaging in an old-fashioned political transaction – vote for me and this is what I will do for you. And since being elected, Trump has arguably gone even farther than he promised, enacting a number of policies that, according to one evangelical advisor "ha[ve] been a dream" (Groppe 2018). Not only did he appoint Neil Gorsuch and Brett Kavanaugh, both pro-life jurists, to the US Supreme Court, he also has made opposition to abortion rights a judicial litmus test for lower-level courts. In addition, he has prohibited US foreign aid from supporting international groups that promote abortion; created a division within the Health and Human Services Department to shield medical professionals who refuse to treat transgender patients or perform abortions; instructed the Justice Department in a prominent Supreme Court case to take the side of a Colorado baker who refused to make a wedding cake for a same-sex couple; recognized Jerusalem as Israel's capital; allowed federal disaster relief to be used to rebuild places of worship

(Groppe 2018); and instructed ambassadors not to fly the rainbow flag at US embassies during Pride Month (Londoño 2019).

Our choice of the word "transactional" is deliberate, as that is precisely how Trump's relationship to evangelicals has been described by one of his evangelical supporters. In the words of Richard Land, former head of the Southern Baptist Convention's Ethics and Religious Liberty Commission, "The relationship that evangelicals have with President Trump is a very transactional one. They feel like their voices are heard and he is keeping their promises to them" (Tackett 2019). Pastor Robert Jeffress also leaves no doubt that he cares more about policy than character. "I can't look into the president's heart to know if he really personally believes these positions he's advocating, or whether he thinks it's smart politics to embrace them because of the strong evangelical influence in the country. But frankly, I don't care. As a Christian, I'm seeing these policies embraced and enacted, and he's doing that" (Weiland 2018). Indeed, Trump himself is not shy about acknowledging the transactional nature of his support among evangelicals. In a speech to a gathering of evangelical leaders at the White House, he said:

The support you've given me has been incredible. But I really don't feel guilty because I have given you a lot back, just about everything I promised. And as one of our great pastors just said, "Actually, you've given us much more, sir, than you promised." And I think that's true, in many respects. (Trump 2018)

Vice President Mike Pence's background stands in sharp contrast to Trump's. Unlike Trump, Pence has long been a religious conservative, with personal bona fides as an evangelical Christian who speaks openly, and often, about his religious beliefs. Pence is famous (perhaps infamous) for following the Billy Graham rule of never being alone with a woman who is not his wife. On policy, Pence has made a career of being a staunch social conservative, including offering strident opposition to abortion. As governor of Indiana, he signed into law a highly controversial "religious liberty" bill that would have sanctioned discrimination against members of the LGBTQ community – a bill that was quickly revised after it met with widespread criticism, including from his fellow Indiana Republicans. In short, Pence's relationship to evangelicals is more than merely transactional. As one of them, he has long been their advocate.

This experiment follows the same methodology as in the previous ones: a pre-test, followed a week or so later by exposure to the "treatment" and a post-test. Once again, the treatment consists of realistic-looking news stories. Each describes a meeting between a group of religious leaders and either Trump or Pence, with subtle differences between them: Trump is portrayed as nonreligious, while Pence is described as having strong religious beliefs and being a frequent church attender. Less subtle than these differences in wording, the news articles feature a pull-out box that emphasizes the religiosity/nonreligiosity of Pence or Trump in a larger font size. In both cases, the story also features a photo of Trump or Pence in prayer with other people.

The experiment also includes two stories about a fictional Republican congressional candidate (with the generic name of Tim Cooper) that parallel the Trump and Pence articles, to see whether national figures like the president and vice president trigger a different type of response than a low-profile politician. The text of each story is identical to those about Trump and Pence, except of course that they feature "Tim Cooper." These stories also include a photo of the candidate deep in prayer within a church, holding hands with two people alongside him.

The control group read a story about a charming group of third-graders visiting City Hall to meet the mayor and learn about local government, complete with an adorable photo of children sitting in the council chambers. Importantly, the story includes nothing about religion. A Closer Look 6.3 has the details, while Figure 6.5 shows what the Mike Pence story looked like.

A Closer Look 6.3:
Content of the Transactional Religion Experiment

Transactional Religion (Trump and Local Member of the House)

<u>Headline</u>
Religious Leaders Show Support for Trump/Republican Candidate
<u>Background</u>
Because he is not known for being personally religious, there was a lot of speculation about what he would say. His critics point out that he does not seem to hold strong religious beliefs and he rarely attends church.
<u>Trump/Representative Quote</u>
I will always put the interests of the religious community first. I promise you that I will only nominate judges who have demonstrated their commitment to the pro-life cause. And I will defend the rights of religious believers like ourselves to exercise our religion freely.
<u>Pastor Quote</u>
It is clear that even if he has not always been a devoted Christian, he will be our advocate.
<u>Photos</u>[*]

(continued)

(*continued*)

Transactional Religion (Trump and Local Member of the House)

* Photo of Trump used by permission of the Associated Press (Jae C. Hong).

Sincere Religion (Pence and Local Member of the House)

Headline

Religious Leaders Show Support for Pence/Republican Candidate

Background

Because he is known for being personally religious, there was a lot of speculation about what he would say. Even his critics concede that he seems to hold strong religious beliefs and he often attends church.

Pence/Representative Quote

As a person of faith myself, I will always put the interests of the religious community first. I promise you that I will only support the appointment of judges who have demonstrated their commitment to the pro-life cause. And I will defend the rights of religious believers like ourselves to exercise our religion freely.

Pastor Quote

It is clear that because he is a devoted Christian, he will be our advocate.

Sincere Religion (Pence and Local Member of the House)

Photos[*]

* Photo of Pence used by permission of the Associated Press (*The Republic*/Joe Harpring).

Control

Headline

Third-Graders Visit City Hall

Background

Yesterday, a class of third-graders at Maple City Elementary School visited City Hall to learn about our city government. They were welcomed by Mayor Tim Cooper, who showed them around the building and his office. The children got to sit in the council chambers and pretend that they were the mayor and city council members.

Quotes

Their teacher, Jessica Riley, said that this was a wonderful experience to teach the children about the importance of democracy. One of the students, nine-year-old Ava Anderson, said that she was happy to meet the mayor and learn about his job. "I am happy that he works hard for our city." Another student,

(*continued*)

(*continued*)

Control

---

    ten-year-old Mason Davis, said that he thought it was "awesome that we got
to pretend to be the mayor."
Mayor Quote
I am proud of these young people. They asked tough questions and really kept
me on my toes. Our future is in good hands.
[Photo redacted because of copyright].

There are high hurdles to this experiment inducing the same effects as the previous two. For one, the treatments are subtler than those in our other two experiments. In the Clerical Campaign Experiment, the candidates were portrayed in religious settings, were endorsed by overtly religious groups, and touted their faith to the entire electorate. Here, the politician is not in a place of worship and is speaking to a group of pastors – a circumstance in which religious language might be expected. In the Political Pastor Experiment, the pastor was engaged in campaigning, while in the Transactional Religion Experiment the politicians are courting the pastors' political endorsement. They are receiving rather than seeking support. Just as importantly, the fact that two of the news stories are about Donald Trump and Mike Pence suggests that respondents might already have strong opinions, making it unpredictable how they will respond within the confines of the experiment.

In light of these hurdles, it is perhaps not surprising that we do not find a backlash effect among the population as a whole, or even among all Democrats. This pattern may suggest that most Americans expect transactions in politics, whether they agree with the currency or not.

We do find backlash among young Democrats (under thirty), which we are able to detect because we significantly increased the number of respondents included in this experiment. Among Democrats under thirty, every one of the stories leads to backlash, thus increasing their likelihood of disclaiming a religious identity.[16] These results provide confirmation of the backlash hypothesis, albeit in only a subset of the population. That subset, however, is precisely where past research suggests an effect should be most likely. It is Democrats who experience cognitive dissonance, while young people are the

---

[16] Technically, the effect of the Trump story for Democrats under thirty falls just short of conventional statistical significance, $p < .13$ (two-tailed test).

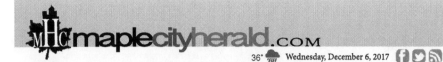

Religious Leaders Show Support For Pence

By Richard Townsend
December 5, 2017 11:19 AM EST

Vice President Mike Pence, in prayer before his speech

WASHINGTON - Yesterday, Vice President Mike Pence spoke to a gathering of conservative religious leaders, who are among his strongest supporters. These religious leaders were eager to hear from the Vice President. Because he is known for being personally religious, there was a lot of speculation about what he would say. Even his critics concede that he seems to hold strong religious beliefs and he often attends church.

In his speech, he told the religious leaders about what they can expect from the administration:

"As a person of faith myself, I will always put the interests of the religious community first. I promise you that I will only support the appointment of judges who have demonstrated their commitment to the pro-life cause. And I will defend the rights of religious believers like ourselves to exercise our religion freely.

> "It is clear that because he is a devoted Christian, he will be our advocate."
>
> *-Pastor Jim Young*

Afterwards, Pastor Jim Young, of Christ Fellowship Church in Sioux Falls, South Dakota, said that he was pleased with the administration's policies. "It is clear that because he is a devoted Christian, he will be our advocate."

FIGURE 6.5 Sample news story from the Transactional Religion Experiment*
* The photo is used by permission of the Associated Press (*The Republic*/Joe Harpring).

most likely to have a weak attachment to a religious identity – one reason why the growth of religious nonaffiliation is more striking among the young (Jones 2017; Putnam and Campbell 2012). As for the primary question posed by the experiment, it does not seem to matter whether politicians employ religion in purely

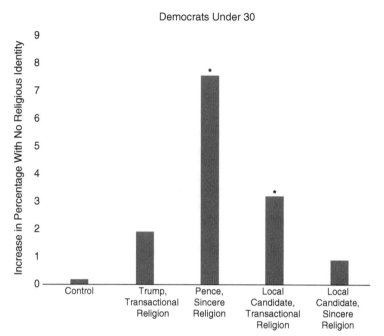

FIGURE 6.6 Young Democrats become Nones when exposed to sincere and transactional religion
* = *Effect of experimental treatment statistically significant at p < .05*
Source: Transactional Religion Experiment

transactional terms or actually are personally devout. Instead, it appears to be *any* mingling of religion with conservative politics that triggers the backlash among young Democrats.[17]

Interestingly, the biggest effect is for the Pence story – a jump in religious non-identification of nearly 8 percentage points (see Figure 6.6). Pence is well known for being overtly and sincerely religious. That we see such a strong effect for Pence suggests that young Democrats are especially allergic to politicians with a track record as candidates of the Religious Right, perhaps especially those associated with opposition to LGBTQ rights.[18]

---

[17] As with the other two experiments, we see no effects on religious behavior or personal secularism.
[18] Intriguingly, the Transactional Religion Experiment produces one more finding of note. The Pence story – in which subjects are reminded of his religious background – leads Republicans to become slightly more likely to identify with a religion. Theoretically, this makes sense. Although our focus has been how politicized religion drives Democrats away from a religious identity, the very same logic suggests that it should draw Republicans to religion, something found by other scholars (Patrikios 2008; Putnam and Campbell 2012). We hesitate to make too much of this one finding in one experiment, especially as religious nonaffiliation is relatively rare among Republicans to begin with, but nevertheless it is a possible counterbalance to the rise in religious nonaffiliation.

CONCLUSION

Based on the rigor of three controlled experiments, we have provided clear evidence that religious disaffiliation is due at least in part to a backlash to the mixture of religion and conservative politics, especially the Religious Right. When coupled with the observational research on people "in their natural habitat" in Chapter 5, the argument for the backlash hypothesis is compelling. Furthermore, our observational research has also shown how personal secularism affects both political attitudes and civic engagement. All of this evidence points to the same conclusion: secularism is shaping the contours of our political environment.

However, if the secular surge is truly transforming the landscape, the real test lies in the extent that secularism and nonreligiosity matter for party politics. Is there a deep – and potentially enduring – partisan fault line between a Secularist Democratic Party and Religionist Republican Party? Chapter 7 takes up that question by examining the secularism gap *between* the two parties. The next two chapters then examine the role of secularism, and nonreligiosity, *within* the Democratic (Chapter 8) and Republican (Chapter 9) parties.

7

Secularism and Party Politics

The secular–religious divide between Democratic and Republican partisans is echoed in the attacks that each party's stalwarts direct at each other. On the one hand, Democratic leaders portray the GOP as a party of fundamentalist zealots demanding adherence to a narrow religious orthodoxy and weaponizing religion for political gain. Democratic strategist John McCarthy, for example, claims that the Republicans have "crafted a political rhetoric to take their political agenda and force-feed it to Faithful America … They'll tell you that Jesus died for America – and ONLY America."[1] Similarly, in criticizing an unabashedly Christian prayer by a fellow Pennsylvania legislator, Democratic state representative Kevin Boyle noted that "I walked off the House floor in protest during today's prayer led by a GOP member. This fire and brimstone Evangelical prayer … epitomizes religious intolerance."[2] In a Democratic debate in 2019, 2020 presidential hopeful Pete Buttigieg claimed that "The Republican Party likes to cloak itself in the language of religion," but "We should call out hypocrisy when we see it."[3]

On the other hand, Republican leaders portray the Democrats as "secular humanist" extremists determined to eliminate religion from American life. Consider Senator Ted Cruz, who, while campaigning for the 2016 Republican presidential nomination, warned that

---

[1] John W. McCarthy, "Republicans Use Religion as a Political Tool," *HuffPost*, September 7, 2012, www.huffpost.com/entry/republicans-use-religion-as-a-tool_b_1862375.

[2] Reis Thebault, "GOP Legislator Prays to Jesus for Forgiveness Before State's First Muslim Woman Swears In," *Washington Post*, March 28, 2019, https://beta.washingtonpost.com/politics/2019/03/27/gop-lawmaker-prays-jesus-forgiveness-before-states-first-muslim-woman-swears/?noredirect=on.

[3] Emma Green, "Pete Buttigieg Takes Aim at Religious Hypocrisy," *The Atlantic*, June 27, 2019, www.theatlantic.com/politics/archive/2019/06/pete-buttigieg-religion/592897/.

We will see Ten Commandments monuments torn down because a radical Supreme Court says that we cannot acknowledge the Ten Commandments. If Hillary Clinton is elected president, we will see a radical Supreme Court ordering veterans' memorials to be taken down all over this country. We are just steps away from the chisels coming out in Arlington, to remove crosses and stars of David from the tombstones of our fallen soldiers. (Quoted in Barnes 2016)

Ben Carson, another candidate for the GOP's 2016 presidential nomination, sounded similar alarms about people "who are trying to push God out of our lives," and claiming the "real question is: Are we willing to stand up for those values and principles? Or will we allow ourselves to be intimidated by the secular progressives?" (quoted in Gass 2015). In a 2019 speech at the University of Notre Dame, Attorney General William Barr darkly warned of "organized destruction. Secularists and their allies have marshaled all the forces of mass communication, popular culture, the entertainment industry, and academia in an unremitting assault on religion and traditional values."[4]

Secularism and religiosity are also becoming key sources of intraparty division. Committed Secularists battle less-secular forces within the Democratic Party while Religionists are pitted against less-religious members of the Republican Party.

The secularism gap within the Democratic Party is highlighted by clear differences in how the candidates for the party's 2020 presidential nomination approached religion. In a March 2019 article entitled "Secular Democrats Are the New Normal," journalist Peter Beinart noted that many of the leading Democratic candidates broke with the time-honored American tradition of invoking God, as in "God bless America," at the end of speeches. Instead, trying to appeal to the Democrats' increasingly secular activist corps, white progressive candidates such as Elizabeth Warren, Bernie Sanders, and Beto O'Rourke "don't only talk about faith less than their predecessors," they "more often cite religion as a source of division" (Beinart 2019). In contrast, the two prominent African American candidates in the race – Senators Kamala Harris and Cory Booker – continued to close their campaign speeches with calls for God's blessings. Beinart contends that "For Harris and Booker, whose path to the Democratic nomination requires winning the black vote, religious language is a necessity." Meanwhile, Pete Buttigieg touted a remarriage of faith and Democratic politics – arguing that "we need to … invoke arguments … on why Christian faith is going to point you in a progressive direction" (quoted in Powers 2019).

Within the GOP, factional competition between religious traditionalists – particularly committed evangelical Christians – and business-oriented and less-

---

[4] "Attorney General William P. Barr Delivers Remarks to the Law School and the de Nicola Center for Ethics and Culture at the University of Notre Dame: South Bend, IN – Friday, October 11, 2019," The United States Department of Justice (website), www.justice.gov/opa/speech/attorney-general-william-p-barr-delivers-remarks-law-school-and-de-nicola-center-ethics.

religious "country club" Republicans has spanned decades. Despite recent accommodation between the two Republican wings (Cohen et al. 2008; Layman et al. 2010), tensions between them have at times been deep. For example, a *New York Times* editorial on "Republican Infighting" in 1998 suggested that "the Republicans have been split into two camps, one obsessing about abortion and family values, the other fixated on the capital-gains tax."[5]

In short, the cleavage between Secularists and Religionists may be a significant source of division both between and within the Democratic and Republican parties. Over the next three chapters, we evaluate the interparty and intraparty secular–religious divides. In this chapter, we focus on the secular–religious gap between the parties and its relationship to partisan ideological polarization. Chapter 8 concentrates on the secularism gap within the Democratic Party, and Chapter 9 turns to similar divisions within the GOP. Over the course of these chapters, we give a central role to party activists as vanguards of partisan change and exemplars of interparty and intraparty secular–religious divisions.

PARTY ACTIVISTS AND THE INTERPARTY DIVIDE

Party activists play an indispensable role in American party politics. They provide the physical, intellectual, and financial resources necessary to sustain party organizations as well as the means to effectively contest elections. As Marjorie Hershey suggests, without millions of volunteer activists, political parties "would not be able to register voters, get out the vote, build support for their policies, or even maintain their Facebook page" (2013, 13). Moreover, because the American parties nominate their candidates through a participatory process, activists exert a great deal of influence over who the nominees – and hence officeholders – are, from the presidency to local government.

All this effort means that activists occupy a central place in the life of the parties. Some theories of political parties view activists as important because of the critical support they provide to the officeholders and candidates at the heart of the party (Aldrich 1995; Schlesinger 1991). Other theories go further and identify activists as the central element in the parties. For example, Gaetano Mosca argues that in between "the highest stratum of the ruling class" and ordinary citizens lies a much larger "second stratum" of elites that "comprises all the capacities for leadership in the country." Mosca contends that "without such a class any sort of social organization would be impossible," and that this second stratum represents the driving force behind political change (1939, 404–405). In more recent work, Kathleen Bawn and her colleagues (2012) see political activists and their policy goals not only as the primary reasons for why

[5] "Republican Infighting," *New York Times*, July 26, 1998.

party organizations develop in the first place, but also as key to defining how and why they evolve over time (see also Cohen et al. 2008).

Whether they are essential or preeminent actors, party activists are unquestionably important to the development of new cleavages between the major parties. In fact, they are a key reason why cleavages between the parties exist at all. The office-seeking view of parties suggests that, left to their own devices, officeholders and office-seekers would position their parties as close as possible to the ideological center, leaving little or no policy difference between the two major parties (Downs 1957). However, because activists hold more ideologically extreme views than do ordinary voters, party leaders are compelled to move away from the center, resulting in interparty cleavages, and in many cases a high level of partisan polarization (Aldrich 1983; Miller and Schofield 2003).

The role of party activists may be even more outsized when it comes to new cleavages. When important new divisions, such as the cleavage between religious and secular Americans, first emerge, officeholders are understandably reluctant to stake out clear positions that might undermine their existing bases of support (Carmines 1991). So, initial support for distinct positions on the new issues typically comes from activists who are strongly motivated by the issues and push hard for these new views to be adopted (Carmines and Stimson 1990; Karol 2009; Wolbrecht 2000).

At that point, activists are important for translating new cleavages between party leaders into parallel cleavages between the parties' voter coalitions. It may take some time for ordinary voters, famously inattentive to politics, to recognize and respond to new policy differences between the parties. This process is accelerated when they have activist friends, family members, and coworkers who are aware of the new political developments and already participate in them (Lazarsfeld, Berelson, and Gaudet 1948). So, changes in the patterns of party activism signal to ordinary voters that the parties have staked out distinct positions on new issues on either side of a new cleavage (Carmines and Stimson 1990).

For example, increases in Republican activity by evangelical Christians and other Religionists tell ordinary voters that the GOP has become the party of religious conservativism. Meanwhile, increases in Democratic activity by atheists and humanists show voters that the Democratic Party has become the political home of secular progressivism. In this way, growing polarization between party activists is translated into parallel differences between the parties' voter coalitions.

This mechanism suggests that a secular–religious divide should emerge earlier and to a larger extent among Democratic and Republican activists than in the parties' voter coalitions. Thus, there should be a greater presence of secularism in the ranks of Democratic activists than among Democratic voters. Likewise, there should be more religiosity among Republican activists than among the GOP's voters.

NATIONAL AND STATE CONVENTION DELEGATE STUDIES

To assess the secular–religious divide among Democratic and Republican activists, we turn to surveys of national and state party convention delegates. The combination of data on delegates to national and state party conventions provides a broad perspective on activists in both parties. National convention delegates comprise a more "elite" group of activists (Miller and Jennings 1986). Because national convention delegates are among the most active participants in party politics and receive considerable attention during presidential election campaigns, they are likely to have greater influence than other activists on the parties' policy positions and the electorate's perception of the parties (Layman 2014). Meanwhile, the delegates to the many state-level party conventions held across the country are more likely to be grassroots activists who are keenly interested in politics and involved in the parties – at least from time to time – but who may not be connected to the highest echelons of national, or even state, parties (Rapoport, Abramowitz, and McGlennon 1986).

Data on national convention delegates come from the latest installments of the long-running series of Convention Delegate Studies (CDS) that began in 1972 and has continued through 2016.[6] Because most of these surveys do not include our indicators of secularism, we cannot employ the full CDS time series. However, we did include some of our secularism measures on both the 2012 and 2016 CDS surveys, allowing us to assess recent changes in levels of secularism in the two parties' activist bases.

Data on delegates to state-level party conventions comes from the 2016 State Convention Delegate Study (SCDS). To our knowledge, the SCDS is the first multistate survey of delegates to state party conventions to be conducted in many years. It was fielded in 2017 and 2018, surveying delegates to the 2016 Democratic Party state conventions in Texas, Minnesota, Washington, and Iowa; and the 2016 Republican Party state conventions in Texas, Illinois,

---

[6] See Kirkpatrick (1976), Layman et al. (2010), Layman and Weaver (2016), and Miller and Jennings (1986), for details on the CDS surveys from 1972 to 2012. The 2016 CDS was conducted by Kimberly Conger, Rosalyn Cooperman, Gregory Shufeldt, Mark Brockway, John Green, Ozan Kalkan, and Geoffrey Layman. As with the earlier CDS surveys, we contacted all of the delegates to the 2016 national conventions through the mail. In January 2018, we sent mailings to 5,126 delegates to the 2016 Democratic National Convention and 2,186 delegates to the 2016 Republican National Convention. We sent postcard reminders to delegates in February and March 2018 (one to Democrats, two to Republicans). After removing delegates who were deceased at the time of the survey or for whom we did not have complete or updated address information, our number of possible mail contacts was 4,745 Democrats and 1,969 Republicans. Unlike CDS surveys conducted before 2012, the mailings to 2016 delegates directed recipients to an online survey administered through the online survey platform Qualtrics from January through May 2018. We received valid responses from 307 Republicans and 806 Democrats, for effective response rates of 15.6 percent for Republicans and 17.0 percent for Democrats.

and Utah.[7] While the geographic makeup of the sample raises some concerns about representativeness, the demographic patterns seem to be relatively consistent across states and parties (Brockway 2019). Because the number of delegates is much larger in the SCDS than in the national CDS survey, we use the SCDS for most of our analyses and reserve the national CDS for over-time comparisons.

The 2012 and 2016 CDS surveys and the 2016 SCDS included most of our measures of secularism and nonreligiosity. The four secular belief statements that appeared on all of the Secular America Studies (SAS) were included on all three delegate surveys, along with our battery of religious and secular identity terms. As in earlier chapters, we treat the "secular," "humanist," "atheist," and "agnostic" labels as secular identities and count the number of secular labels selected.[8] Our secularism measure for the delegate surveys is a simple additive index of the four belief items and the secular identity count.[9] Two indicators of nonreligiosity – religious attendance and the amount of guidance individuals receive in their lives from religion – were present in all three delegate surveys. Our nonreligiosity measure is simply the sum of religious attendance and religious guidance (with each indicator and the resulting scale coded to range

---

[7] The SCDS was conducted by Mark Brockway, Geoffrey Layman, Rachel Blum, John Green, and Hans Noel. We contacted the executive offices of each state party that held a statewide convention in 2016 and we received lists of delegates from these seven state parties. We sent letters inviting participation in the survey to all 32,275 state convention delegates for whom we had complete contact information (15,131 Democratic delegates and 17,594 Republican delegates). As with the 2016 national CDS, the invitation letter directed delegates to a website on which they could take the survey through the Qualtrics online survey platform. We sent the initial letters to delegates in Minnesota, Washington, Iowa, Utah, and Illinois in September 2017, with three sets of postcard reminders sent in two-week intervals after the initial mailing. Because of extreme weather in Texas in September 2017, we delayed our mailings to both Democratic and Republican delegates in Texas until December 2017 and January 2018. We sent only one postcard reminder to Texas delegates – two weeks after the initial mailing – because the delegate lists for both Texas parties included e-mail addresses for all delegates. So, we sent four rounds of e-mail reminders to Texas Democratic and Republican delegates in two-week intervals following the postcard reminder. Our online survey was active from September 2017 through May 2018. We received completed surveys from 5,627 respondents (2,837 Democratic delegates and 2,790 Republicans) for effective response rates of 18.7 for Democrats and 15.9 for Republicans. The number of Republican respondents by state was 1,578 from Texas, 247 from Illinois, and 965 from Utah. The number of Democratic respondents by state was 1,740 from Texas, 236 from Iowa, 460 from Minnesota, and 401 from Washington.

[8] As in the SAS surveys, there were two places on our delegate surveys where respondents could identify themselves as atheists or agnostics: the battery of religious or secular labels and the religious affiliation question, which included "atheist" and "agnostic" as options. Our secular identity count variable includes respondents identifying themselves as atheist or agnostic in response to either question.

[9] We code all of our indicators to range from zero to one and sum each respondent's scores on the three belief items worded in a secular direction and our secular identity count. We then subtract the respondents' scores on both of the belief items worded in a nonsecular direction from that sum and rescale the resulting index to again range from zero to one.

from zero to one).[10] We use these measures to create our four secular-religious categories (described in Chapter 2) – Religionists, Non-Religionists, Religious Secularists, and Secularists – for national and state party activists.[11]

To compare secularism and nonreligiosity in the parties' activist and electoral coalitions, we created parallel indices of secularism and nonreligiosity – and the four secular-religious groups – in the 2017 SAS and the 2011 wave of the 2010–2012 SAS panel.

THE SECULAR–RELIGIOUS DIVIDE BETWEEN THE PARTIES

How well are our four secular-religious categories represented within the parties' activist bases and electoral coalitions? Figure 7.1 shows the four categories for each party's citizen identifiers (in the 2017 SAS), national convention delegates, and delegates to various state conventions (both in 2016). This evidence reveals a sharp secular–religious divide *between* the two parties. Among the delegates to the 2016 Democratic National Convention and the 2016 state conventions in Iowa, Minnesota, Texas, and Washington, Secularists were far and away the largest group of delegates. Secularists, in fact, represented a near majority of national Democratic delegates, nearly half of Iowa Democratic delegates, and roughly three fifths of the delegates to the Washington state Democratic convention. Even among Democratic citizen identifiers, Secularists are a plurality at over 35 percent of the Democratic coalition.

In contrast, Religionists comprised a substantial majority of every Republican delegation in 2016. Nearly 70 percent of Illinois Republicans were Religionists, and the numbers go up from there – over 70 percent of Republican national convention delegates, nearly 80 percent of Texas GOP delegates, and over 90 percent of delegates to the Republican convention in Utah. The Republican voter coalition is not as uniformly religious, but Religionists still represent a plurality – over 40 percent – of all GOP identifiers.

At the same time, it is important to recognize the secular–religious diversity *within* the two parties – especially within their voter coalitions, which are far less homogenous than the parties' activist corps. Secularists represent just a slight plurality of Democratic citizen identifiers, while Non-Religionists are

---

[10] All of our activist surveys also allow us to identify people with no religious affiliation. However, because religious affiliation was asked about in very different ways across our delegate and SAS surveys – sometimes with open-ended questions, other times with closed-ended branching questions – we limit the nonreligiosity measure to only attendance and guidance.

[11] Because we are comparing the size of the four categories across different surveys and over time, we use a standard cut point, rather than means within particular survey samples, to define the four groups. Religionists score below .5 on both the secularism and nonreligiosity scales. Non-Religionists score above .5 on nonreligiosity and below .5 on secularism. Religious Secularists score above .5 on secularism but below .5 on nonreligiosity. Secularists score above .5 on both the secularism and nonreligiosity indices.

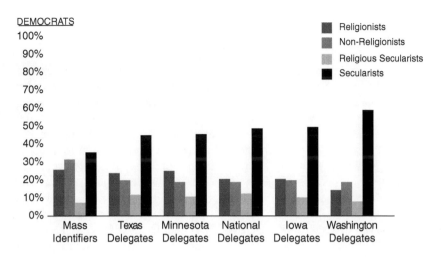

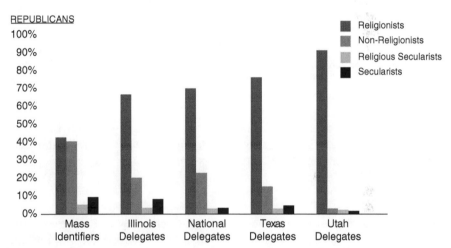

FIGURE 7.1 Party activists: Democrats are very secular, Republicans are very religious
Source: 2016 Convention Delegate Study; 2016 State Convention Delegate Study; 2017 Secular America Study

almost as prevalent. Religionists are not too far behind, at over one quarter of the Democratic coalition. A similar situation exists for Religionists in the Republican coalition: they represent just a slightly larger share of the Republican base than do Non-Religionists, although there is little presence of Secularists and Religious Secularists in the GOP.

In short, the Democratic and Republican voter coalitions have very different tendencies: the Democratic coalition clearly leans secular while the Republican base is much more religious. However, the division of the party system between

Secularist Democrats and Religionist Republicans is far from unqualified among citizen identifiers.

How comprehensive is this pattern among party activists? The answer depends on the party. In the GOP, Religionists represent an overwhelming majority of delegates to national conventions and party conventions in every state. The die appears to have been cast in favor of religiosity among Republicans – and mostly of a highly traditional variety.

In short, secularism represents a potential source of division within the Democratic Party – the topic of the next chapter. For now, we should not lose sight of the impressive and consistent pattern of interparty cleavage that Figure 7.1 highlights. Despite the demographic differences between the populations of Iowa, Minnesota, Texas, and Washington state, Secularists are clearly the largest group of Democratic Party activists in each of those states. And, even though there are clear differences in the social and religious profiles of Illinois, Texas, and Utah, Republican activists in each of those states fall overwhelmingly into the Religionist category.

Focusing on the Democratic and Republican state conventions in Texas paints a particularly powerful picture of the secular–religious divide between the parties' activists. The numbers of Secularists and Religionists at the two Texas state conventions could hardly have been more different. Texas Republicans were overwhelmingly in the Religionist category. And while a healthy number of Texas Democrats were Religionists, a large plurality were Secularists. Texas Democrats and Texas Republicans look far more like their partisan brethren in other states – and at the national level – than they look like each other. The secular–religious cleavage between Democratic and Republican activists is wide and consistent across the United States.[12]

IS THE SECULAR–RELIGIOUS DIVIDE GROWING?

To understand the implications of the secular–religious divide between the Democratic and Republican activist corps and voter coalitions, it is important to have information on whether or not it is growing over time. If it is expanding, perhaps as part of the secular surge, then its continuing importance for interparty politics may be greater than if it is holding steady or growing smaller.

Ideally, an examination of trends in the partisan divide would involve data over numerous election cycles so that we might distinguish short-term shifts, idiosyncratic to a particular campaign, from true long-term patterns.

---

[12] This same pattern holds if we examine the positions of party delegations on our full secularism and nonreligiosity indices. The mean of every Democratic delegation was above .62 on non-religiosity and above .55 on secularism (both ranging from zero to one), while the mean of every Republican delegation was below .37 on both scales. In Texas, the Democratic means were .62 on nonreligiosity and .57 on secularism. The Republican means were .27 on nonreligiosity and .31 on secularism.

Unfortunately, we do not have that luxury, as our measures of secular beliefs and identities are the first of their kind. However, because we included our secularism indicators on the 2012 and 2016 national CDS surveys, and in our 2010–2012 and 2017 SAS surveys, we can gain some insight into recent changes in secular–religious cleavage between the party's activist corps and voter coalitions.

In Figure 7.2, we examine these changes for both parties by showing the presence of our secular-religious categories at each party's 2012 and 2016 national conventions as well as among each party's citizen identifiers in the 2011 and 2017 SAS surveys. To indicate that the difference in the presence of our four categories between the second period (2016 for activists, 2017 for party identifiers) and the first period (2012 for activists, 2011 for identifiers) is statistically significant, we place a star above the bar for that group at the second time point.[13]

The picture for activists is a growing partisan cleavage. Of course, there is considerable stability in the secular-religious profiles of the parties' convention delegates over this very short period, but the interparty divide still clearly grew. The change was clearest among Democratic activists. There was an increase of over 10 percentage points in the presence of Secularists between the 2012 and 2016 national conventions, and there was a decline of almost the same size in the representation of Religionists. Given the strong showing of "not particularly religious" Bernie Sanders in the 2016 Democratic presidential nomination contest, this change is not surprising, but it is nonetheless impressive in a period of just four years.

Change among Republican activists was not as marked. However, despite the 2012 Republican presidential nominee (Mitt Romney) being a person of far deeper religious faith than the GOP's nominee in 2016 (Donald Trump),

[13] To assess whether the difference in the presence of a group in the two time periods was statistically significant, we first pooled the data from the two time periods (2012 and 2016 for convention delegates, 2011 and 2017 for party identifiers). Then, for Democrats and Republicans separately, we regressed a dummy variable for the group on a dummy variable for respondents in the second time period (2016 or 2017) and a number of control variables. The controls included for both activists and identifiers were education, income, sex, age, race, region of residence, and dummy variables for members of the three largest religious traditions (evangelical Protestants, mainline Protestants, and Catholics). For party activists, we also controlled for number of years active in party politics, whether or not the respondent was a first-time national convention delegate, and official delegate classification (dummy variables for super-delegates and at-large delegates for Democrats and a dummy for at-large delegates for Republicans, with congressional district delegates as the comparison category for both parties). The significance level of the coefficient on the dummy variable for the second time period is our gauge of whether the difference between the two time periods is statistically significant. Because the data were pooled from separate surveys, we computed the standard errors by clustering on the survey year. Finally, because the dependent variables in these regressions were binary, we estimated them with logistic regression as well as OLS. The results were very similar for the two methods.

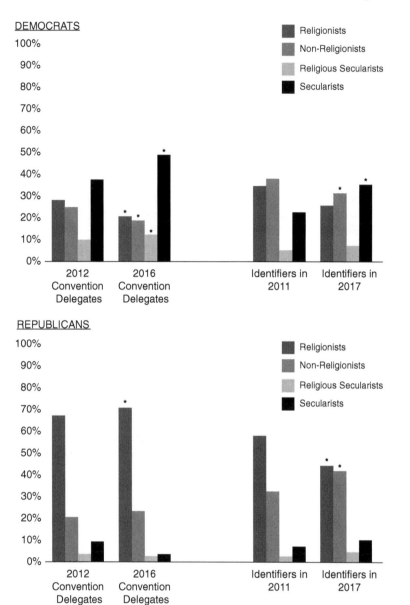

FIGURE 7.2 Democrats are growing more secular, Republicans remain highly religious
* = *Difference between proportion in group in 2016/2017 and 2012/2011 statistically significant at p < .10 with controls*
Source: *2012 and 2016 Convention Delegate Studies; 2011 and 2017 Secular America Studies*

the presence of Religionists actually increased slightly between 2012 and 2016.

Change in the parties' voter coalitions was not as dramatic. The Republican coalition, in fact, became significantly less religious between 2011 and 2017. Importantly, however, the Secularist presence in the Democratic voter coalition grew significantly and substantially over these years.[14] Thus in this time period, we do not have evidence of the GOP's voter coalition continuing to follow the Religionist trajectory of its activist corps, but we do have evidence of secularism in the Democratic electoral coalition growing *alongside* the rising secularism in its activist corps. The secular surge also may be linked to a closer relationship between secularism and party identification in 2017 than in 2011.[15] As Democratic activists become more secular and stand in sharper contrast to their highly religious counterparts in the GOP, secularism seems to be growing more strongly related to citizens' partisan attachment.

THE SECULAR–RELIGIOUS DIVIDE AND PARTISAN POLARIZATION

In Chapter 5, we saw that a growing secular–religious cleavage between the Democratic and Republican parties may increase ideological and affective polarization between those two parties. The progressivism of Secularist Democrats should encourage their party to move leftward ideologically, while the staunch conservatism of Religionist Republicans should spur the GOP to become even more conservative. Meanwhile, the diametrically opposed worldviews of Secularist Democrats and Religionist Republicans may exacerbate the levels of hostility and distrust that each party's supporters direct at their opponents.

Does our admittedly limited evidence for an increase in the secular-religious interparty cleavage coincide with evidence that the parties' activist corps are growing more ideologically polarized and more divergent in their feelings about key groups in each party's coalition? The answer is yes. The expansion of the secular–religious divide between 2012 and 2016 did occur alongside increases

---

[14] There also were statistically significant changes over the two time periods in the parties' positions on the full secularism and nonreligiosity indices. Among both activists and identifiers in the Democratic Party, there were statistically significant increases in both nonreligiosity and secularism. Among Republican activists, the decreases in secularism and nonreligiosity both were statistically significant. For Republican identifiers, there were significant increases in secularism and nonreligiosity.

[15] To assess that, we used our pooled 2011–2017 SAS data and regressed party identification on the secularism scale, the nonreligiosity scale, a dummy variable for 2017 respondents, and interactions between secularism and the 2017 dummy and between nonreligiosity and the 2017 dummy (and the same control variables included in our other models with pooled data). The interaction term coefficients indicate whether the positive relationships in 2011 between secularism and nonreligiosity on the one hand and Democratic Party identification on the other hand grew stronger or weaker over time. They suggest that the connection between secularism and Democratic partisanship grew stronger, while the association of nonreligiosity with partisanship became weaker.

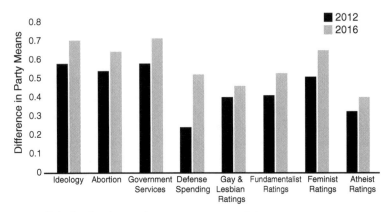

FIGURE 7.3 Polarization is growing among party activists
Note: The difference between 2016 polarization and 2012 polarization is statistically significant at p < .05 for every variable.
Source: 2012 and 2016 Convention Delegate Studies

in the levels of ideological, issue, and affective polarization between Democratic and Republican activists.

In Figure 7.3, we show the difference between the mean values of Democratic national convention delegates and Republican national convention delegates in 2012 and 2016 on liberal–conservative ideological identification for three policy issues (abortion, levels of government services and spending, and spending on national defense), and in affect toward three groups more closely associated with the Democratic Party (gay men and lesbians, feminists, and atheists) and one group closely associated with the GOP (Christian fundamentalists).[16] Party differences grew on every indicator. Democratic and Republican activists were more divided in ideological identification, their views on policy issues, and their feelings about party-relevant social groups in 2016 than in 2012. As polarized as party activists were in 2012, they were even more polarized in 2016.[17]

We cannot say for sure that the deeper secular–religious divide between party activists in 2016 was causally connected to greater ideological or affective polarization. But it is possible that the two patterns are related. An expanded secular–religious cleavage between party activists may make them more

---

[16] Ideology, all three policy issues, and feelings toward all four groups were asked about identically in the 2012 and 2016 CDS surveys. Neither CDS survey included feeling-thermometer ratings of the Democratic and Republican parties, so we cannot assess polarized affect toward the two parties directly. All of these indicators are coded to range from 0 to 1.

[17] We assessed whether the increases in party polarization on each indicator between 2012 and 2016 were statistically significant by regressing each indicator on a dummy variable for Democrats, a dummy variable for 2016 respondents, and their interaction (as well as control variables). The interaction was statistically significant for each dependent variable.

polarized in their political orientations, and that polarization also may encourage greater party division along secular–religious lines.

CONCLUSION

The division between Secularists and Religionists in the United States has clearly made its way into party politics, generating a strong interparty cleavage. Secularists are the ascendant group in the Democratic activist corps, and to a lesser extent in the Democratic voter coalition. In a parallel fashion, Religionists are clearly predominant among Republican activists, but less so in the Republican voter coalition. It appears that the secular–religious divide between the parties' activists is growing, with ideological and affective polarization expanding along with it. More time and data are needed to determine whether and how the secular–religious division contributes to other forms of party polarization. But for now, we can say that the growth of secularism among Democratic activists and of staunch religiosity among Republican activists is part and parcel of the contemporary political landscape.

At the same time, the growing readiness of the two parties' activists to battle along the secular–religious cleavage also means that secularism and religiosity may be continuing sources of division *within* the parties' activist corps and voter coalitions. In the next chapter, we examine the intraparty cleavages that secularism creates among Democrats – in not only ideology and policy positions, but also political style and candidate preference.

8

Secularism and the Democrats

There is a sharp secular–religious divide within the Democratic Party. It was evident in the campaign for the party's 2020 presidential nomination, as hopefuls such as Bernie Sanders, Elizabeth Warren, and Beto O'Rourke avoided "God talk," while candidates such as Kamala Harris, Cory Booker, and Pete Buttigieg trumpeted their faith and, in the words of Buttigieg, explained "why faith is going to point you in a progressive direction" (quoted in Powers 2019). It was also noticeable in the 2016 campaign, when Sanders was open about not being "particularly religious," while Hillary Clinton, the party's eventual nominee, sometimes emphasized her Methodist upbringing (Burke 2016; Luo 2017).

The secular–religious divide was especially clear in a battle over the 2012 Democratic Party platform. While platforms rarely draw much attention beyond the true party insiders, for many activists the platform has great meaning as an expression of the party's priorities and values. Party activists spend many hours, mostly out of the spotlight, seeking consensus among different factions. But in 2012 consensus was threatened when an initial draft of the Democratic platform did not include any mention of God.

This fact was not unprecedented, as Democratic platforms prior to 1996 often did not mention God. However, the initial omission of God from the 2012 platform stood in contrast to Democratic platforms earlier in the 2000s. The 2008 platform supported government giving everyone "the chance to make the most of their God-given potential." In 2004, there were at least seven references to God, including one proclaiming a "common purpose to build one nation under God."[1] And, even the 2012 platform did not ignore religion entirely, devoting an entire section to faith, and noting "We know that our nation, our communities, and our lives are made vastly stronger and richer by faith and the countless acts of justice and mercy it inspires" (Sullivan 2012). Still, the absence

---

[1] Platforms available from The American Presidency Project: www.presidency.ucsb.edu/platforms.php.

of God in the draft document triggered consternation among party leaders and President Obama's reelection campaign – especially when Republicans began to highlight the Democrats' "Godless platform." Republican nominee Mitt Romney, for example, claimed that the Democrats "purposely removed God from their platform," which "suggests a party that is increasingly out of touch with the mainstream of the American people" (Fox News 2012).

Fearing that the platform would unnecessarily alienate religious voters, party leaders, including President Obama himself, acted to amend the platform on the convention floor (Landler 2012). Ohio Governor Ted Strickland, head of the platform drafting committee, introduced an amendment calling for the platform to refer once again to Americans' "God-given" potential and another amendment restoring language that recognized Jerusalem as Israel's capital. The chair for that session of the convention, Los Angeles Mayor Antonio Villaraigosa, called for a voice vote on the amendments. The first voice vote was inconclusive, so he called for another – and then another. After the third try, he declared that the amendment had passed, even though a charitable account would say that the vote was still too close to call. Many observers felt that the nays had the edge. When Villaraigosa announced that the amendments had passed, he was met with boos.

It is unclear whether the booing was due to inappropriate protocol, opposition to the language on Jerusalem, or the phrase "God-given" returning to the platform. Nonetheless, many news outlets reported the story with headlines like "Democrats Boo God" (Murashko 2012). Meanwhile, secular activists expressed disappointment over the outcome. The spokesperson for American Atheists, for example, said that "What appeared to be a bold move by the Democrats to be inclusive has been pulled away. It sends a mixed message. Many, many people who are nonbelievers fall in the lines of the Democrats" (Cirilli 2012).

This dustup over God in the 2012 platform reflects a broader cleavage within the Democratic Party over secularity and religiosity. Like all new fault lines in American politics, secularism has the potential to divide the political parties internally at the same time that it creates greater separation between them. The divisive potential of secularism is particularly strong for the Democratic Party because while Secularists are ascendant in the party's activist and electoral coalitions, Religionists are still well represented in those bases – especially among working-class Democrats and Democrats of color.

In this chapter, we examine the secular–religious divide within the Democratic Party and its relationship to activists' and citizen identifiers' ideological orientations, political goals, norms, and candidate preferences. We also juxtapose the secular–religious divide with other divisions among Democrats, comparing their relative political importance and assessing how they interact with each other. We find that secularism is connected to greater liberalism, commitment to ideological goals, opposition to political compromise, and support for progressive candidates. Thus, our results suggest that the secular–religious divide is important not only for skirmishes over "God talk" on the campaign trail, but also for the broader intraparty clash between the stridently "progressive" wing of the party and its more-pragmatic "moderate" segments.

ACTIVISTS, SECULARISM, AND INTRAPARTY CONFLICT

When new activists, motivated by new issues, emerge within the parties, they not only spur greater divergence between the parties. They also may encourage new divisions within them, as the new activists clash with their party's existing activists. This intraparty discord may result partly from ideological differences. The policy positions championed by the new activists may not be shared by the party's old activists, who were attracted to party politics by older policy concerns and may be more centrist on newer issues (Miller and Schofield 2003; Sundquist 1983).

Fanning the flames of policy differences between old and new activists may be differences in political style – the political goals and norms of the rivals. The literature on parties has long distinguished between "amateur" activists, motivated more by ideological goals than by the success of the party, and "professional" activists motivated more by party success than by ideological goals (Soule and Clarke 1970; Wilson 1962). Closely related is the distinction between political "purists," who place ideological principles over party and disdain compromise for the sake of electoral victory, and "pragmatists," who prioritize compromise to achieve party unity and electoral victory over ideological principles (Wildavsky 1965). Amateurs and purists typically oppose compromise with the other party after the election as well.

New party activists, motivated by new issues and cleavages, are more likely than existing activists and leaders to be political amateurs and purists. With little history of loyalty to the party and zealous commitment to their stands on the emerging issues, new activists are typically "more concerned with victory for their position on the new issue than with their party's electoral success" (Sundquist 1983, 308). The uncompromising political style of new activist groups may exacerbate intraparty tensions and increase conflict over party nominations and platforms. Of course, this dynamic also makes the parties more hospitable to ideologically extreme nominees, and less likely to compromise with each other on important policy issues (Fiorina, Abrams, and Pope 2011; Layman, Carsey, and Horowitz 2006).

A final source of tension between newer and older party activists may be demographic differences. The social cleavage that underlies new issues and increasingly separates the two parties is a likely source of divergence. However, that separation may be related to other social discrepancies. An example is found in the Republican Party of the 1980s. There, the religious differences between the newer Christian Right activists and the GOP's traditional business-oriented "country club" activists were linked to other social differences. The evangelicals were less wealthy and educated than GOP regulars. And while the regulars dressed for corporate boardrooms and enjoyed a good drink, the evangelicals were teetotalers whose sartorial style suggested a tent revival (Oldfield 1996). In fact, Freeman (1986) described this as a conflict between the "ultrasuedes" and the "polyesters."

Secularism among Democratic Party activists should be associated with all three types of intraparty divides: ideological differences, differences in political style, and demographic differences. Because secularism is connected to staunch liberalism in the general public, there is every reason to expect secular activists to have the most liberal ideological and policy orientations of activist Democrats. Secularism also should be associated with amateur and purist political tendencies, just as past research on Democratic activism has shown (Kirkpatrick 1976; Layman 2010). The commitment to secular beliefs, sense of secular identity, and consistent liberalism that characterizes committed secularism should make secular Democratic activists particularly dedicated to their ideological goals and less inclined to compromise on those goals for the sake of electoral success. This combination should spur intraparty tensions with less-secular activists for whom intraparty unity and broad appeals to centrist voters are a higher priority.

Finally, the demographic profiles of Secularist and nonsecularist Democratic activists should differ in important ways, particularly along the lines of race and class. White Americans are markedly more secular than African Americans and Latinos. And, Peter Beinart suggests a racial element to the Democrats' secularism gap, noting that white Democratic presidential candidates generally avoid "God talk" while African American candidates continue to discuss faith openly (2019). Meanwhile, secularism is more prevalent among upper-status citizens than among lower-income white voters. In short, the growth of secularism in the Democratic activist base may antagonize the party's traditional bases of support among people of color and working-class whites.

SECULARISM AND THE POLITICAL PERSPECTIVES OF DEMOCRATIC ACTIVISTS

To evaluate secularism as an intraparty dividing line for the Democrats, we turn to the 2016 State Convention Delegate Study (SCDS) and assess the extent to which secularism and nonreligiosity are associated with differences in Democratic activists' ideological orientations, political style, and candidate preferences. We marshal the evidence in Figure 8.1, where we show how strongly secularism and nonreligiosity are connected to political orientations when we control for other social and political factors.[2]

[2] Specifically, the bars in the figure represent the standardized coefficients for secularism and nonreligiosity from regression models that include controls for demographic variables (education, income, sex, age, and race), dummy variables for the three largest religious traditions (evangelical Protestants, mainline Protestants, and Catholics), how long delegates have been active in party politics, and whether 2016 was the first year in which the respondent had been a delegate to a state party convention. To capture differences in the levels of and variance in our dependent variables across states, we include dummy variables for the state delegations in Iowa, Minnesota, and Washington, and compute standard errors by clustering on state. All variables are coded to range from zero to one.

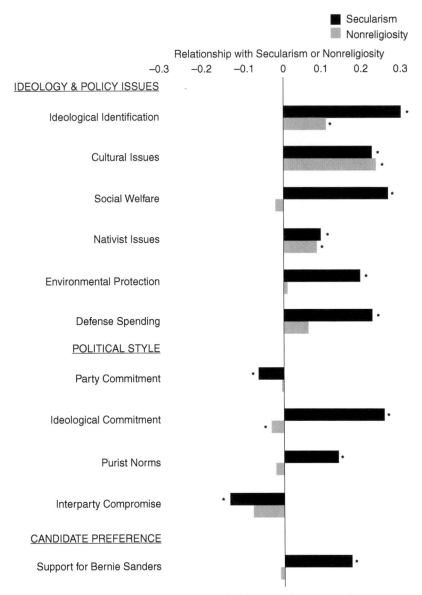

FIGURE 8.1 Democratic activists are divided by secularism, and sometimes by nonreligiosity

* = *Statistically significant at p < .05*

Note: Bars represent the impact, measured as the standardized regression coefficient, of nonreligiosity and secularism on political orientations. Both independent and dependent variables are coded to range from 0 to 1. Models are estimated with control variables that are described in the text.

Source: 2016 State Convention Delegate Study

Ideology and Policy Attitudes

The first set of bars in Figure 8.1 represents the connections of secularism and nonreligiosity to activists' ideological identifications and attitudes toward several areas of public policy. The policy areas are cultural issues (views on abortion, whether same-sex marriage should be legal, and whether businesses should be required to provide services for same-sex weddings); social welfare issues (overall levels of government services and spending, and federal spending to provide a free college education for all Americans); "nativist" issues (the building of a wall on the Mexican border, requiring that English be spoken in the United States, and banning travel to the United States from countries often associated with Islamic terrorism); environmental protection; and spending on national defense.[3] All of our measures have been coded so that a higher value means either more secular or more liberal. Thus, a bar on the positive side of the scale indicates that more secularism or nonreligiosity corresponds to a more liberal attitude.

Immediately evident is a secularism gap in ideological identification. Secularists are significantly more likely than less-secular activists to call themselves liberals. Nonreligiosity is also linked to liberal ideology, but the connection is only about half as strong as that for secularism.

Such a divergence in secularism's and nonreligiosity's political connections is not present for cultural and nativist issues. Both orientations are strongly linked to liberal views on abortion and same-sex marriage. Secularism and nonreligiosity are also similarly connected to unfavorable views on nativist policies such as a Mexican border wall and English as the official US language. These connections are weaker than those for cultural issues, but both are statistically significant.

The contrast between the political relevance of secularism and nonreligiosity returns for social welfare issues, environmental protection, and defense spending. On each dimension, secularism is significantly related to liberal attitudes while nonreligiosity is not. There is, in short, a secular–religious divide in the ideological and issue orientations of Democratic Party activists, with secularism significantly connected to liberalism in ideology and on a wide range of issues. Nonreligiosity also is connected to liberalism, but the differences between nonreligious and religious Democrats are less consistent and generally weaker than the divide between secular and less-secular activists.

Political Style

Are secular Democrats more likely than other Democratic activists to be political amateurs and purists? Are they less committed to the party and

[3] Exact question wording is presented in the online appendix: see secularsurge.com.

more committed to ideological goals? Are they less willing to compromise on ideological principles for the sake of party unity and electoral victory? Are they less inclined to seek common ground with political rivals to advance common policy goals? If you are interested in how we measured the delegates' political priorities, please see A Closer Look 8.1.

The next set of bars in Figure 8.1 shows secularism's and nonreligiosity's connections to political style, with the first two measures tapping into activists' priorities – how committed they are to supporting partisan and ideological goals. We find that secularism is negatively related to party commitment and positively related to ideological commitment. Secularism's negative association with party commitment is not very strong and just misses statistical significance (p = .08), but its positive link to ideological commitment is both strong and statistically significant. Secularists, in other words, are less motivated by party loyalty and more driven by ideological priorities than are other Democratic Party activists. Nonreligiosity, by contrast, is not associated with prioritizing ideology over party – indeed, it has no connection to party commitment, while its significant relationship with ideological commitment is negative. Nonreligious Democrats are less motivated than religious Democrats by ideological goals.

Does the tendency of Secularist Democrats to be political amateurs mean that they also have a distaste for compromise? To answer that, we examine the degree to which delegates have "purist" or "pragmatist" norms about decision-making within the party. As we expected, secularism is positively and significantly related to political purity. Even beyond Secularists tending to be younger and less politically experienced than other activists,[4] they are more purist. In other words, they are less likely than their less-secular counterparts to prioritize intraparty unity and broad electoral appeal. In contrast, nonreligiosity is not connected at all to purist–pragmatist political norms.

A final aspect of political style is support for compromise between the two parties as opposed to ideological constancy among elected officials. Both secularism and nonreligiosity are negatively associated with support for interparty compromise. Secularists and Non-Religionists are more likely than their less-secular and more-religious counterparts to favor principled steadfastness over pragmatic compromise with the GOP. However, secularism's connection here is about twice as large as that of nonreligiosity. Secularists, it seems, are opposed to political pragmatism when it comes to both intraparty politics and interparty governing relationships.

All in all, our evidence suggests that secularism is connected to the "aggressive liberalism" that is ascendant in the contemporary Democratic

---

[4] Among state Democratic delegates in our sample, secularism's correlation is –.13 with years of experience in politics and –.20 with age.

A Closer Look 8.1:
Measuring Activists' Political Styles

Our analysis includes four elements of activists' political styles: party commitment, commitment to ideological goals, purist–pragmatist political norms, and support for compromise between the parties.

Party and Ideological Commitment

Our indicators of party commitment are:

- Delegates' self-reports of how strongly they support their party (on a sliding scale ranging from "not very strongly" to "very strongly")
- How important party attachment is as a reason for being involved in politics
- Delegates' ranking of how important the party organization was as a group they represented at the 2016 state party convention (relative to a candidate support group, a geographic place, a demographic group, an organized group, or an ideological group).

Our indicators of ideological commitment are:

- The importance of getting "the party and its candidates to support the policies in which I believe" as a reason for political participation
- Delegates' ranking of ideological groups as entities they represented at the 2016 state party convention (relative to the groups listed above for the ranking of party organization).

In a factor analysis of these indicators of political priorities, the party commitment variables loaded strongly on one factor and the indicators of ideological commitment loaded strongly on another factor. The scores for these two factors are our measures of party and ideological commitment.

Purist–Pragmatist Political Norms

Delegates were asked for their levels of agreement with five norms:

- It is best to minimize disagreement within the party
- One should stand firm for a position even if it means resigning from the party
- The party should play down some issues if it will improve the chances of winning
- The party should select a nominee who is strongly committed on the issues
- Choosing a candidate with broad electoral appeal is more important than consistent ideology.

Our measure of activist norms (with higher scores representing greater pragmatism) is the score from a factor analysis of levels of support for these five political norms. For both parties' respondents, there was only one factor with an eigenvalue greater than one.

Interparty Compromise

Our measure of support for interparty compromise is based on a single question asking delegates to place themselves on a scale ranging from "Democratic elected officials should stand up for their principles no matter what" to "Democratic elected officials should compromise with Republicans in order to get things done for the country."

Party. Secularists are among the most liberal activists in the Democratic camp, they prioritize ideological goals, they blanch at calls for intraparty harmony and compromise, and they zealously oppose compromise with the GOP.

Candidate Preference

There is every reason to expect that the secular–religious divide among Democratic Party activists was related to preferences for the party's 2016 presidential nominee. At times, Bernie Sanders was openly secular while Hillary Clinton was openly religious. Moreover, given Secularists' strong and consistent liberalism and their distaste for political pragmatism, Sanders' staunch progressivism and unconventional, anti-establishment political style should have made him an ideal candidate.

We assess that expectation in the last set of bars in Figure 8.1, which shows the connection of secularism and nonreligiosity to the likelihood of preferring Sanders over Clinton.[5] The effect of secularism is substantial: Secularists were significantly more likely than other Democratic activists to support Sanders over Clinton. In contrast, nonreligiosity had no connection to presidential nominee preference among state Democratic delegates in 2016. Again, the politically relevant divide in the Democratic activist base is principally along the lines of secularism rather than between nonreligious and religious Democrats.

---

[5] We estimated a logit model in which the dependent variable was support for Sanders or Clinton and the independent variables were secularism, nonreligiosity, and the control variables. The bars represent the effects of increasing secularism/nonreligiosity from one standard deviation below its mean to one standard deviation above its mean – holding all other variables at their observed values – on the predicted probability of preferring Bernie Sanders as the Democratic Party's 2016 nominee.

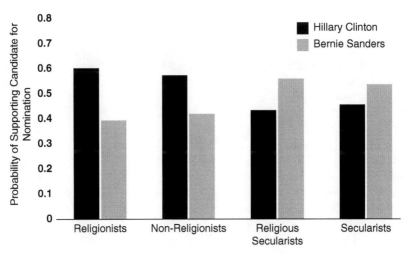

FIGURE 8.2 2016 presidential preference: Secularists preferred Sanders, Religionists favored Clinton
Note: Bars represent the predicted probabilities of supporting Clinton or Sanders from a logistic regression model.
Source: 2016 State Convention Delegate Study

To illustrate that further, we estimated a slightly different statistical model that replaced our full secularism and nonreligiosity indices with dummy variables for our secularist-religious groupings.[6] In Figure 8.2, we show the probability of support for Clinton and Sanders. The gap in nominee preference is clearly based on secularism and not nonreligiosity. Both Religionists and Non-Religionists were noticeably more likely to support Hillary Clinton than Bernie Sanders. In contrast, both Secularists and Religious Secularists favored Sanders over Clinton.

SECULARISM AND OTHER DEMOCRATIC DIVIDES

There is a secularism gap within the Democratic Party and it matters for ideology, policy, political style, and candidate preference. But how does it compare to other intraparty fault lines? The most important dividing lines within the Democratic Party traditionally have been class and race (Brewer and Stonecash 2001; Mayer 1996). The Democrats' blue-collar, labor-union wing has long vied with better-educated and higher-income liberal activists for intraparty control (Stonecash 2000; Wilson 1962). Meanwhile, intraparty competition between white Democrats and Democrats of color harkens back to the one-party Democratic South, and continues to the present as Latinos have

---

[6] This was a logistic regression model that included dummy variables for Religionists, Non-Religionists, and Religious Secularists, with Secularists serving as the comparison category.

joined African Americans as a key party constituency (Conger et al. 2019; Frymer 2010). Gender and age also have been important factional lines among Democrats (Kirkpatrick 1976). They may have been particularly important for intraparty politics in 2016, as Hillary Clinton garnered robust support from women in her successful bid to become the party's first female presidential nominee. Meanwhile, Bernie Sanders, her chief competitor, appealed strongly to young, male activists (Golshan 2019).

In Figure 8.3 we address the relative importance of the secularism gap and these other fault lines for Democratic activists' ideological identifications, attitudes on social welfare policy, purist–pragmatist political norms, and presidential nominee preferences. We employ the same statistical models used in Figure 8.1 and show the predicted differences between activists who are secular and nonsecular, white and nonwhite, well-educated and poorly educated, younger and older, and female and male.[7]

Overall, the secularism gap among Democratic Party activists is as large as or larger than other intraparty gaps. The ideological distance between secular and nonsecular activists is clearly larger than that between activists who are white and nonwhite, highly educated and less-educated, younger and older, and male and female. In fact, only secularism and gender are significantly associated with ideology. The same pattern holds true for social welfare attitudes: the secularism gap among Democrats is noticeably larger than the racial, education, age, or gender gaps. In fact, only secularism and education are significantly connected to welfare liberalism.

The pattern changes somewhat for purist political norms and support for Bernie Sanders. In both cases, the largest divide in the Democratic activist base is between younger and older activists. This is not surprising, given that activists are more likely to be ideological idealists when they are young, typically growing more politically pragmatic with age (Stone and Abramowitz 1983). Importantly, however, the secularism gap in both political norms and presidential nominee preferences is nearly as large as the age gap.

The other statistically significant fault lines are a gender gap in political norms, and gender and education gaps in presidential preferences. Women are more politically purist than men. Not at all surprisingly, women were less likely than men to support Sanders. Somewhat surprisingly, less-educated activists were more likely than better-educated activists to support Bernie Sanders. But all of these differences are noticeably smaller than the norm and nominee

---

[7] For secularism, education, and age, we define low values as one standard deviation below the mean value for all state Democratic delegates and high values as one standard deviation above the mean value. For the racial and gender dummy variables we simply set the values of the variables to zero and one. All other independent variables are held at their observed values. For the figure, we have reversed the coding of education (ranging from high to low) and age (ranging from oldest to youngest) in order to highlight the way in which those variables traditionally have been related to Democratic partisanship (with less-well-educated and younger people more likely to be Democrats).

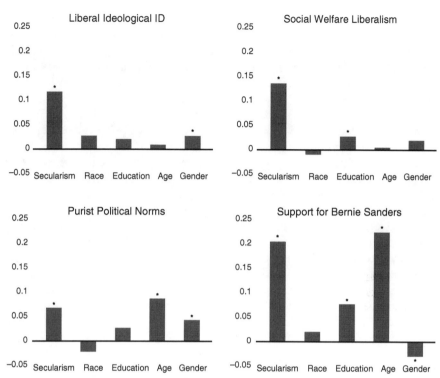

FIGURE 8.3 Secularism and other gaps among Democratic activists
* = *Effect of independent variable on dependent variable (in models shown in Figure 8.1) is statistically significant at p < .05*
Note: *The bars represent the following group differences: secularism (high vs. low), race (white vs. nonwhite), education (low vs. high), age (young vs. old), and gender (women vs. men).*
Source: *2016 State Convention Delegate Study*

differences based on secularism and age. Secularism, in short, is as closely connected as any demographic factor to political divisions within the Democratic Party.

Given the relative importance of the secularism divide within the Democratic Party, it is important to ask whether it is related to and interacts in important ways with other gaps within the Democratic coalition, namely those based on race and socioeconomic class. Race and class not only have been the defining traditional fault lines within the Democratic Party, but also remain crucial to Democratic electoral success. Two of the most common explanations for Hillary Clinton's 2016 loss in the Electoral College to Donald Trump have been her lack of appeal to white working-class voters, particularly in the Midwestern states that loomed particularly large in 2016, and that African

Americans' lack of enthusiasm for Clinton may have led them to turn out at lower rates than they had for previous Democratic candidates (Coontz 2016; Frey 2017). So, understanding how secularism's ascent in Democratic politics is related to the party's appeal to people of color and to white working-class voters is crucial to understanding its implications for Democrats' ability to win elections.

We explore the class and racial aspects of differences in secularism within the Democratic Party in Figure 8.4. Because of the relative lack of less-educated people among state convention delegates, we turn back to our 2017 SAS survey of the American electorate. Here we show the presence of our four secular-religious (see Chapter 2) categories for African American and Latino Democratic identifiers as well as for college-educated and non-college-educated white Democratic identifiers.

Not surprisingly, Secularists are concentrated most heavily among college-educated white Democrats. They are much less prevalent among non-college-educated white Democrats. These Democrats are not strongly religious – Religionists are nearly as rare here as they are among upper-status white Democrats. However, they are not strongly secular either. Rather, Non-Religionists are clearly the modal category among white working-class Democrats. Meanwhile, nonwhite Democrats look different from both groups of whites: Religionists represent a plurality of both black and Latino Democrats, and are a near majority of African American Democrats.

There is, in short, a distinct racial and socioeconomic face to the rise of secularism in the Democratic Party, and it is not the face of the party's

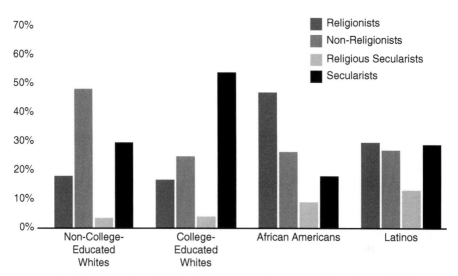

FIGURE 8.4 Democratic secularism is concentrated among college-educated whites
Source: 2017 Secular America Study (Democrats only)

traditional working-class and minority base. Rather, Democratic Secularists are mostly white and mostly well-educated. Thus, ascendant secularism may represent a double-edged sword for the Democratic Party. It may attract new support from well-educated whites, but threaten the parties' long-time backing from working-class and minority voters.

CONCLUSION

For much of the early twenty-first century a battle has been raging within the Democratic Party. That battle was particularly evident in the 2020 presidential primaries. On one side of this battle were progressives such as Bernie Sanders and Elizabeth Warren, who promulgated unabashedly liberal visions on a range of policy issues and unapologetically aggressive postures toward President Trump and conservative Republicans. On the other side were candidates such as Joe Biden, Pete Buttigieg, and Amy Klobuchar who called for a more centrist approach that seemed more likely to appeal to swing voters, and embodied a policymaking style that emphasized pragmatic interparty compromise.

Our findings suggest that secularism is at the very heart of such battles for the soul of the Democratic Party. Secularists have the most liberal ideological identities and policy positions among Democratic activists. They are motivated more by ideological goals and less by party loyalty. They are more likely to spurn intraparty and interparty compromise in favor of principled battles over correct ideology and policy visions. And, Secularists are more likely than other active Democrats to support aggressively liberal candidates who share their vision. It is no wonder then that highly progressive candidates like Sanders and Warren mostly avoid "God talk," while candidates who are not quite as liberal – candidates like Biden and Buttigieg – are more forthcoming about matters of faith.

Secularism, in short, represents an important fault line within the Democratic Party, with significant electoral implications for the Democrats. Secularism brings new, largely white and better-educated activists into the party. However, it also may dampen the enthusiasm of traditional working-class and minority constituencies for the Democratic Party and its candidates. In the next chapter, we turn to the internal politics of the Republican Party.

9

Nonreligiosity and the Republicans

One of the defining characteristics of the contemporary Republican Party is its staunch religiosity. Traditional religiosity has been growing among Republican activists since the early 1980s (Layman 2010). And, as we showed in Chapter 7, Religionists became an even larger share of GOP activists between 2012 and 2016.

This does not mean that there are no Secularists in the Republican Party. Secularists comprised nearly 10 percent of delegates to the 2012 Republican National Convention (see Chapter 7), heavily supporting Ron Paul, the libertarian hero who sought the party's presidential nomination in 2012 (Layman and Weaver 2016). Paul's appeal to Secularists is not surprising given that Secularists and Non-Religionists have long represented a large share of activists in the Libertarian Party – which gave Paul its presidential nomination in 1988 – as well as Republican activists with a libertarian bent (Guth and Green 1996). In fact, as we show below, Secularists disproportionately supported Rand Paul, Ron Paul's son and another libertarian favorite, for the GOP's presidential nomination in 2016.

However, secularism is unlikely to represent the sort of fault line among Republicans that it does for Democrats. One reason is simply the predominance of Religionists and the small number of Secularists in the GOP. In fact, while Religionists' share of Republican delegates grew between 2012 and 2016, the presence of Secularists declined to just a smidgeon, as Rand Paul fared less well in 2016 than his father had in 2012.

In such a religious party, secularism has often served more as an enemy against which forces should be amassed than as a serious participant in intraparty debates. Conservative politicians and pundits warn of the dire threats that "secular humanism" and its allies in Hollywood, the media, academia, and the Democratic Party pose not just to traditional religious values, but to the American way of life. Conservative commentator Bill

O'Reilly calls attention to "the committed forces of the secular-progressive movement that want to dramatically change America, molding it in the image of Western Europe" (2006, 2). In the provocatively titled *Godless*, conservative author Ann Coulter warns that secular progressives have much bigger goals than limiting the public role of religion. Rather they seek to establish a "state religion of liberalism" and "demand total indoctrination" into its beliefs (2007, 1).

A second reason why secularism may be a less important fault line for Republicans than Democrats lies in the political styles of secular and religious activists. Secularists play the part of ideologically motivated political amateurs in the Democratic Party, but in the GOP it has long been true-believing Religionists, particularly devout evangelical Christians, who have played that role. Decades of research have shown that committed evangelicals are less motivated by party loyalty, more driven by ideological goals, and less willing to compromise for the sake of party victory than are other Republican activists (Layman and Brockway 2018; Oldfield 1996). In fact, even Senator Barry Goldwater, the famous proponent of conservative orthodoxy,[1] found evangelical Republican activists to be frustratingly unwilling to compromise. Goldwater warned that:

[I]f and when these preachers get control of the party, and they're sure trying to do so, it's going to be a terrible damn problem. Frankly, these people frighten me. Politics and governing demand compromise. But these Christians believe they are acting in the name of God, so they can't and won't compromise. I know, I've tried to deal with them. (Quoted in Dean 2006)

If Republican Secularists are themselves political purists – Ron Paul's Secularist delegates in 2012 seemed to adopt the contrarian political style and weak party commitment of their candidate (Layman and Weaver 2016) – they will not be alone in the GOP. The much larger group of Religionists in the party has long shunned compromise and demanded ideological purity. Thus, if there is a divide over political style in the Republican Party, it is likely to be defined more by differences between Religionists and other kinds of Republican activists than by secularism.

Although secularism may be a less important fault line within the GOP, our theme of growing nonreligiosity and secularism still may be important for intraparty Republican politics. That is because there may be a newly important dividing line between Religionists and Non-Religionists in the Donald Trump–era Republican Party. In the race for the party's presidential nomination in 2016, Trump attracted an impressive level of support from nonreligious voters. In the early days of the Republican primaries, Trump's base among evangelical voters was not among the devout, but among those who

---

[1] Goldwater, of course, was famous for proclaiming – in his speech accepting the 1964 Republican presidential nomination – that "extremism in the defense of liberty is no vice! And . . . moderation in the pursuit of justice is no virtue." "Goldwater's 1964 Acceptance Speech," *Washington Post*, www.washingtonpost.com/wp-srv/politics/daily/may98/goldwaterspeech.htm.

rarely attended church (Layman 2016) and were less committed to traditional evangelical beliefs (Margolis 2019). In fact, among Republicans in three of the major Christian faith traditions – evangelical Protestants, mainline Protestants, and Catholics – Trump's spring 2016 support was noticeably higher among infrequent church attenders than among frequent attenders (Martinez and Smith 2016). Of course, by the 2016 general election, Trump was the overwhelming favorite of evangelical Christians and other GOP Religionists.

As we discuss below, there are numerous reasons why less-religious Republican and independent voters may have been attracted to Trump's candidacy. However, what is certain is that Non-Religionists are less conservative on, and less concerned about, the moral and cultural issues that have been at the heart of the GOP's appeal to Religionists over the last several decades. If the presence of Non-Religionists in the Republican coalition grows, the potential for intraparty tension between this group and Religionists should grow as well.

In this chapter, we examine the fault lines between Secularists, Religionists, and Non-Religionists within the Republican Party's activist corps and voter coalition. We focus first on differences in political attitudes and styles among delegates to state Republican conventions, finding that secularism is of limited importance to Republican intraparty politics. Next, we employ survey data from January 2016 to assess whether Religionists and Non-Religionists were early supporters of Donald Trump for the 2016 Republican presidential nomination. We find that Non-Religionists were significantly more likely than Religionists to back Trump. Trump's appeals to nativism and white racial grievance plus his bleak portrayal of the collapse of economic prosperity in the United States were more attractive to nonreligious Republicans than to their religious copartisans.

RELIGION, SECULARISM, AND REPUBLICAN ACTIVISTS

We begin by examining the connections between secularism, nonreligiosity, and the political orientations of delegates to the 2016 state Republican Party conventions. Based on recent Republican politics, we expect the dividing lines within the GOP to be multifaceted, with Religionists, Secularists, and Non-Religionists all diverging in potentially unique ways. In Figure 9.1, we show political orientations for Republican state delegates in our four secular-religious categories (created in Chapter 2), predicted from a statistical model that mirrors the one we used for Democrats in Chapter 8, and thus accounting for other potentially confounding demographic characteristics.[2]

---

[2] We employed the same regression models of political orientations for Republicans as we used for Democrats in Chapter 8, but with dummy variables for Religionists, Non-Religionists, and Religious Secularists (with Secularists as the comparison category) as the key independent variables. The models include dummy variables for delegates to the GOP conventions in Utah and Illinois and produce standard errors by clustering on state.

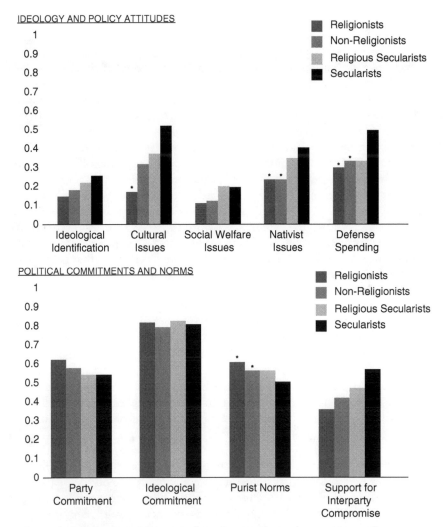

FIGURE 9.1 Secular Republicans are less conservative and more pragmatic
* = *The difference between the particular group and Secularists in regression models (with control variables described in text) is statistically significant at p < .05*
Note: *Higher scores on ideological identification and policy attitudes represent greater liberalism.*
Source: *2016 State Convention Delegate Study*

In overall ideological identification, the differences between Secularists and other GOP activists – even Republican Religionists – are not statistically significant and pale in comparison to the differences among Democratic activists. The same is true for attitudes on social welfare issues, with

Secularists differing little from Religionists or any other group of Republican activists.

On other issues, however, there is greater variation across the secular-religious groups. Not surprisingly, Secularists are the most liberal group of activist Republicans on cultural issues such as abortion and same-sex marriage, and there is a statistically significant difference between Religionists and Secularists. The same pattern holds, though to a lesser degree, on "nativist" issues such as a Mexican border wall and a ban on travel from certain Muslim-majority countries. Secularists are significantly less supportive than both Religionists and Non-Religionists of these policies proposed by Donald Trump. Finally, in keeping with the libertarian bent that they displayed by supporting Ron Paul in 2012, Secularists are less enamored than any other group of Republican activists with buildups in defense and military spending.

Secularists, in short, do offer support within the GOP for less-conservative positions on a range of issues. However, that support is tempered by Secularists' negligible presence in the GOP activist corps as well as the fact that they are no less conservative than other Republicans – even Religionist activists – on social welfare and overall ideology.

It also may be tempered by the political commitments and norms of Republican Secularists. Although the Secularist backers of Ron Paul in 2012 displayed an amateur and purist political style (Layman and Weaver 2016), secular Republicans in 2016 were – relative to their fellow partisans – less ideologically committed and more pragmatic than were Secularists in the Democratic Party. There is no difference across our four secular-religious categories in the GOP in devotion to party or ideological commitment.

Meanwhile, it is the Republican Religionists who are least willing to compromise with intraparty or interparty political opponents. Both Religionists and Non-Religionists are significantly more purist than Secularists in norms about intraparty politics. In willingness to compromise with Democrats "to get things done for the country," Religionists are the least accommodating GOP activists and Secularists are the most willing to seek common ground.[3] In the Republican Party, it is still religiosity, not secularism, which encourages ideological orthodoxy and discourages political concession.

As we show in Figure 9.2, secularism also had relatively weak connections to Republican activists' preferences for the party's 2016 presidential nominee.[4] Because our Republican delegates come overwhelmingly from Texas – where native son Ted Cruz was the clear favorite – and Utah – where the

---

[3] In the regression estimates for interparty compromise, the difference between Republican Religionists and Secularists is close to standard levels of statistical significance (p < .08).

[4] The bars in Figure 9.2 represent predicted probabilities from a multinomial logit model of Republican delegates' support for Donald Trump, Ted Cruz, Rand Paul, or other Republican candidates. The model included the same control variables as our other regression models.

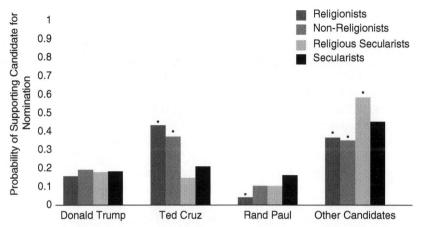

FIGURE 9.2 Republican activists: Secularism is weakly connected to Republican presidential preferences
* = *The difference between the particular group and Secularists in regression models (with control variables described in text) is statistically significant at p < .05*
Note: *Higher scores on ideological identification and policy attitudes represent greater liberalism.*
Source: *2016 State Convention Delegate Study*

overwhelmingly Mormon core of Republican activists was unenthusiastic about Donald Trump's candidacy (Campbell 2016), support for the eventual party nominee was quite low in our sample. But there was no difference across secular-religious groups in preference for Trump. There were differences in support for other candidates. Ted Cruz performed best among Religionists, while Non-Religionists were significantly more likely than Secularists to back Cruz. Meanwhile, Rand Paul, following in his father's footsteps as the libertarian voice in the GOP, received his strongest backing from Secularists and appealed least to Religionists.

There were, in short, differences between Secularists, Non-Religionists, and Religionists in preferences for the Republican nominee in 2016. However, those differences were of relatively little political consequence because they emerged in support for also-ran candidates and not in support for eventual nominee Donald Trump.

NONRELIGIOSITY AND SUPPORT FOR DONALD TRUMP

Once he became the GOP's presidential standard bearer, Republicans of all religious and secular stripes became Donald Trump backers. For example, by the general election in November 2016, devout evangelicals had caught up to – and, in fact, overtaken – less-religious evangelicals in support for Trump (Margolis 2019). And now that Trump is president, more frequent church attendance is associated with stronger support for him (Djupe and Burge 2018). So, to really understand how Trump and his brand of populist politics appeal to our four secular-religious categories within the Republican Party, it is necessary to look back to before Trump became the GOP presidential nominee. Which of our four secular-religious groups in the Republican electorate were most enthusiastic at that point about both Trump and *Trumpism* – as political style and substance?

From the perspective of early support for his candidacy, Trump's strongest support among Republican voters seemed to come from Non-Religionists. Less-religious Republicans – whether they were evangelicals or otherwise – were more enthusiastic than their devoted brethren about Trump (Martinez and Smith 2016; Margolis 2019). And, these core Trump supporters were not, it appears, Secularists. Rather, they were people who identified with a religion yet were not especially devout. For example, in her discussion of the "five types of Trump voters," Democracy Fund pollster Emily Ekins (2017) shows that Trump's strongest support in the Republican primaries came from "American Preservationists," a group of people who rarely attend religious services, but attach considerable importance to their religious identities.

What Ekins shows empirically, J. D. Vance suggests anecdotally in his best-selling memoir *Hillbilly Elegy*, often described as a guide to the white working-class people who see Trump as their tribune. Vance poignantly describes his grandmother (Mamaw) as one of these Americans for whom religious identity and belief are important, but who display low levels of religiosity:

"Mamaw, does God love us?" She hung her head, gave me a hug, and started to cry. The question wounded Mamaw because the Christian faith stood at the center of our lives, especially hers. We never went to church, except on rare occasions in Kentucky or when Mom decided that what we needed in our lives was religion. Nevertheless, Mamaw's was a deeply personal (albeit quirky) faith. She couldn't say "organized religion" without contempt. (2016, 85)

Although Vance does not use this term to describe her, Mamaw's belief system fits the definition of what sociologists call "cultural religion," in which "religious symbols retain some emotive and cultural power for individuals even as they disengage from actively practicing religious communities" (Baker and Smith 2015, 17). In other words, people like Mamaw are clearly not committed to Secularist beliefs, but they also are not committed to the conventional practices of organized religion. They are, in short, neither Secularists nor Religionists. They are, most likely, Non-Religionists – albeit of a special kind.

And Non-Religionists were, we expect, the group of Republican partisans most enthusiastic about Donald Trump and his campaign before supporting Trump became synonymous with supporting the Republican Party. To see if that is true, we turn to the 2016 American National Election Studies (ANES) Pilot Study – fielded in January 2016, at the height of the primary season – and develop plausible proxies for our secular-religious groups.[5] We limit our analysis of the pilot study data to Republican identifiers and independents who lean Republican – in other words, the respondents most likely to participate in Republican presidential primaries or caucuses. There were very few Secularists among this group of respondents. So, while we do include a dummy variable for Secularists in our statistical models, we focus on comparisons between Religionists and Non-Religionists in the Republican electorate.[6]

The ANES pilot asked respondents which Republican presidential candidate they preferred ("regardless of whether you will vote in the Republican primary this year") and we show candidate preferences among Republican Religionists and Non-Religionists in Figure 9.3. To simplify the presentation, we group GOP candidates other than Donald Trump into three groups: Christian Conservatives (Ted Cruz and Ben Carson), Establishment Republicans (Jeb Bush, John Kasich, and Marco Rubio), and "other candidates."

Both the Christian Conservative and Establishment candidates fared better among Religionists than among Non-Religionists in the GOP electorate. Meanwhile, Trump was the plurality favorite among both Religionists and Non-Religionists, but he attracted noticeably more support from Non-Religionists (46 percent) than from Religionists (34 percent). Just as other analyses have suggested, the core of Trump's early support in the Republican nomination contest seems to have been nonreligious people.

Why were nonreligious Republicans drawn to Donald Trump's candidacy? An obvious first place to look is socioeconomic status, given that the less-committed members of major faith traditions tend to have lower income and education levels than their devoted counterparts (Wilcox et al. 2012), and Trump appealed uniquely to working-class whites (Sides, Tesler, and Vavreck 2018). That is, in fact, part of the story. Non-Religionists in the Republican coalition do have lower education and income levels than Republican

---

[5] The pilot study interviewed a nationally representative sample of 1,200 Americans from January 22–28, 2016. For more information about the survey, see https://electionstudies.org /project/anes-2016-pilot-study/. For these data, we define Secularists as people who identify themselves as atheists or agnostics in the survey's religious-affiliation question and attend religious services infrequently (a few times a year or less often). Non-Religionists are respondents who attend worship services infrequently, but do not identify as atheists or agnostics. Religionists are people who attend worship services frequently (once or twice a month or more often) and do not identify as atheists or agnostics. Because there were only three Religious Secularists – respondents identifying as atheists or agnostics and attending religious services frequently – among pilot-study respondents (none among Republican respondents), we exclude this group from the analysis.

[6] Of the 381 Republican identifiers or Republican-leaning independents in the ANES pilot study, we classify 163 (43 percent) as Religionists, 208 (55 percent) as Non-Religionists, and 10 (under 3 percent) as Secularists. Among the Non-Religionists in this Republican sample, under 20 percent claimed no religious affiliation. Nearly 45 percent of the Republican and Republican-leaning Non-Religionists identify as Protestants and over 25 percent are Catholics.

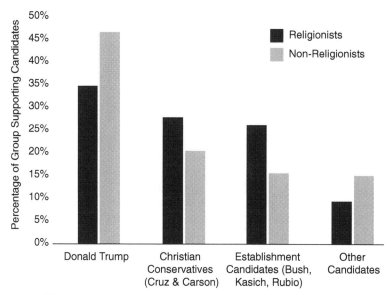

FIGURE 9.3 Non-Religionists were Trump's strongest early supporters
Source: 2016 American National Election Studies Pilot Study

Religionists.[7] And, lower-status Republican voters were more likely than upper-status Republicans to back Trump in the early stages of the 2016 nomination campaign.[8] However, this pattern is only part of the story. Even when we control for income, education, and other sociodemographic variables, Non-Religionists are significantly more likely than Republican Religionists to prefer Donald Trump as the Republican presidential nominee.[9]

If the relative enthusiasm of Non-Religionists for Donald Trump and his candidacy cannot be attributed only to economic class, then what else explains

---

[7] Among Republican identifiers and leaners in the ANES pilot study, 27 percent of Religionists and 44 percent of Non-Religionists had a high school diploma or less education while 32 percent of Religionists and 44 percent of Non-Religionists had family incomes of less than $40,000 per year.

[8] Fifty-four percent of Republicans with no college education and 48 percent of Republicans with family incomes under $40,000 per year backed Trump. Only 30 percent of Republicans with a four-year college degree and 34 percent of Republicans with family incomes of $70,000 or higher supported Trump.

[9] Using the 2016 ANES pilot study, we estimated a logit model in which the dependent variable was coded one for Trump supporters and zero for Republican identifiers and leaners backing other candidates. The independent variables were dummy variables for Non-Religionists and Secularists (with Religionists as the comparison category), education, family income, region, gender, age, race, and marital status. The coefficient on the dummy variable for Non-Religionists is positive and statistically significant. The predicted probability of supporting Trump (holding all control variables at their actual values) is .47 for Non-Religionists and .36 among Religionists.

it? The answer may lie in *Trumpism* – in the sorts of policy issues on which Trump focused, the positions he took on those issues, and the social groups he embraced and attacked. Specifically, Trump's hard-line positions on immigration, his appeals to nativism and white racial grievance, and his relative inattention to the traditional moral and cultural agenda of the Religious Right and the GOP may have been more attractive to nonreligious Republican voters than they were to their religiously devout counterparts.

Ekins's description of the "American Preservationists" – the core Trump constituency that attaches importance to religion but generally avoids participation in it – is suggestive. The Preservationists:

appear more likely to desire being around people like themselves ... [and] are far more likely to have a strong sense of their own racial identity. They take the most restrictionist approach to immigration ... and intensely [support] a temporary Muslim travel ban. They feel the greatest amount of angst over race relations: they believe that anti-white discrimination is as pervasive as other forms of discrimination, and they have cooler feelings ... toward minorities. (2017)

The fact that this group of Trump enthusiasts combines antipathy toward racial, ethnic, and religious "out-groups" with low levels of religious devotionalism squares with research showing that, among people claiming a religious affiliation, those who are more devout tend to be more generous, more trusting of people different from themselves, and more tolerant toward immigrants and minority groups (Burge 2013; Ekins 2018; Knoll 2009; Putnam and Campbell 2012). In contrast, the less-devout religious affiliates often cling tightly to the unique identities of religious bodies without being exposed to the messages of universal love, acceptance of strangers, and generosity toward the disadvantaged that most religions promote (Wald and Calhoun-Brown 2018). That, in fact, may explain the negative relationship between nonreligiosity and humanitarianism that we uncovered in Chapter 5. From this perspective, Donald Trump's strident calls to "make America great again" may have been particularly appealing to such nonreligious people.

Adding to the allure of Trump and Trumpism for Non-Religionists may be the fact that, as we showed in Chapter 4, nonreligious people are more likely than both Religionists and Secularists to be civic dropouts, not deeply involved in community or political life. Trump's entreaties to people disenfranchised by rapid economic and cultural change may have related particularly well to Non-Religionists' sense of disconnection from the civic and political lives of their communities (Wilcox et al. 2012). Moreover, because, as we found in Chapter 5, nonreligiosity is not closely connected to a consistently liberal or conservative ideological outlook, Trump's departure from conservative orthodoxy on trade, foreign policy, and even some moral issues may have enhanced his appeal to Republican Non-Religionists.

To see how attractive Trumpism was to Religionists and Non-Religionists in the Republican electorate, we turn back to the 2016 ANES Pilot Study and compare religious and nonreligious Republicans on a range of variables. We do so while controlling for a host of demographic factors and show the results in Figure 9.4.[10]

We start with feeling thermometers, gauging Republican Religionists' and Non-Religionists' affect toward three groups on the cultural left – gays and lesbians, feminists, and transgender people – and three racial and religious minority groups – African Americans, Hispanics, and Muslims. The results suggest that less-religious people are more accepting than Religionists of nontraditional lifestyles, but are less tolerant toward racial, ethnic, and religious minority groups.

Religionists, on average, rate all three cultural-left groups lower than do Non-Religionists. All of these differences are statistically significant and they are pretty substantial for gay men and lesbians, as well as for transgender individuals. This suggests that Non-Religionists are, not surprisingly, less supportive than Religionists of the moral traditionalism that has been GOP orthodoxy since the 1980s. Thus, the fact that Donald Trump placed less emphasis on moral traditionalism than most Republican candidates, and even touted his support for LGBTQ rights – saying in his acceptance speech at the 2016 Republican National Convention that "As your president, I will do everything in my power to protect our LGBTQ citizens from the violence and oppression of a hateful foreign ideology" – may have been a selling point for him among Republican Non-Religionists. In fact, nonreligious Republicans are not only more liberal than their religious copartisans on cultural matters, but also find moral and cultural matters to be less salient.[11]

The pattern flips, however, for feelings about racial, ethnic, and religious minority groups. Non-Religionists have less favorable views than Religionists toward African Americans, Hispanics, and Muslims. The differences are not

---

[10] The bars in Figure 9.4 represent the values for Religionists and Non-Religionists predicted by regression models that control for education, family income, region, gender, age, race, and marital status.

[11] The ANES pilot study presented respondents with a set of political issues and asked them "Which of the following issues are the most important to you in terms of choosing which political candidate you will support? Please rank which four of these are the most important to you." Three of the issues in the list were abortion, gay rights, and "morality and religion in society." We took each respondent's mean ranking of these three issues – coded one through four for the corresponding importance ranking of the issue and five for respondents who did not rank the issue – to form a "moral values importance" scale, and then compared the mean of Republican Religionists and Non-Religionists on it. Among Republican identifiers and leaners, the mean moral values importance scores are 4.54 for Religionists and 4.90 for Non-Religionists and the difference in means is statistically significant (p < .001). The only other issue agendas on which there was a statistically significant difference in salience between Republican Religionists and Non-Religionists were social welfare issues (respondents' mean ranking of health care, income inequality, unemployment, and social security) and issues of economic growth (mean ranking of national debt, economic growth, and taxes). Non-Religionists attached slightly more importance than Religionists to social welfare issues and slightly less to economic growth.

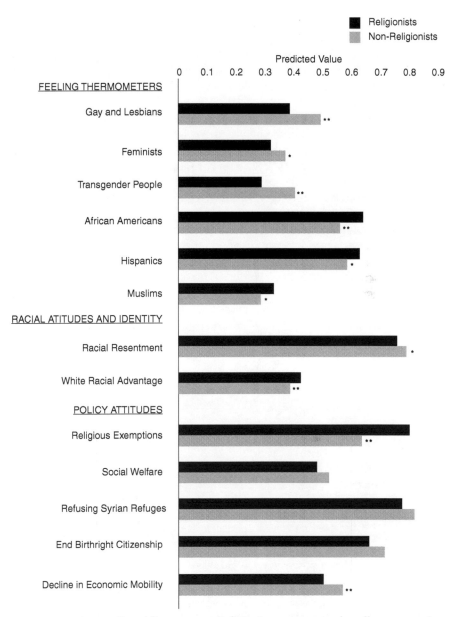

FIGURE 9.4 Among Republican voters, Religionists are more culturally conservative, Non-Religionists are more racially conservative

Note: *Bars represent the values predicted from regression models with control variables*
Source: *2016 American National Election Studies Pilot Study*
** = *The difference between Non-Religionists and Religionists is statistically significant at p < .05*
* = *The difference between Non-Religionists and Religionists is statistically significant at p < .10*

particularly large, but they are all statistically significant. And they suggest that Trump's call for a ban on travel to the United States from predominantly Muslim countries, his attacks on undocumented Latino immigrants, and his earlier championing of the "birther" questions about President Obama would have played better with nonreligious Republicans than with religiously devout affiliates of the GOP.

In the next set of bars, we turn from feeling thermometers to other indicators of racial attitudes and identity. First, we form the traditional measure of anti–African American "racial resentment" or "symbolic racism" (Kinder and Sears 1981).[12] Next, to tap into a sense of white racial grievance, we employ a series of questions that the pilot study asked to white respondents about whether being white was an advantage or disadvantage to them in today's society. Higher scores represent a greater sense of white racial advantage – that white people tend to be advantaged by the color of their skin.[13] Whites with a stronger sense of racial grievance should score lower on this scale.

In fact, Republican Non-Religionists do score significantly lower than Religionists on white racial advantage and they have higher levels of racial resentment than do their more-religious copartisans. Thus, Trump's appeals to white racial animosity had more traction with Republican Non-Religionists than with the more traditionally religious elements of the GOP base.

Finally, we turn to the attitudes of Religionists and Non-Religionists on several issues of public policy. These issues include views about exemptions

[12] We measure racial resentment with the score from a factor analysis of respondents' reactions to two statements worded in a resentful direction – "Irish, Italians, Jewish and many other minorities overcame prejudice and worked their way up. Blacks should do the same without any special favors" and "It's really a matter of some people not trying hard enough; if blacks would only try harder they could be just as well off as whites" – and two statements worded in a nonresentful direction – "Generations of slavery and discrimination have created conditions that make it difficult for blacks to work their way out of the lower class" and "Over the past few years, blacks have gotten less than they deserve."

[13] The pilot study split its sample and asked two slightly different sets of questions about white racial advantage to randomly selected halves of the sample. The first half of the sample received four questions: (1) "Does your skin color make your everyday life easier for you, make it harder, or does it not make any difference?", (2) "How much does being white grant you unearned privileges in today's society?", (3) "To what extent do white people have certain advantages that minorities do not have in this society?", and (4) "Does having white skin generally give whites more opportunities in their everyday lives, fewer opportunities, or does it not make any difference?" The other half of the sample were asked four different questions: (1) "Does being white help you, hurt you, or make no difference for you personally in today's society?", (2) "How many advantages do white people have that minorities do not have in this society?", (3) "How many disadvantages do white people have that minorities do not have in this society?", and (4) "Compared to other groups, do white people generally have an advantage, a disadvantage, or does it not make any difference?" For each set of respondents, we took their mean value across the items and that mean value represents a respondent's white racial advantage score.

from aspects of state or federal law on religious grounds,[14] social welfare issues,[15] allowing Syrian refugees to come to the United States, ending birthright citizenship for children born in the United States to unauthorized immigrants, and respondents' views on whether levels of economic mobility in the United States are increasing or decreasing.[16]

There are substantial and statistically significant differences between Religionists and Non-Religionists on religious exemptions to the law. As we would expect, Religionists are noticeably more supportive of allowing exemptions on same-sex wedding services for religious people and exemptions on contraceptive coverage for religious employers. And Republican Non-Religionists are significantly more likely than Religionists to believe that the opportunities for upward economic mobility are on the decline in the United States (even controlling for differences across respondents in socioeconomic status).

None of the other differences between GOP Religionists and Non-Religionists are statistically significant. However, they all come close to significance and they are consistently in the direction of Non-Religionists supporting policies that Donald Trump has either supported or publicly considered supporting. These differences include social welfare policies, where Trump has flirted with breaking with Republican orthodoxy on paid parental leave and single-payer health insurance – and where Non-Religionists are a bit more liberal than Religionists. They include greater support by Non-Religionists for Trump's calls to refuse US asylum for Syrian refugees. And they include more enthusiasm for ending birthright citizenship – an idea sometimes floated by Trump and his allies.

In short, the policy attitudes, social group affect, and white racial grievance that are characteristic of Trumpism are nearly all more prevalent among Non-Religionists in the Republican voter coalition than they are among Republican Religionists. Thus, Non-Religionist Republicans should have been the core of voter support for Donald Trump during the 2016 Republican nomination contest – and in fact, they were.

---

[14] Our scale of religious-exemption attitudes is the mean of respondents' views on two issues: whether business owners should be allowed to refuse wedding-related services to same-sex couples if same-sex marriage violates their religious beliefs, and whether employers who object to birth control on religious grounds should be exempt from the requirement that health insurance for their workers cover contraceptive prescriptions. Higher scores represent more support for religion-based exemptions.

[15] Social welfare attitudes are a factor score of respondents' views on government services and spending, paid parental leave, raising the federal minimum wage, federal spending on health insurance, and federal spending on child care.

[16] Economic mobility attitudes are a factor score of responses to questions about whether there is more or less opportunity today "for the average person to get ahead," whether it is easier or harder for people to "move up the income ladder" compared to their parents, and whether "people's ability to improve their financial well-being" is better or worse today than it was twenty years ago.

CONCLUSION

Secularism is not a major fault line in the Republican Party in the way it is in the Democratic Party. There are relatively few Secularists in the Republican activist corps and voter coalition. And the Secularists who are active in the GOP are not as distinct in ideological orientations or political norms as their counterparts in the Democratic Party.

Instead, the fault line that may be emerging within the Republican Party is between Religionists and Non-Religionists. Non-Religionists – people who are not Secularists and who may identify with religion but do not participate actively in it – were more enthusiastic than Religionists about Donald Trump early in his bid for the 2016 Republican presidential nomination. Non-Religionists continued to support Trump through the 2016 general election and have remained loyal to him throughout his presidency. These nonreligious Republicans do not differ hugely from the Religionists at the core of the GOP voter coalition, but they do differ in ways that make them consistently more favorable than Religionists to Trumpism – Trump's nativism, staunch anti-immigration positions, critique of racial and religious minority groups, and populist battle cry against the loss of the American economic dream.

If Non-Religionists' numbers in the Republican voter coalition grow and they become more influential in Republican inner circles, there may be new political tensions with the Religionist core of the party base. These tensions may become particularly intense when Donald Trump leaves the White House and the GOP faces the question of whether to continue on a path consistent with populist Trumpism or return to the economic and cultural orthodoxy that has defined the Republican Party since Ronald Reagan.

With this possibility in mind, we turn to the impact of secularism and nonreligiosity in electoral campaigns in Chapter 10.

10

Secularism on the Stump

In the previous chapters, we have seen that many party activists and voters have secular orientations, presenting a high-value political target to some enterprising office-seekers. How might such candidates seek to convert this potential energy to a kinetic political force? A first step would be more secular politicians stepping out of the shadows to acknowledge their own secularity. And that would only happen if they were convinced that doing so was politically advantageous. But just as politicized religion has generated backlash, it is widely believed that politicized secularity has a similar effect. So enterprising candidates might well tread cautiously in this regard. Up to this point, our analysis has focused on politics as it is; this chapter now turns to consider what might be. How ready are Americans to support candidates who wear their secularity on their sleeves?

As an example of voters' willingness to vote for an "out" secular candidate, consider the case of US Senator Kyrsten Sinema (Democrat-Arizona). She holds the distinction of having been the first member of Congress to affirmatively describe herself as not having a religious affiliation (Sandstrom 2017a). Yet while, as a newly elected member of the US House of Representatives, Sinema passively disclaimed a religious affiliation, she also pushed back at other, more affirmatively secular labels. When she was described in the *New York Times* as a "nontheist," her office issued a statement disavowing such a description (Oppenheimer 2012). "Kyrsten believes the terms 'nontheist' 'atheist' or 'nonbeliever' are not befitting of her life's approach or personal character." Although resisting a secular label, she nonetheless has offered a secular perspective on governance. That same statement went on to say, "She believes that a secular approach is the best way to achieve ... good government" (Flock 2013).

In other words, Sinema is like many Americans: not identifying with the religion of her childhood (in her case, Mormon), believing in a clear separation of church and state, but unwilling to adopt an explicitly secular identity. In avoiding an overtly secular label, she is also like nearly all politicians in the United States. However, Sinema's self-description as religiously unaffiliated does not appear to have caused her any political harm, as Arizonans elected her to the US Senate in 2018.

Sinema is much like Bernie Sanders. As noted in Chapter 1, he described himself as "not particularly religious" during his run for the Democratic presidential nomination in 2016 (Feldman 2015). Similarly, when asked by talk-show host Jimmy Kimmel whether he believes in God, Sanders demurred, saying "I am who I am. And what I believe in, and what my spirituality is about, is that we're all in this together" (Sellers and Wagner 2016). While other presidential candidates have no doubt been covertly secular, Sanders was the first to defy the norm that, while on the campaign trail, American politicians put their personal religious devotion on public display. While he describes himself as culturally Jewish, Sanders had "come out" as being secular. Sanders's self-description as not being religious did not generate much political commentary and did not appear to hurt him with voters, at least in the Democratic primaries.

Sanders's acknowledgment of his own secularity is perhaps not surprising for a politician from Vermont, one of the least religious states in the country. Sanders is actually the second presidential candidate in recent years to hail from Vermont, Howard Dean being the other. Like Sanders, Dean ran an incandescent campaign for the Democratic presidential nomination by appealing to the progressive wing of the party. And like Sanders, Dean was a highly secular candidate. Unlike Sanders, though, he was criticized for his irreligious worldview. The left-leaning magazine *The New Republic* even named him "one of the most secular candidates to run for president in modern history," lamenting that his secularity is "a warning flag that will mark him as culturally alien to much of the country" (Foer 2003). Why the difference in the reactions to Dean and Sanders? One reason is likely the effects of the secular surge, particularly within the ranks of the Democratic Party.

Yet there are still limits to what degree of secularity is considered politically acceptable. Importantly, Sanders did not describe himself as an *atheist*. This distinction became important when emails from officials with the Democratic National Committee (DNC) were leaked in the summer of 2016. In one email thread, the DNC's chief financial officer wrote to other party staffers, "I think I read he [Sanders] is an atheist. This could make several points difference with my peeps. My Southern Baptist peeps would draw a big difference between a Jew and an atheist" (Boorstein and Zauzmer 2016). When news of this email broke, Sanders was quick to deny it. On CNN he plainly told Jake Tapper, "I am not an atheist" ("Sanders: 'I'm Not Atheist . . . It's an Outrage'" 2016).

Both Sinema and Sanders illustrate the emergence and growing acceptance of secular political candidates. They also demonstrate that some labels are still politically radioactive.

This chapter is about the boundaries of acceptance for secular Americans, particularly in the political arena. It is an article of faith that, going all the way back to Thomas Jefferson, "atheist" is an especially damaging epithet to be hurled at a political opponent. None other than Alexander Hamilton mobilized anti-Jefferson sentiment by referring to him as "an atheist in religion and a fanatic in politics."[1] What, though, about other secular terms that are more common? In past years, the Secular Coalition for America had a website listing a number of overtly secular candidates around the country. These candidates – some who won, many who lost – described themselves using a wide range of terms: atheist, agnostic, unaffiliated, and even "a humanist and universalist Christian who draws inspiration from the life and teachings of Jesus." Their secular identities are as diverse as the secular population writ large.

This chapter examines how voters react to such a diversity of secular self-descriptions. It starts with data from national surveys, showing how people react to neighbors, coworkers, family, and politicians who are described as nonreligious or secular in different ways. It then presents the results of two experiments in which voters reacted to political candidates who acknowledge being either nonreligious or overtly secular (e.g. an atheist). The results show that candidates who describe themselves as not religious can win favor among voters, especially Democrats, without necessarily alienating Republicans. However, voters in both parties have a strong aversion to candidates who directly state that they do not believe in God.

WHAT'S THE MATTER WITH ATHEISTS?

The aversion to atheists is both well known and long-standing. In John Locke's *Letter Concerning Toleration*, still cited today as a seminal argument for tolerance as a democratic virtue, he nonetheless singles out atheists as an exception: "No one should be tolerated who denies the existence of God." In the centuries since, atheists continue to be viewed with disfavor. But why? The answer is far from obvious. Atheists are a relatively small group with little formal organization, and the organizations that do exist have a low profile. They are certainly not known for marching in the streets or advocating violence.[2]

Among scholars who have studied the matter, two complementary explanations for such animus have been offered. Sociologists Penny Edgell, Joseph Gerteis, and Douglas Hartmann argue that atheists are moral

---

[1] Letter from Alexander Hamilton to John Jay, May 7, 1800. https://founders.archives.gov/documents/Hamilton/01-24-02-0378.

[2] For more details on the characteristics of American atheists, see Lipka (2019). The major difference between atheists and our Secularists is that atheists are more likely to express hostility toward religion. This feature may help account for the stereotype of the "angry atheist." On this issue see Wolpe (2011).

outsiders, "the symbolic representation of one who rejects the basis for moral solidarity and cultural membership in American society" (2007, 230). Consistent with this view of atheists as beyond the boundaries of a shared national identity, in the 2017 Secular America Study (SAS) roughly half of Americans said that believing in God is essential to being a "true American" (Jacobs and Theiss-Morse 2013). A second explanation of unease with atheists is that of psychologist William Gervais and his collaborators, who reason that atheists are viewed as untrustworthy because they do not believe in a deity who monitors their moral behavior, now and into eternity. In contrast, religious groups such as Muslims may be disliked but, because they believe in God, are more likely to be trusted than atheists (Gervais 2013; Gervais, Shariff, and Norenzayan 2011).

It is not difficult to reconcile these two explanations, as being a moral outsider goes hand in hand with not being trustworthy. Indeed, John Locke fuses them together as he explains why atheists are not deserving of toleration. By his reasoning, someone who does not believe in God cannot be trusted to swear an oath or keep a promise, and thus falls outside of the moral community. "Promises, covenants, and oaths, which are the bonds of human society, can have no hold on an atheist: this all dissolves in the presence of the thought that there is no God."[3]

Empirically, Locke's anti-atheist sentiment is reflected in a Gallup Poll question that asks respondents whether they would vote for an atheist presidential candidate, even if this atheist were a well-qualified member of their own party. Gallup has asked this question periodically for nearly six decades, and has consistently found widespread reluctance to vote for an atheist – although in recent years that resistance has declined. As seen in Figure 10.1, in 1959, 78 percent of Americans said that they would not vote for an atheist. Forty years later that had dropped to 51 percent, falling further to 42 percent by 2015. That puts atheists roughly on a par with Muslims, who also face widespread political opprobrium. In contrast, both are well below other religious groups, such as Jews and even Mormons – another group viewed with suspicion by many voters (Campbell, Green, and Monson 2014).

In the 2017 SAS, we find evidence that the same anti-atheism expressed by John Locke over 300 years ago is alive and well today, although the depth of discomfort depends on the situation. We asked our representative sample of Americans whether they would be comfortable with an atheist in three situations: as a coworker, marrying their child, and as a candidate for political office. For comparison, we also asked about their comfort level with other types of people in each of these settings. In addition to an atheist, respondents were randomly assigned to be asked about one other person:

---

[3] John Locke, *A Letter Concerning Toleration and Other Writings*, ed. and introduction by Mark Goldie (Indianapolis, IN: Liberty Fund, 2010). Text found at http://oll.libertyfund.org/titles/locke-a-letter-concerning-toleration-and-other-writings.

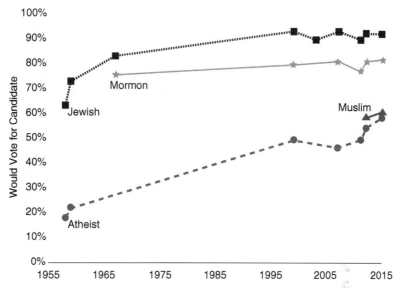

FIGURE 10.1 While the numbers are rising, many Americans are unwilling to vote for an atheist

Note: Lines represent affirmative responses to the question "If your party nominated a generally well-qualified person for president who happened to be ____, would you vote for that person?"

Source: Gallup Polls

- someone who is "deeply religious," but with no religious affiliation specified
- a deeply religious Catholic
- a deeply religious evangelical Christian
- a deeply religious Muslim.[4]

Relative to their feelings about various types of deeply religious people, Americans' comfort level with atheists is generally in the middle of the pack – roughly the same as with someone who is simply described as either deeply religious in general or a deeply religious evangelical.

Of the different scenarios, Americans are most likely to approve of an atheist as a coworker than as an in-law or elected official.[5] This relative comfort with

---

[4] The description as "deeply religious" was to make this an apples-to-apples comparison. Since a self-described atheist is more than just nominally secular, we ensured the comparison was with someone who is more than nominally religious.

[5] Specifically, 17.5 percent of Americans are either "not at all" or "not very" comfortable with an atheist coworker. For a coworker who is deeply religious/not further specified this figure is 14 percent, and 17 percent for a deeply religious evangelical. In comparison, 28 percent are uncomfortable with a deeply religious Muslim, and only 11 percent say the same about a deeply religious Catholic.

an atheist coworker is likely because, whatever one's feelings about atheists, sharing a place of employment does not necessarily imply a close relationship. Americans express greater concern about a much closer relationship, an atheist marrying their child. Roughly 40 percent of Americans are uncomfortable with an atheist in-law.[6] While this figure is lower than the discomfort with a deeply religious Muslim, it is considerably higher than the concerns raised about the other three types of deeply religious people.

As we turn to elections, it is telling that slightly more Americans are uneasy voting for an atheist than having their child marry one. However, as prelude for a motif repeated throughout this chapter, atheists are perceived through a partisan lens. While many Democrats express reservations about an atheist politician, this pales in comparison to the disapproval among Republicans. One in three Democrats are uncomfortable with an atheist candidate, compared to three in five Republicans.[7]

Our data dovetail with those of others who have also found negative attitudes toward atheists.[8] Anti-atheism is so pervasive that the canonical questions used for decades as a barometer of social tolerance include atheists alongside other groups that have long faced hostility, such as communists, and "homosexuals" (Stouffer 1992; Sullivan, Piereson, and Marcus 1993). Nor is this aversion to atheists merely hypothetical, as other studies have documented the discrimination faced by atheists in their lives (Cragun et al. 2012; Hammer et al. 2012). In the 2017 SAS, four fifths of self-identified atheists say that nonbelievers experience discrimination, no doubt based on their personal experience.[9] Within the political realm, anti-atheist animus is manifested in the seven state constitutions that explicitly prohibit nonbelievers from holding public office, notwithstanding the unequivocal prohibition on religious tests in the federal constitution (Bulger 2012).

Even if attitudes toward atheists are experiencing a slight thaw, they are still viewed negatively. Perceptions of atheists, though, are only a small part of the larger story about the place of Secularists within American society and politics. While atheists are met with strong disapproval, keep in mind that relatively few Americans either apply that label to themselves or disavow a belief in God.

---

[6] This figure is the percentage who were "not at all" or "not very" comfortable. Note that it is nearly identical to results from Edgell et al. (2016b), who found that 43.7 percent of Americans would object to their child marrying an atheist. By comparison, 15.5 percent are uncomfortable with their child marrying someone who is deeply religious, 19 percent would object to a deeply religious Catholic, 20 percent to a deeply religious evangelical. Over half – 53 percent – of Americans would be troubled if their child married a deeply religious Muslim.

[7] Again, these figures combine the "not at all" and "not very" comfortable responses.

[8] For examples, see Cook, Cohen, and Solomon (2015); Edgell et al. (2016b); Edgell, Gerteis, and Hartmann (2007); Franks (2017); Franks and Scherr (2014); Gervais (2011, 2013, 2014); Gervais, Shariff, and Norenzayan (2011); Ritter and Preston (2011); Swan and Heesacker (2012).

[9] More precisely, 80 percent said that they experienced either "a lot of" or "a little" discrimination. The survey specifically asked whether "nonbelievers" face discrimination.

A full reckoning must include attitudes toward people who are secular but do not describe themselves as atheists. If the objection to atheists were simply the lack of religion in their lives, we should expect that other secular labels would elicit the same sort of reaction. However, this parallel seems unlikely.

As we have shown throughout this book, many Americans describe themselves in secular terms: they do not have a religious affiliation or do not often (or ever) attend religious services. People who are themselves nonreligious are unlikely to be troubled by politicians who describe themselves similarly. Nor is acceptance of "softly secular" candidates likely to be limited only to voters who share their secularity. The vast majority of Americans have social networks, often including their own family members, that cross religious lines (Putnam and Campbell 2012). Given the increasing size of the secular population, most Americans – even those who are highly religious – will be acquainted with neighbors, coworkers, friends, and family (even spouses) who exhibit some signs of secularity. Indeed, as we saw in Chapter 4, many Secularists have numerous nonsecular friends. Many Americans may not know people who describe themselves as atheists but they almost certainly know people who are not regular churchgoers, do not claim a religious identity, or who describe themselves as not being particularly religious. Just as interacting with people of a different faith fosters acceptance of other religions, we would expect that regular contact with secular people leads to tolerance of people with little to no religion in their lives.

Most Americans likely draw a bright line between atheism and other forms of secularity. The word "atheism" has a hard edge to it and is a term that few Americans use to describe themselves. Since it is relatively rare to encounter a self-described atheist, a large majority of Americans are not acquainted – at least, not knowingly – with one. The absence of social relationships with atheists fans the flames of animus toward them, leading many Americans to harbor suspicions that atheists are immoral and untrustworthy. It may even be that some people think of atheists as "beyond salvation." Secularism with softer edges, though, is not likely to be viewed so pejoratively. For some voters, a politician's candid self-description as secular might even be a plus. Secular voters could see such a candidate as sharing a common identity with them. Whatever their personal level of religious commitment, many voters might view a secular candidate as not beholden to religious dogma and thus as open-minded.

As evidence that many Americans view atheists differently than those who are not religious, the 2017 SAS found that when asked about a wide variety of people, atheists stand out as being viewed as particularly untrustworthy. They are trusted less than people who are described as being "not religious." They are even trusted less than "deeply religious Muslims," as predicted by Gervais et al. (2011). Attitudes on the trustworthiness of atheists differ by partisanship, albeit modestly – 28 percent of Republicans do not trust them at all, compared to 21 percent of Democrats. That modest difference takes on more significance given that there is no partisan gap whatsoever in perceptions of people who are simply described as not religious.

Furthermore, the partisan divide in views toward atheists is widening, as shown by feeling-thermometer scores. In 2011, there was a 7-point difference between Republicans' and Democrats' feeling-thermometer rating for atheists, both of which were well below the neutral point – 35 points for Republicans, 42 for Democrats.[10] By 2017, that had grown to a 19-point gap. Republicans barely budged, increasing by an inconsequential 2 points. Democrats' assessment of atheists, however, rose substantially to 56 points. By way of comparison, this figure is higher than Democrats' assessment of Mormons (46) and evangelicals (42), two groups widely associated with the Republican Party. It is markedly lower than their assessment of Jews (68), who are closely identified with the Democratic Party, and modestly lower than their rating of Catholics (61), a group that, historically, was heavily Democratic but in recent years has been split between the parties. They have about the same opinion of atheists as of Muslims (57), a group that in recent years has leaned heavily toward the Democrats (Pew Research Center 2017).

Not surprisingly, it appears that Democrats respond positively to the groups they see as politically comparable, including atheists. As we mentioned in Chapter 5, Americans are far more likely to indicate that atheists are "mainly Democrats" than to say that they are "mainly Republicans," and the percentage who make that association increased from 2010 to 2017 (Campbell, Green, and Layman 2011).[11] Nonetheless, it is important to note that, in 2017, less than half of Americans connected atheists with the Democrats, suggesting that this pattern is far from a universally held group association. The pattern is the same for people described as nonreligious rather than as atheists – many more Americans see them as Democrats than as Republicans; the percentage linking the nonreligious population to the Democrats has increased between 2010 and 2017, but it is still far less than a majority who make the connection.

Thus far, two themes emerge. First, while atheists are viewed negatively, the same is not true for people whose secularism is described in a less strident way. Atheists are seen as untrustworthy, but there is no trust deficit for people who are simply "not religious." Second, while there is a sharp partisan divide in the assessment of atheists, this division is less sharp in the assessment of people who are described as not religious. Even though more Americans – accurately – see the nonreligious as more likely to be Democrats than Republicans, that does not mean Republicans have a lower opinion of them. To the contrary, Republicans and Democrats share the same view of people described as not being religious.

Given all this evidence, we have some clear expectations and a few matters of ambiguity for Americans' reception of secular candidates. We clearly expect voters to react differently to atheists than to those who describe themselves in less strident terms. To return to the distinction we have made between

---

[10] The 2011 results are taken from the third wave of the Faith Matters survey (Putnam and Campbell 2012).

[11] The 2010 data are taken from the SAS Panel.

individuals' type of secularism, we hypothesize that voters will have a sharply negative reaction to candidates who use overtly secular language to describe themselves versus a more sanguine response to those who are not religious. We are also interested in whether it matters if the candidate uses the label "atheist," or if voters care more about a candidate who explicitly expresses unbelief in God. For this our expectations are unclear.

However, while it is important to know how voters react to atheist candidates, given the resistance of actual candidates to being described in such stark terms (see Sinema and Sanders), we stress that any analysis limited to atheists does not reflect the real world of today's politics. We are just as interested in understanding how voters will react to candidates who are at different points on the secular spectrum.

We also expect Republicans and Democrats to have different reactions to secular candidates of all stripes – Democrats being more favorable toward them than Republicans. Less clear is the degree of acceptance among Democrats, especially of overtly secular candidates. On the one hand, atheists are increasingly associated in the public mind with the Democratic Party, and Democrats' attitudes are warming toward them. On the other hand, though, atheists still have a relatively negative reputation, even among Democrats. Recall from Chapter 8 that the Democratic coalition is highly diverse, containing sizable fractions of both highly secular and religious supporters.

THE SECULAR CANDIDATE EXPERIMENT

While informative, previous research into voters' reaction to secular candidates has suffered from some limitations. The bulk of it has been observational, meaning that survey respondents are simply asked whether they would vote for a candidate described in a certain way. This approach is what the Gallup Poll has done for decades, and is also what we did in the SAS. The problem with such observational data is the inability to isolate the effect of describing someone as secular. To determine the relative influence of a secular label, it is necessary to randomly assign respondents to read about one of the candidates. When candidates' descriptions are assigned by sheer chance, we can compare respondents' attitudes toward one candidate versus another, confident that any differences are due solely to what varies between the descriptions. In other words, by changing the secularity of the candidate while holding everything else constant, we can pinpoint its effect on voters' reactions.

Another limitation of past research has been its focus on atheist candidates, who, as we have noted, are virtually unheard of in contemporary American politics.[12] Of course, there are good reasons for studies that feature deeply

---

[12] Even the exception proves the rule, which we can safely say because our own work is that exception. In a previous experiment, we tested voters' reactions to a fictional candidate who, while not described as an atheist per se, was nonetheless presented as far more secular than

secular candidates, as they demonstrate a boundary condition – how do voters respond when politicians are described in stridently secular terms? Having established the boundary, we can now test the reception of candidates described as not being religious, thus more closely resembling the real world.

The remainder of the chapter discusses two experiments. In the first, the Secular Candidate Experiment, respondents react to a candidate in a nonpartisan race, allowing an analysis of voters' responses without party labels. The second, the Partisan Secular Candidate Experiment, replicates the first, but identifies the candidate as either a Republican or Democrat.

The two experiments have the same straightforward design.[13] After answering a few demographic questions, a national sample of respondents were randomly assigned to read a realistic-looking news story about a candidate for the school board in the fictional community of Maple City. Following the story, respondents indicated how likely they were to vote for that candidate on a 0–100 scale. The story describes a town hall meeting the candidate has held with voters. As with our previously described experiments (see Chapter 6), the candidate's personal details are as innocuous as possible. He has a common name (Jim Lee) and a well-regarded occupation (pediatrician). The candidate is described as having been married for twenty years. He and his wife, who is a local veterinarian, have two children in the community's public schools. His platform is vague and nonideological, as he says that he "will always put our young people ahead of special interests." He is not identified as either a Democrat or Republican, which is realistic given that most school board elections are not partisan.

In the control condition – that is, the one without a religious or secular cue – the candidate is asked by a voter, "Mr. Lee, what influences your thinking? For example, can you tell us where you grew up?" The candidate is then described as "taking the question in stride" because he responds by admitting that he was "born and raised over in Fairview" (that is, not in Maple City). After this confession, he goes on to say "But, what matters is that I am willing to listen to and learn from everyone. I hope voters will see that I have an open mind." While, in the context of the story, the candidate feels the need to tread gingerly when acknowledging that he was born in a different city, the point was to keep

---

a prototypical candidate like Kyrsten Sinema or Bernie Sanders. We found that Republican voters find an overtly secular candidate, even one who is a fellow Republican, an anathema (Castle et al. 2017).

[13] Both this experiment and the Partisan Secular Candidate Experiment were conducted by Qualtrics, an online survey firm. We commissioned Qualtrics to provide a sample of subjects that matched the demographic profile of the national population for gender, age, and race. In addition, the sample had a quota of 40 percent Republicans, 40 percent Democrats, and 20 percent Independents. For both experiments, each treatment (cell) has at least 200 cases. For the Secular Candidate Experiment, this means a total of 1,200 cases. For the Partisan Secular Candidate Experiment there were 2,400 total cases.

the information provided inoffensive and nonpartisan. Presumably there is no animosity toward a generic-sounding city like Fairview.

We succeeded in our objective of presenting a candidate equally attractive to both Democrats and Republicans. The control condition elicited an average of 67 on the 100-point likelihood of voting scale, which was much higher than the 50-point neutral point, and there was no statistical difference between the reactions to the candidate of Republicans and Democrats.[14]

In the other versions of the story, the candidate is not asked the noncontroversial question about where he was raised. Instead he is asked "can you tell us about your religion?" He responds with one of the following statements, all prefaced with "To be honest with you . . ."

- I do not currently identify with a religion
- I am not particularly religious
- I am an atheist
- I do not believe in God
- I am personally quite religious

The statement is also shown as a pull-out quote, in larger font, so that the respondent would be sure to see it (as was the case for the admission that he was raised in a different city). To parallel the control condition, the candidate follows up on this admission by noting that he has an open mind. A Closer Look 10.1 recaps the differences across the different versions of the story (i.e. the treatments).

Having the candidate's secularism elicited by a question from a visitor captures the way a candidate's secularism might actually be broached in a campaign, since it is highly unlikely that a candidate would broadcast this fact. The descriptions have varying degrees of secularity. The phrase "I do not currently identify with a religion" represents the growing population of religious nonaffiliates. By including the word "currently," the candidate implies that either he has identified in the past or may in the future (or both), thus reflecting the fluidity of many Americans' religious affiliations. The self-description as "not particularly religious" is a similar version of soft secularism, but encompasses more than affiliation. Recall that this formulation is the precise language used by Bernie Sanders to describe himself in 2016.

In addition to these self-descriptions of being nonreligious, the candidate also describes himself using more explicitly secular language. In one version, the candidate identifies as an atheist, enabling us to see how voters react to the "a-word," when applied to an otherwise innocuous, even appealing, candidate.

---

[14] This chapter focuses only on Republicans and Democrats, and thus does not include any discussion of Independents. This is primarily because we do not have theoretical expectations for the reactions of Independents to secular and religious candidates. Also, "pure" Independents – those who do not lean to one party or the other – are a small slice of the overall population, making it difficult to draw conclusions about them.

A Closer Look 10.1:
Content of Secular Candidate Experiments

Both versions of the Secular Candidate Experiment are identical, save that the Partisan Secular Candidate Experiment identifies the candidate as either a Democrat or Republican.

Candidate Characteristic	Statement from Candidate in the News Story
Religious	I am personally quite religious
Nonaffiliation	I do not currently identify with a religion
Not religious	I am not particularly religious
Atheist	I am an atheist
Nonbeliever	I do not believe in God
Control	I was born over in Fairview

In another version, the candidate does not describe himself with the term atheist, but instead says that he does not believe in God. Functionally, these self-descriptions should be considered the same, since the definition of atheism is nonbelief in God. By distinguishing between them, we can see whether the oft-observed negative reaction to atheism is owing to negative connotations associated with the term in particular or with atheism's defining characteristic – disbelief in God – without the baggage of the word. The existing literature suggests that it could go either way (Swan and Heesacker 2012), but no previous study has made the direct comparison in the context of a political campaign.

For the sake of comparison, in one version of the story the candidate describes himself as "personally quite religious." This condition enables us to see how the various degrees of the candidate's secularity compare to a candidate who uses language far more familiar in American politics. While conventional wisdom – and common practice – might suggest that being described as religious is generally a political plus, the politicization of religion could also lead some voters to respond negatively.

Using a school board race enables the race to be plausibly nonpartisan. Furthermore, public schools are often the front line for battles over the separation of church and state, and so some voters would consider a candidate's religious – or secular – views to be a reasonable consideration. Figure 10.2 provides an example of the news story used in the experiment. In this case, the candidate describes himself as "not particularly religious."

It is important to acknowledge what can and cannot be learned from such an experiment. Having randomized who read which story, we can be confident that we are recording the reaction to the candidate's self-description and

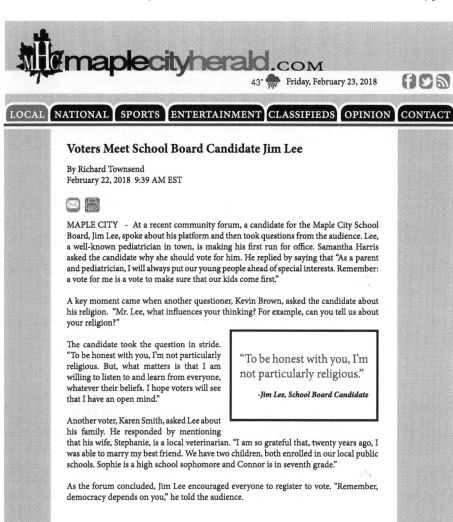

FIGURE 10.2 Sample news story from the Secular Candidate Experiment

nothing else (and thus the experiment has high internal validity). Keep in mind, though, that a respondent's immediate response to a single news story does not fully capture a real political campaign, as there would be myriad other factors at

TABLE 10.1 *How voters respond to religious and secular candidates*

	All Voters	Republican Voters	Democratic Voters
Candidate's Self-Description			
Personally quite religious	**+5**	+3	**+6**
Does not currently identify with a religion	+3	−3	**+9**
Not particularly religious	+1	**−6**	**+8**
Atheist	−3	**−12**	+6
Does not believe in God	**−8**	**−15**	−2

Results are the increase or decrease in likelihood of voting for the candidate, relative to the control condition (no mention of secularity or religiosity). Numbers in bold are statistically significant at p < .10.
Source: Secular Candidate Experiment

play as voters make their decision (thus limiting external validity). Our experiment is best interpreted as testing how voters form their initial impressions of candidates based on a secular label. However, because voters typically have little information about most races – especially for low-salience elections like those for a school board – it is informative to see what first impressions are made.

Table 10.1 presents the results from the Secular Candidate Experiment. The number in each cell indicates how respondents reacted to that description compared to the control story, where the candidate "confesses" to having been raised in Fairview instead of Maple City.[15] The discussion references the size, direction, and statistical significance of the results, which means we sometimes highlight results that do not clear the bar for conventional statistical significance. This limitation is because, even with a large sample size, the number of cases per "cell" (experimental group) is still relatively small, making conventional statistical significance a high threshold. Of course, the nonsignificant results should be interpreted with caution, as it is less clear that they can be distinguished from a noneffect.

Note the positive response to the candidate who is "personally quite religious." This finding comports with the generally accepted view that if

---

[15] For both experiments discussed in this chapter, the randomization was successful, as Tukey's Honestly Significant Difference tests indicate that subjects assigned to different treatments do not vary by gender, age, race, education, or income. There is thus no need for control variables. Throughout the chapter, each analysis we report consists of regressing a set of dummy variables representing each treatment (minus the control group) on the dependent variable, in this case the likelihood of voting for the candidate.

religion comes up in a political campaign, it is better to be seen by voters as religious than not. When the candidate is described as "not particularly religious," it elicits essentially no reaction – positive or negative – from voters in general. It appears that the Bernie Sanders approach is politically viable, at least for a school board candidate. Similarly, there is a modestly positive – though not statistically significant – reaction to a candidate who describes himself as not currently identifying with a religion.

In contrast to these positive reactions, voters react negatively to candidates who are either atheists or affirmatively state that they do not believe in God. Interestingly, the effect for the atheist candidate, while negative, is relatively small in magnitude, and fails to reach statistical significance. The decline in support for a candidate who does not believe in God is over twice as large and highly significant ($p < .01$). In fact, the negative effect for nonbelief in God is slightly larger than the positive effect for a "personally quite religious" candidate, although it is of course in the opposite direction.

With these results, we can start to see how voters react to varying degrees of a candidate's secularity. Expressions of nonreligiosity do not hurt a candidate – and might even help. While the centuries-old epithet of "atheist" does elicit a negative reaction, it is weaker than voters' aversion to candidates who affirmatively state that they do not believe in God.

While a start, these findings raise as many questions as they answer. In particular, since religiosity and secularity are closely associated with the two major parties, it is natural to wonder if Democrats and Republicans differ in their reactions to the various descriptions. Remember that, by design, the part of the story that stays constant contains no information that would enable voters to infer the candidate's partisanship. Therefore, if the reactions of Republicans and Democrats vary, it is solely because of the candidate's self-description as either secular or religious, which of course was randomly assigned. Any partisan differences may indicate that being identified as secular or religious leads voters to assume the candidate is from one party or the other.

Table 10.1 also displays the results from the Secular Candidate Experiment broken out by Republican and Democratic respondents. The differences are striking. Perhaps surprisingly, while Republicans have a slightly positive reaction to the candidate's description as personally religious (again, compared to the control condition), the effect fails to reach statistical significance. From there, though, we see increasingly negative reactions to the different secular labels. Republicans have a mildly negative and nonsignificant reaction to religious nonidentification, and a more pronounced but still not quite significant ($p = .12$) response to "not particularly religious." Their reaction to both an atheist and nonbeliever in God is much more negative, as both are unequivocally significant. While the effect for nonbelief in God appears to be a little larger, statistically there is no meaningful difference between them.

There are two mutually reinforcing reasons why Republicans respond the way they do to secular candidates. The first is based on identity. Since many

Republicans are themselves religious, they likely see secular candidates – especially those who are atheists and/or nonbelievers – as "unlike them," and thus not deserving of their political support. And "unlike them" may mean a perceived difference in religious identity. It also may mean a perceived difference in partisan identity, as Americans tend to see nonreligious people as being Democrats. The second explanation is rooted in policy preferences. It could be that, whatever their own religious background, Republicans infer that a secular candidate will hold policy positions that differ from theirs.

Granted, neither of these explanations illuminate why the "personally quite religious" candidate *does not* trigger a more positive response from Republicans. Given our religion-saturated political environment, perhaps it is because they assume candidates for office will be religious, and so providing that information does little to sway them. Or maybe it is because they have an asymmetric reaction to religion and secularism. It could be that they do not see the presence of religion as all that relevant, but the absence of religion is worrying or even threatening. Or it could be that they care less about whether a candidate is religious, and more about the candidate's specific religious affiliation.

At the risk of understatement, Democrats react very differently than Republicans. Three of the secular self-descriptions increase Democrats' support for the candidate – religious nonidentification, not particularly religious, and atheist. The effects for all three are roughly the same size and all are statistically significant. The only nonsignificant effect is for nonbelief in God. It is essentially zero, meaning that Democrats are not swayed either way by a candidate who openly acknowledges not believing in God.

In sum, while Republicans respond negatively to a candidate's secularism, all but nonbelief in God increases support among Democrats. As with the Republicans, one reason for Democrats' reactions may be their identity – either because many Democrats are personally secular or because they view nonreligious candidates as likely being Democrats themselves. In addition, whatever their own degree of secularity, many Democrats will infer shared policy positions with secular candidates.

Yet Democrats' affinity for secular candidates does not translate into hostility for a religious candidate. Democrats are more likely to support a candidate who describes himself as religious – an effect that is larger than observed among Republicans, and is statistically significant. In fact, among Democrats the increase in support for a religious candidate is almost exactly the same as for an atheist (+6 points). This result may reflect the religious-secular diversity within the Democratic coalition. Recall from Chapter 8 that while few Republicans are secular, many Democrats are highly religious. It is thus understandable that they would be supportive of candidates who, absent any other partisan cues, describe themselves as religious. Chapter 8 also shows that highly religious Democrats are largely African Americans and Latinos, thus leading to the question of whether the Democrats' positive response to a "personally quite religious" candidate is limited to minorities. It is not. There are no racial differences among Democrats.[16]

We can draw three conclusions from the Secular Candidate Experiment results:

• *Not All Forms of Secularity are Seen as Equal by Voters*

Voters react very differently to varying levels of candidate secularity. While both the label of atheist and expression of nonbelief in God are viewed negatively – the latter more than the former – descriptions of candidates as being nonreligious do not elicit the same degree of animus.

• *Republicans and Democrats Perceive Secular Candidates Differently*

In general, Republicans see a candidate's secularism as a negative, while Democrats see it as a positive. The one exception to the Democrats' general favor toward Secularists is a candidate who explicitly says he does not believe in God, which triggers neither a positive nor a negative reaction. In contrast, Republicans are especially averse to a nonbeliever.

• *Democrats are Fine with Religious Candidates – to a Point*

Contrary to the storyline that Democrats are universally hostile toward religion, they are supportive of a highly religious candidate – about as much as Republicans are.

THE PARTISAN SECULAR CANDIDATE EXPERIMENT

The Secular Candidate Experiment adds to our understanding of how Americans perceive secular political candidates, but it is difficult to generalize the results to most elections since the candidate's description was missing the one ingredient found in nearly all US political races, and which dominates voters' decision-making: a party label. There is no way to know whether voters are responding to the secularism alone, or if they are inferring the candidate's partisanship from his secularism or religiosity. What happens when party cues are added to the description of a secular candidate? One possibility is that, given the high state of partisan polarization in the American electorate, party trumps secularism. That is, when making judgments about candidates, it could be that voters look primarily to the party label, which overshadows any other details.

If this insight is correct, then the secular labels will have no effect when accompanied by a partisan affiliation. A second possibility is that a secular candidate amplifies the voters' tendencies – so that, say, an atheist Democrat will

---

[16] In other words, we have tested whether the results differ when the analysis is limited to whites, African Americans, or Latinos. There are no systematic differences across the groups.

draw even more opposition from Republicans and greater support from Democrats than a nonpartisan atheist. A third possibility is that voters' reactions to a candidate's secularism have an impact in addition to the party label, whether the label is Republican or Democrat. This possibility would mean that the secular labels will have the same effect regardless of the candidate's party.

Because past studies of candidates' secularism have not included party labels, the existing literature does not lead to a strong expectation among these three potential outcomes, although the long-standing Gallup Poll question about an atheist presidential candidate does provide a hint. That question specifies that the atheist candidate in question is from the respondent's own party. Assuming that Gallup's respondents are paying attention to this stipulation, it means that the results are effectively controlling for the candidate's party label. In spite of describing the candidate as coming from the same partisan tribe, Gallup still finds that atheists meet with strong disapproval. Thus, at least for the atheist label, partisanship does not supersede secularism.

What, though, about other ways of describing a candidate's secularity? It could be that a candidate self-description such as "not particularly religious" does not in and of itself elicit a particular reaction from voters. Instead, voters might be inferring that the candidate is a Democrat. If so, explicitly identifying candidates with a party label should negate any effect.

To find out how candidate partisanship and secularity interact, the second experiment is identical to the Secular Candidate Experiment, except that the candidate portrayed in the news story is identified as either a Democrat or Republican. This change was done in three places: the headline, the first sentence, and the pull-out quote. While each reference is relatively subtle, in combination they ensured that respondents would not miss that the fictional candidate, "Jim Lee," was either a Republican or Democrat. Figure 10.3 provides an example, with the mentions of the candidate's party affiliation underlined.

Portraying a school board race enabled us to maintain verisimilitude when adding a partisan label. As previously noted, most school board elections in the country are nonpartisan, but there are nonetheless some jurisdictions where candidates run under a party banner (Burnette 2017). Besides the addition of a party label, everything else about this study echoed the previous one, as respondents were randomly assigned to read about a candidate who described his secularity, religiosity, or place of birth (the control) using exactly the same language as in the Secular Candidate Experiment. As before, they indicated their likelihood of voting for the candidate on a 0–100 scale.

Table 10.2 displays the results when the candidate is described as either a Democrat or Republican, separating out the reactions of Democratic and Republican voters. When interpreting this figure and the next, remember that the *overall* level of support for the respective candidates varies between Democratic and Republican respondents, as voters, not surprisingly, favor candidates from their own party. Here our interest is not in the overall level

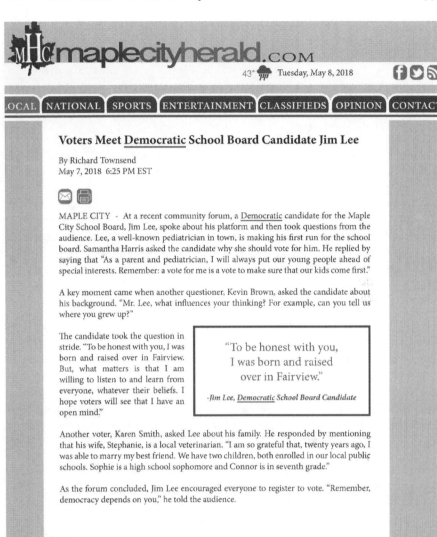

© 2018 The Maple City Herald and MapleCityHerald.com

FIGURE 10.3 Sample news story from the Partisan Secular Candidate Experiment (with emphasis added)

of support for each candidate, but rather the reaction each secular or religious label elicits from Democrats and Republicans, respectively, relative to the control condition. For example, how does support from Democratic voters

TABLE 10.2 *How voters respond to religious and secular candidates with a party label*

	Democratic Candidate		Republican Candidate	
	Republican Voters	Democratic Voters	Republican Voters	Democratic Voters
Candidate's Self-Description				
Personally quite religious	+1	+0.1	**+3**	**−3**
Does not currently identify with a religion	−3	**+7**	**+4**	**+4**
Not particularly religious	+1	**+4**	+2	−2
Atheist	**−8**	−2	**−13**	−1
Does not believe in God	**−13**	**−7**	**−15**	**−7**

Results are the increase or decrease in likelihood of voting for the candidate, relative to the control condition (no mention of secularity or religiosity). Numbers in bold are statistically significant at p < .10.
Source: Partisan Secular Candidate Experiment

vary when, holding constant the fact that the candidate is a Democrat, he is described as having varying levels of secularity?

How do voters react to a Democratic candidate described using different secular terms? For Republicans, the candidate's Democratic affiliation lessened the effect of one label in particular: not particularly religious. Recall that with no party label associated with the candidate, the negative effect was moderately large.[17] When the candidate is identified as a Democrat, the effect drops to nearly zero – suggesting that Republicans' negative reaction to a nonreligious politician is because they inferred that such a candidate is a Democrat. Adding the Democratic label, however, does little to affect Republicans' reaction to the other labels. There are small but insignificant effects for a candidate who is personally religious (positive) and does not identify with a religion (negative). Like the nonpartisan version of the experiment, there are large and significant effects for an atheist or nonbeliever, although they are slightly smaller in magnitude than in the first experiment. The diminished magnitude hints that some of the negative reaction was because of an assumption about the candidate's partisanship rather than a negative reaction to either form of secularism per se. Still, the results clearly show Republicans' antipathy to atheists, whether defined by the label or by an affirmative statement of nonbelief in God.

[17] Recall also that it was just beyond the level of conventional statistical significance, p = .12.

Among Democrats, we again see the lack of hostility to a religious candidate, as the Democratic candidate's self-description as "personally quite religious" registered essentially no effect either way. The two nonreligious descriptions – nonidentification and not particularly religious – produced increases in support, especially the lack of a religious affiliation. This pattern suggests that Democrats feel an affinity toward Nones, although this experiment leaves unanswered whether this is because of a shared identity, the assumption of shared policy preferences, or a mixture of the two. Unlike in the nonpartisan experiment, Democrats do not respond either way to a Democratic atheist – the effect is essentially zero. Their positive reaction in the nonpartisan experiment was thus likely because they were relying on the atheist label to deduce that the candidate is a fellow Democrat.

In the absence of a party label, Democrats' response to a candidate who does not believe in God seems also to be due to an inference about his partisanship, but in this case identifying the candidate as a Democrat amplifies the negative reaction. It appears that there are two countervailing factors affecting Democrats' response: (a) an aversion to an overtly nonbelieving candidate, and (b) the inference that a nonbeliever is a fellow Democrat. On balance, the nonpartisan experiment suggests that they cancel each other out, leading to a null effect. Now, however, when the candidate is explicitly identified as a Democrat, voters are no longer making any inferences about the candidate's party, leaving only their reaction to the candidate's nonbelief. Democrats do not look favorably on a fellow Democrat who disavows a belief in God – the negative effect is both large and significant.

In short, the one consistency between the two experiments for Democrats and Republicans alike is their mutually negative reaction to a candidate who says that he does not believe in God.

What differs when a secular candidate is identified as a Republican, cutting against the groups typically associated with the GOP? The answer is not much. Adding a Republican party label produces nearly the same effects as when the candidate is identified as a Democrat. For the most part, the differences are minor. For example, Republicans have a modestly positive reaction to a Republican who says he does not identify with a religion (perhaps they give him credit for being forthcoming). Similarly, Democrats now have a slightly negative reaction to the "personally quite religious" candidate, probably because this description reinforces the association of the GOP with religion. Still, neither of these effects achieve statistical significance. Most notably, Democrats and Republicans react alike to atheists and nonbelievers, regardless of their party. In fact, the negative reaction by Democrats to a nonbeliever is nearly identical, whether the candidate is a Republican or a Democrat (–7 in either case).

To return to the three possibilities for how party and secularism might interact, we find the most evidence that, whatever their own partisan leanings, voters react similarly to a candidate's secularism – especially atheism and disbelief in God – regardless of the candidate's party. However, this pattern does not mean that a candidate's secularism has no net effect. Recall that we have presented the results in comparison to the control condition, the one that did not mention the candidate's secular or religious background. This method shows the relative size of the effects for each of the other descriptions but it obscures the raw level of support for each candidate. These raw – or absolute – scores are also illuminating.

Most notably, inspection of the raw scores reveals that for Republicans the negative association with nonbelief in God either matches or outweighs the effect of a candidate's party. Their likelihood of voting for a fellow Republican who does not believe in God is nearly identical to their likelihood of voting for the generic Democratic candidate (that is, with no secular or religious label) – 57 in both cases. In other words, among Republicans, the statement that a candidate does not believe in God wipes out the effect of partisanship, the most powerful informational cue voters have when casting a ballot. Similarly, Democrats and Republicans are equally likely to vote for a Republican atheist.

The difference in partisans' reactions to secular candidates naturally leads to the question of why they have the reactions they do. The extant literature on perceptions of secular people suggests some possible explanations, including that atheists are seen as untrustworthy and not truly American. At the same time, we should not assume that other kinds of secular candidates are only viewed negatively. We have also seen that some forms of secularism are an electoral advantage. Among the positive attributes that might be associated with secular candidates are being open-minded and caring – the latter might be especially true for people who have a secular orientation themselves.

To illuminate why voters react to secular candidates the way they do, we asked our respondents to the Partisan Secular Candidate Experiment to rate the candidate in the news story on four traits: patriotism, trustworthiness, being open-minded, and caring about people like yourself.[18] We again used a 100-point scale, enabling us to detect even relatively small effects. There are myriad

---

[18] Specifically, after answering a host of other questions, including their likelihood of voting and campaigning for the candidate, as well as items about their personal levels of secularism and religiosity, respondents were asked about their perception of the candidate's traits. To ensure that the critical information about the candidate was fresh in their minds, the question reminded them of what the candidate had said about his religious background (or, for the control, where he grew up). Here is an example:

Next we will ask some more questions about Jim Lee, the Republican school board candidate featured in the news story. As a reminder, here is the key exchange he had with a voter: Kevin Brown asked the candidate about his background. "Mr. Lee, what influences your thinking? For example, can you tell us about your religion?" The candidate took the question in stride. "To be honest with you, I'm not particularly religious. But, what matters is that I am willing to listen to and learn from everyone, whatever their beliefs."

Based on what you know about Jim Lee, please rate him on the following characteristics:

Trustworthy/Can't be trusted
Cares about people like me/Does not care about people like me
Patriotic/Unpatriotic

combinations of secular labels, candidate party, and respondent's party identification – enough that we would expect some statistically significant effects simply by chance. For that reason, we will focus only on those effects that do not appear idiosyncratic but instead indicative of a broader trend.

As confirmation that the Republican and Democratic parties are identified with, respectively, religiosity and secularity, we find that Republicans and Democrats differ in their perception of religious and secular candidates. Democrats rate a fellow Democrat who does not identify with a religion higher (than the control) on all four traits; likewise, Republicans rate the Republican who is "personally quite religious" higher on all of the characteristics. The explanation for these mirror images is not hard to see – partisans have a positive perception of candidates who align with their party's image.

For Democrats and secularism, though, we do not see the same positive associations when the candidate is described as not particularly religious, an atheist, or a nonbeliever. Nor do they have negative associations with these other secular labels. Rather, they generally have a neutral reaction. In parallel fashion, Republicans also do not typically associate secularism with negative traits. But there are two notable exceptions, both of which confirm the evidence about the way atheists are perceived by the general public.

The first example of a negative trait associated with secularism is that Republicans view the Democratic candidate as unpatriotic if he identifies as an atheist or says he does not believe in God (with a slightly larger effect for the latter). Republicans do not question the patriotism of an atheistic or nonbelieving Republican candidate, suggesting that it is not the candidate's secularity alone that triggers the response, but instead a secular label that also reinforces a partisan stereotype. See Figure 10.4 for the details. Republicans are apparently unwilling to label a fellow Republican as unpatriotic no matter his belief in God, but are willing to apply that label to a Democratic politician.

Second, as shown in Figure 10.5, Republicans view a candidate who does not believe in God as untrustworthy, *whether that candidate is a Democrat or Republican*. This distrust of nonbelievers is consistent with the work of Gervais et al. (2011), who find that atheists are generally not trusted, mostly because they do not believe in a deity who monitors morality. Our findings add nuance to Gervais et al.'s results. They conclude that distrust of atheists is widespread while we find that, at least for political candidates, Democrats do not see atheists or nonbelievers as untrustworthy – even if the candidate in question is a Republican.

Republicans' unwillingness to vote for a nonbeliever, whether a Democrat or Republican, is thus easily explained by their lack of trust. The puzzle, however,

Open-minded/Close-minded

Each word or phrase was placed at opposite ends of the scale. Respondents indicated their opinion of the candidate by selecting a position on the scale – all the way to one term or the other, or somewhere in between.

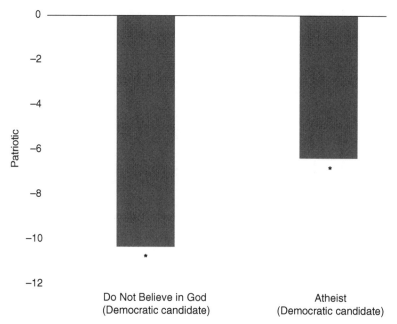

FIGURE 10.4 Republicans see nonbelieving and atheist Democrats as unpatriotic (Republican respondents only)
* *Effect of experimental treatment statistically significant at p < .05*
Note: *Bars represent the difference in ratings of the candidate on the "patriotic vs. unpatriotic" scale, relative to the control condition (no mention of secularity or religiosity).*
Source: *Partisan Secular Candidate Experiment*

is why Democrats are reluctant to vote for a nonbeliever (as seen earlier in this discussion) even while their assessment of his trustworthiness is unchanged. It suggests that Democrats do not link nonbelief and distrust. Their wariness stems from something else – perhaps the perception that such a candidate is unelectable. Just what that something else is will be a fruitful question for future scholars, or perhaps for political consultants managing the campaign of a nonbelieving candidate.

An obvious question from the experimental results is the degree to which the reactions we have attributed to voters' partisanship are actually due to their own degree of secularity. To answer that, we focus on Democratic candidates, since they are the most likely to identify as secular. To do so, we have divided Republicans and Democrats into those who are high and low in secularism.[19] For the most part we find that secularism matters far more than partisanship.

---

[19] This is operationalized as either above or below the global mean on the Personal Secularism Index.

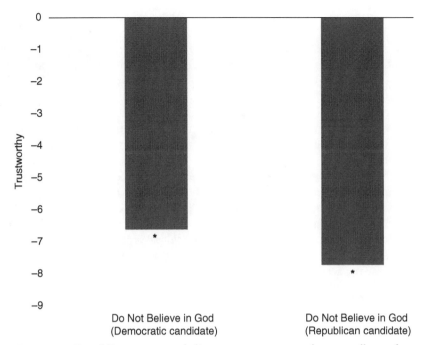

FIGURE 10.5 Republicans see nonbelievers as untrustworthy regardless of party (Republican respondents only)
* Effect of experimental treatment statistically significant at p < .10
Note: Bars represent the difference in ratings of the candidate on the "trustworthy vs. can't be trusted" scale, relative to the control condition (no mention of secularity or religiosity).
Source: Partisan Secular Candidate Experiment

Regardless of voters' party, if they score high on secularism, they react positively to all of the nonreligious and secular labels.[20] Those voters low in secularism react with comparable negativity toward an atheist or nonbeliever, whether they are Republicans or Democrats, while not registering much reaction at all to the other secular descriptions.

These results indicate that voters' reactions to the secular descriptions are driven more by their secularism than their party affiliation. The same is not true, however, for the description of a Democratic candidate who is

---

[20] There is a difference between Republican and Democratic respondents in whether the effects of candidate secularity are statistically significant. For Democrats, all of these effects are either significant or, in the case of the atheist, close to it (p = .135). For Republicans, none of these effects reach statistical significance, suggesting greater variability among highly secular Republican voters (compounded by the fact that the much smaller number of secular Republicans makes statistical significance harder to achieve).

"personally quite religious." Democrats high in secularism are neutral toward such a religious candidate, again belying the assumption that Secularists are inherently hostile to religion. As further evidence, highly secular Republicans actually grow more supportive of the Democratic candidate when he is described as religious,[21] perhaps inferring that the candidate shares their policy preferences.

The conclusion to be drawn from these results is that, even in a time of partisan polarization, voters' own partisanship is not the whole story. Their secularism also shapes reactions to secular candidates in similar ways within the two parties.

The reader may wonder why this chapter has placed so much emphasis on comparing how Republicans and Democrats react to secular candidates, when their reactions – at least to a seemingly innocuous candidate in a low-salience race – are largely shaped by their level of secularism. After all, isn't secularism the "real" story? From a theoretical perspective, it is important to know what lies behind partisans' attitudes toward politicians who describe themselves in secular terms. Indeed, the finding that Republican and Democratic voters with comparable levels of secularism react similarly to secular candidates – accounting for their differing baseline levels of support – reinforces a theme of this whole book: secularism shapes political preferences.

However, we are also interested in the practical implications of a candidate's secularism. The world of campaigning is largely organized along partisan lines. If you are a candidate for office, you do not see voters as high or low in secularism; you see them as Republicans and Democrats. Virtually every function of a political campaign – voter mobilization, outreach, advertising – is filtered through the lens of partisanship. While it is important for the sake of theory to know that equally secular Republicans and Democrats behave similarly, to speak of an equivalence between the two parties is just a theoretical construct. In reality, of course, far fewer Republicans than Democrats have a secular worldview. To understand the electoral impact of politicians' secularism requires knowing how Republicans qua Republicans, and Democrats qua Democrats, respond when faced with candidates with varying degrees of secularity.

To summarize, the most important points from the Partisan Secular Candidate Experiment are:

• *Nonreligion Can Help, Not Hurt – For Democratic Politicians*

For Democratic candidates, nonreligious labels (don't identify, not particularly religious) are more likely to be a political plus than minus. They attract support from

---

[21] Although the effect falls short of significance, p = .18.

Democrats while being neutral among Republicans. The same labels do little, among either Republicans or Democrats, for Republican candidates.

• *Nonbelief in God Is a Political Nonstarter in Both Parties*

Both Democrats and Republicans react negatively to candidates who say they do not believe in God, regardless of their party label (although Democrats are not bothered by a candidate who describes himself as an atheist).

• *Partisanship Matters, but So Does Secularism – in Both Parties*

While we see predictable differences between the parties – Democrats are more likely than Republicans to vote for a Democratic candidate – the role of voters' secularism is comparable within the parties. That is, if Democrats and Republicans have comparable levels of secularism they react similarly to secular candidates, reinforcing the importance of secularism as a worldview that shapes the American political landscape.

CONCLUSION

Americans' reactions to secular candidates are more varied and nuanced than the top-line antipathy toward atheism would suggest. For one, Democrats and Republicans differ in their reaction to the label of atheist. It is a negative for Republican voters, but much less so for Democrats. Yet both Republicans and Democrats react with comparable negativity toward a candidate who explicitly claims to not believe in God. It is unclear why a statement of nonbelief engenders more opposition than the term atheist. We leave it to future research to find out why.[22]

For now, it is clear that in a country where – notwithstanding the rise in religious nonaffiliation – belief in God remains high, a candidate who explicitly denies believing in God is simply a bridge too far. Yet even when it comes to their unease with unbelief, there is an important difference between Republicans and Democrats. For Republicans, an unbelieving candidate is untrustworthy, regardless of his party. Distrust of nonbelievers transcends partisanship. Among Democrats, their reluctance to vote for a nonbeliever is not accompanied by distrust, suggesting that perhaps there is hope for an openly nonbelieving candidate within Democratic ranks. At the same time, Democrats are untroubled by a candidate who describes himself as highly religious, contrary to the assumption that Democrats are hostile to candidates of faith. In some cases, being religious can help a candidate draw support from Democrats.

Democrats are sanguine about candidates who are not religious as compared to openly secular. In fact, the evidence consistently shows that Democrats react

---

[22] It is probably not because people do not know what "atheist" means, as Pew finds that 85 percent of Americans can accurately define the term (Pew Research Center 2010).

positively when candidates describes themselves as not identifying with a religion, with a similar – if slightly more muted – positive reaction to candidates who are "not particularly religious." In other words, to be nonreligious is not a political liability, and may even be an asset with some voters. This chapter thus confirms the political instincts of both Kyrsten Sinema and Bernie Sanders, each of whom describe themselves as not being religious, while being careful to avoid the label of atheist.

Given the nation's recent secular surge, Sinema and Sanders are only the beginning. Just as religion's salience in American politics has led many candidates – especially Republicans – to signal their religious bona fides, the growth of secularism suggests that it will soon be common for politicians to wear their lack of religion on their sleeves.

11

Beyond the Secular Surge

Pick up any sociology of religion textbook and you will read how, when compared to other advanced, industrialized democracies, the high level of religiosity in the United States is an outlier. That assertion is certainly true, but the comparison misses the fact that there is more secularism among Americans than meets the eye – and it is growing. The best-documented trend has been the increasing number of Americans without a religious affiliation, an example of what Charles Taylor calls "subtraction stories" (2007). But the "rise of the Nones" is hardly the only indicator of America's turn away from religion. In their exhaustive analysis of the existing data on religious trends, David Voas and Mark Chaves conclude, "the evidence for a decades-long decline in American religiosity is now incontrovertible. Like the evidence for global warming, it comes from multiple sources, shows up in several dimensions, and paints a consistent factual picture" (2016, 1524).

The growth of nonreligiosity has received far and away the most attention. But it is not the whole story of American secularization. To borrow from Taylor, there is also an "addition story." A growing number of Americans have actively embraced a secular worldview and secular identities. This secular surge, we have seen, has both political causes and consequences.

Throughout the course of our investigation we have come to four major conclusions:

• *All Secular People Are Not Alike*

To be "nonreligious" is not the same as being "secular." The former – personal non-religiosity – is merely the absence of religiosity; the latter – personal secularism – is an affirmative embrace of a secular worldview. Indeed, it is possible for a person to simultaneously score high in religiosity *and* secularism (Chapter 2).

• *Secularism Affects Politics – and Politics Affects Secularism*

The secular surge results, at least in part, from an allergic reaction to politicized religion. Many Americans (mostly Democrats) have dropped their religious affiliation because of a backlash against the Religious Right (Chapter 6). And beyond helping to spur the growth of Non-Religionists, politics also has contributed to the expansion of Secularists. At the same time, secularity also influences politics, as Secularists have strong and distinctive political views. This includes their views on public secularism, or the separation of church and state (Chapter 3). However, it extends beyond church and state to Democratic Party affiliation, liberal ideology, and progressive positions on a wide variety of policy issues. Secularism, in fact, is not just connected to these political orientations, but appears to spur citizens to greater liberalism and stronger Democratic ties (Chapter 5). Furthermore, Secularists are not sitting on the civic sidelines, as they are very politically engaged (Chapter 4).

• *A Secular–Religious Divide Is Becoming Embedded in Party Politics*

Secularists are highly engaged in politics, mostly on the political left. Both among party activists and rank-and-file voters, Religionist Republicans strengthen the conservative wing of the GOP, while Secularist Democrats bolster the progressive wing of the "party of the people" (Chapter 7). Yet within the Democratic Party, the rise of secularism has created tension. Secularist Democrats find themselves at odds with Religionist Democrats, many of whom are African Americans and Latinos (Chapter 8). There is a trace of a similar tension within the GOP, as there is a small wing of libertarian Secularists who are at odds with the Religionists. Far more significant, though, is the fact that Donald Trump has attracted more Non-Religionists to the Republican Party, making them uneasy allies with the Religionist base of the party (Chapter 9).

• *For Political Candidates, Secularity Is Not Necessarily Fatal*

Contrary to conventional political wisdom, voters do not necessarily react negatively to candidates who describe themselves in secular terms – although many are suspicious of politicians who say they do not believe in God. This suggests that atheist candidates may do well to describe themselves in "softly secular" terms, not unlike the way religious candidates are often careful in how they describe their beliefs (Chapter 10).

In sum, the secular surge has the potential to change the American social and political landscape. The major force and agency of this change is personal secularism and Secularists, operating in a society with a growing population of Non-Religionists, who are sometimes allies but often bystanders. Thus, for those who advocate for a greater presence of secularism in American politics, converting these bystanders to Secularists is both an opportunity and a challenge.

What follows beyond the secular surge? Think of secularism as a geologic fault line. It is there, but is mostly subterranean. It can be seen on the surface in some places, but until and unless the ground shifts it will remain largely unseen. However, given the right conditions it could cause an earthquake – a dramatic change in the political landscape. The question is one of political seismology.

How likely is it that the ground will shift? One possibility is the emergence of a new Secular Left movement. Such a movement would make the fault line more visible, thus increasing the likelihood of more political polarization. However, such polarization need not increase if political actors seek common ground between Secularists and Religionists. Secularity surely adds to pluralism but not inevitably to polarization.

A SECULAR LEFT MOVEMENT?

The partisan divide between Religionists and Secularists suggests the possible birth of a Secular Left analogous to the Religious Right. Note that to speak of a collective movement is different than the observation – reinforced throughout this book – that there are already many individual Secularists on the political left. A movement is comprised of people who share a common identity, have common objectives, and are organized to achieve a common purpose. The Religious Right is one example. Prior to the emergence of the Religious Right as we now know it, plenty of individual churchgoers were socially conservative. They did not become a political movement, though, until those individuals came to see themselves as part of a collective effort.

There is evidence both for and against the imminent rise of a Secular Left. For example, Secularist organizations are both growing in size and becoming more politicized (Cimino and Smith 2014). At colleges and high schools, the Secular Student Alliance (SSA) has grown by leaps and bounds – from forty-two chapters in 2003 to hundreds today (Moore and Kramnick 2018, 174). Beyond college campuses, there are myriad Secularist organizations, such as the American Humanist Association (AHA), which we have featured in previous chapters, as well as American Atheists, Center for Inquiry, and the Freedom From Religion Foundation (Cragun, Fazzino, and Manning 2017). Many of these groups are focused specifically on being a political voice for Secularists. The AHA – the oldest of these groups, with a founding date of 1941 – shifted its focus in the 2000s. "From being primarily an organization of secular nontheists committed to liberal causes like human rights, international peace, church–state separation, and reproduction rights, it has become an activist, identity-focused group, deeply committed to the rights of nontheists" (Moore and Kramnick 2018, 166). In 2018, the Secular Coalition for America represented nineteen Secularist organizations in lobbying for secular policies in state and national government (Secular Coalition for America 2019).

There are still other examples of secularism's political emergence.

- During the Obama administration, a group of secular leaders held a lengthy meeting with members of the White House staff – the first time a president's staff had ever met with an explicitly secular delegation (Niose 2013, 135).
- In 2018, four members of Congress formed the Congressional Freethought Caucus, which has among its goals, "public policy formed on the basis of

reason, science, and moral values" and promoting the "secular character of government" (Manchester 2018).

- Three state Democratic parties have secular caucuses (Secular Coalition for America 2019) as does the national Libertarian Party (Mehta 2018). In 2016, a session held by the secular caucus at the Texas state Democratic convention far exceeded the anticipated attendance, causing delegates to be turned away (Brockway 2019).
- There are more and more openly secular candidates running for office at different levels of government. As of spring 2020, a number of Democratic presidential candidates have quietly signaled a secular orientation by avoiding the use of religious rhetoric (Beinart 2019).
- In the fall of 2019, the Democratic National Committee passed a resolution recognizing "the value, ethical soundness and importance of the religiously unaffiliated demographic" and stating that they "should be represented, included, and heard by the Party" (Gage 2019).

Yet for all the evidence suggesting a Secular Left is right around the corner, there is also reason to think that secularism will remain inchoate and thus politically ineffectual. Yes, Secularist leaders had a meeting with White House staff, but that meeting took place in 2010, under a Democratic president. No comparable meeting has been held, or is likely to be held, with a Republican in the White House. Yes, there is a Freethought Caucus in Congress, but it only has four members, fewer than the Friends of Kazakhstan Caucus (which has ten members). Yes, there are a few state-level secular caucuses, but these are still small drops in a large bucket. Yes, there are more "out" secular politicians than ever before, but it is still a very small number. Yes, there are Democratic presidential candidates who steer clear of religious language, but none of them advertise themselves as Secularists – and there are others who are very comfortable quoting scripture. Yes, the Democratic National Committee (DNC) has passed a pro-secular resolution, but it was in an off year and has gone largely unnoticed.

Furthermore, despite efforts to build a broad coalition among Secularist organizations, rank-and-file activists may not follow their leaders. For example, just 40 percent of the AHA activists have a favorable view of the Secular Coalition for America – of which the AHA is a member – compared to 95 percent favorability of their own organization.

It thus remains an open question whether a Secular Left will form. The answer, we suggest, lies in whether politicians, and Secularist activists, see a strategic advantage in forging such a movement. The parallel with evangelical Protestants – the heart and soul of the Religious Right – is instructive. As with evangelicals in the past, Secularists today are a large but disparate share of the population, and thus a prime group to mobilize.

One condition for the successful mobilization of a Secular Left movement would be the creation of a shared Secularist identity. While Secularists are politically active, they are a disparate group, lacking a common identity around which they can be mobilized. Many left-handed Americans are politically active, but few (if any) think of themselves primarily as lefties. Not being a deep-seated identity, left-handedness has very little political relevance.

In politics, mobilization always centers on identity of one sort or another. It could be a partisan identity, for example "Turn out and vote for the Democratic ticket to stop Donald Trump." Or mobilization can occur around an occupational category, for example steelworkers or teachers. Often, voters are mobilized through an appeal to their identity, such as gender, race, or sexual orientation – or of course religion. In today's politics, white evangelical Protestants are widely recognized as one such identity group.

In contrast to evangelicals, Secularists do not have a sense of common identity. They include people who either do not think of themselves as having a Secularist identity or, if they do, they have adopted one of a cluster of identities, such as humanist, atheist, or freethinker. Either way, they are not generally united under a single superordinate identity. What do we mean by a superordinate identity? It refers to an overarching identity that incorporates a set of subidentities. One example is "Latino," which spans a host of nationality groups such as Mexican Americans and Cuban Americans. One can identify both as a Mexican American and a Latino, but it is the latter that constitutes the superordinate identity (Mora 2014). Nor is this the only example – Asian Americans also include a variety of nationality groups, while the LGBTQ community includes people who have an array of sexual orientations and gender identities. Political mobilizers draw on these common identities in their political appeals, and in so doing reify the superordinate status of that identity. The more they invoke a shared identity, the more that identity is reinforced in the public mind.

It is not only that Secularists lack the breadth of a superordinate identity; the disparate identities they do hold typically lack depth as well. We draw this conclusion based on a strength-of-identity index that we included in the 2017 Secular America Study. Recall that we asked respondents whether any of a long list of identities describe them, including the four terms included in the Personal Secularism Index: atheist, agnostic, humanist, and secular. In addition to secular labels, the list contains religious terms, including "born-again /evangelical Christian." Respondents could select any or all of these terms that apply to them; many chose more than one. Respondents then selected which of the terms *best* described them, followed by a short battery of questions, drawn from previous research, to gauge the strength of our respondents' identification with that term (Huddy 2003).[1]

---

[1] They indicated their level of agreement or disagreement with each statement, with higher numbers indicating a greater strength of identity. The specific items are as follows.

- I think of myself as being a member of this group
- When talking about this group, I often use "we" instead of "they"

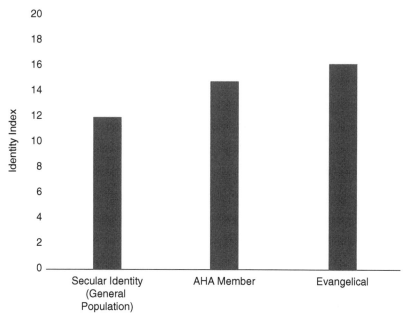

FIGURE 11.1 Evangelicals have a stronger sense of identity than Secularists
Source: 2017 Secular America Study; AHA Member Survey

When evangelicals[2] are compared to Secularists, we see that the former have a greater strength of self-identity. As shown in Figure 11.1, the mean score for evangelicals on a 20-point scale is 16, compared to only 12 for Secularists, a statistically significant difference. Nor is identity much stronger when we look only at people who self-identify as atheists – arguably the most sharply defined secular group – as their identity score is only 12.7.[3] Nor do we find a level of identity comparable to evangelicals among members of the AHA who, recall from previous chapters, otherwise score very highly on the Personal Secularism Index and, by virtue of their membership in the group, are self-identified Secularists. While the AHA members have a stronger sense of identity than Secularists in the general public, they still lag behind evangelicals.

   - Being part of this group is important to me
   - When someone criticizes this group, it feels like a personal insult to me
   - There is a lot of prejudice against this group.

[2] Evangelicals are defined as people who said that the term "born-again/evangelical" best describes them. The figure includes all evangelicals regardless of race. When limited to white evangelicals, their identity score is slightly higher: 16.4.

[3] Of the four identity groups in the active secularism index, atheists had the highest identity score. Just behind them are those who identify as humanists, at 12.6. Those who chose the term secular to describe themselves scored 11.9 on the identity index, while agnostics were only at 10.7.

That Secularists do not have a strong sense of identity is not surprising given the internal diversity among them. They are a disparate group, filled with people who have many different opinions and are likely to be individualistic. The very fact that the Personal Secularism Index combines people who use multiple terms to describe themselves underscores their heterogeneity. As Susan Jacoby puts it "American secularists have a hard time deciding what to call themselves today" (2004, 364).

The diversity of identities within the secular population presents a challenge for political mobilization. David Niose, president of the Secular Coalition for America, describes the difficulty of forging a secular identity by contrasting Secularists with supporters of the Religious Right.

While the Religious Right also used identity politics with its emphasis on proud Christian identity, in the early years its primary opposition lacked that strong sense of identity. Members of groups like PFAW [People for the American Way], the ACLU [American Civil Liberties Union], and Americans United [formerly, Americans United for the Separation of Church and State] certainly had identity, calling themselves civil libertarians, liberals, and a host of other descriptive terms, but there was nothing comparable to the strong, unifying sense of Christian identity that can be seen in the Religious Right. (2013, 128)

Niose is describing the Religious Right as it is, but not as it was. The "Christian identity" that he describes is largely an evangelical phenomenon, but evangelicals have not always had such a strong sense of shared identity. Indeed, it is remarkable that evangelicals have such a strong sense of identity, given that evangelicalism is not a single denomination with a clearly defined membership, like Mormons (Campbell, Green, and Monson 2014) or Catholics (D'Antonio, Dillon, and Gautier 2013), or a group with an ethnic dimension like Jews (Wald 2019). Indeed, there is no universal way to determine who is an "evangelical." To be an evangelical is entirely a matter of self-definition.

There is thus a parallel between evangelicals in the past and Secularists now. Just as many Secularists today do not have a shared identity, the same was true of evangelicals forty years ago. At that time, the people who are now described as, and generally identify themselves as, evangelicals were much more likely to see themselves as members of particular denominations (such as Southern Baptists or Assemblies of God) or theological "movements" (such as Fundamentalism or Pentecostalism) than as part of a broader evangelical tradition (Wilcox and Robinson 2010). Indeed, some of the subgroups within evangelicalism have, historically, been at odds over deep theological differences. The reification of evangelicals' identity did not happen by accident, as it was largely due to the deliberate strategy of political actors. When Jimmy Carter made much of his evangelical beliefs while running for president, it demonstrated that this was a large, and largely untapped, political constituency, but one internally diverse and largely depoliticized.

To win over this potential bloc of voters, prominent religious leaders, such as Jerry Falwell and Pat Robertson, formed an alliance with Republican politicians, such as Ronald Reagan. Like Carter, Reagan reached out to evangelicals by describing himself as being born-again (Wills 1992, 21). Unlike Carter, he also tapped into the organizational networks of religious congregations, and received the support of new Religious Right organizations like the Moral Majority and Religious Roundtable. As he famously told a gathering of evangelical leaders during the 1980 presidential campaign, "you can't endorse me, but I can endorse you" (Milkis and Tichenor 2018). Following Reagan, evangelicals have become a core constituency for many Republican presidential candidates. George W. Bush is a particularly interesting case, as he signaled to evangelicals that he was one of them by using words and phrases from evangelical culture that went unnoticed by nonevangelicals (Albertson 2015).

Today, evangelicals are a landmark of the American political landscape. Political advisors strategize on winning the evangelical vote. Pundits routinely speculate on which candidates will win key evangelicals' endorsements. Polls regularly report the attitudes of evangelicals. All of which only further reinforces that they are a politically critical group, which then further reifies them as a salient social identity, and so on in a self-reinforcing cycle (Wuthnow 1989).[4]

The question is whether Secularists will echo the evangelical experience, by forming a superordinate identity that transcends the thesaurus-like list of terms that Secularists currently use (if they use any term at all). There are certainly many possibilities, including atheists, humanists, skeptics, freethinkers, brights, nonbelievers, and, of course, Secularists. No single term thus far has risen to the top, but it is not clear whether this situation means none will, or if the right term has yet to catch on. Will Secularists find their version of "evangelical"?

The AHA activists illustrate the possibilities. When asked to choose the label that fit them best from a long list, just 37 percent chose "humanist," or "secular humanist," with another 25 percent picking "atheist," and 6 percent selecting "freethinker." The remaining one third of these activists chose a wide variety of other labels, a pattern made even more complex because many activists adopted more than one label when allowed to do so. Interestingly, just 4 percent of the AHA activists said the term "secular" fit them best, but 60 percent included the term among the multiple labels they chose.

We do not mean to suggest that the only thing standing in the way of a Secular Left is the adoption of a common label. A name is merely

---

[4] While the forging of an evangelical identity has united a wide variety of Protestant groups, more recently the circle of shared identity has been stretched even further to include non-Protestants too. The terms of art are often "Christian conservatives" or "people of faith," both of which refer to religious believers of many stripes, the latter obviously extending beyond Christianity (Hunter 1991).

a reflection of what truly matters, a common sense of identity and belonging. A shared identity has a visceral appeal, enabling collective mobilization to advance or defend the group's interests. By forging a new superordinate secular identity, a Secular Left could even expand the base of Secularists in the nation – another case of identity-stretching. Recall that many Non-Religionists have no clear sense of what they are, only what they are not. For those who share the same political views as Secularists, however, they could come to share the same secular identity, and thus come to have an affirmative self-definition. They would know who they are. Put another way, it could be politics that draws them into the movement and, along the way, they come to adopt a secular identity – being baptized by politics, they undergo a secular conversion.

The potential opportunity to forge a new social identity is thus a parallel between the origin story of the Religious Right and the current conditions portending a potential Secular Left. However, it is important to note the differences between evangelicals then and Secularists now. Forty years ago, evangelicals were a new constituency to be courted by the Republican Party. Many were apolitical, and if they were politically engaged, they leaned Democratic. Strategic Republican politicians peeled evangelicals away from the Democrats by emphasizing a new set of issues – opposition to abortion, to feminism, and to gay rights – that had not previously been part of the national political agenda. These issues galvanized evangelicals, as they all share the common DNA of cultural embattlement. From abortion devaluing motherhood, to women's rights upending gender roles, to LGBTQ rights transforming the legal definition of the family, many evangelicals felt (and still feel) that their values were under attack. In contrast, Secularists are already politically energized, typically on the left wing of the Democratic Party, with views that are largely indistinguishable from those of other progressive activists.[5]

How, then, might a Secular Left arise? Unlike evangelicals, who were mobilized around issues that were new to the national political agenda, it seems more likely that Secularists would be mobilized by an appeal to their secular worldview – not just their positions on the issues, but the secular reasoning behind those positions. For example, a candidate could emphasize climate change by advocating policymaking based on science and rationality. An especially sharp-edged version of such an appeal would be accompanied by criticism of those who are guided by religious faith. More broadly, advocacy for

---

[5] Granted, there are some issues that resonate specifically with Secularists, namely those related to the separation of church and state. However, they seem unlikely to inspire much passion. We say this because disputes over the relationship between church and state have been a staple of American law for decades, and yet the Secular Left has yet to emerge. This could be because the stakes in any given case seem relatively low. Can a county courthouse post a copy of the Ten Commandments? Can a church receive recycled tire scraps to resurface a playground from a state-funded program? We do not question the important constitutional issues raised by such questions, but none have the visceral impact of a case like *Roe* v. *Wade*.

science and rationality could potentially serve as an overarching frame to mobilize secular voters, comparable to the theme of cultural embattlement that so motivates evangelicals.

Whether or not we see a Secular Left may depend on whether ambitious politicians have the strategic incentive to lead such a movement. One potential scenario is that an entrepreneurial politician sees Secularists as a constituency to be mobilized *within the Democratic coalition*. Unlike evangelicals being courted to support a new party, Secularists would be energized inside their existing party. There is even a historical precedent for outreach to Secularists. When George McGovern ran for the Democratic presidential nomination in 1972, his winning coalition attracted many secular supporters (Layman 2001). In enlisting these secular activists, he won the battle for his party's nomination but then lost the war of the general election, not least because the American electorate was not nearly as secular as many of McGovern's supporters. Perhaps, though, McGovern was simply ahead of his time – not unlike the way that Barry Goldwater's unsuccessful presidential campaign in 1964 presaged today's Republican Party.

There are numerous progressive candidates today who, like Bernie Sanders and Elizabeth Warren, strongly appeal to Secularists' policy perspectives. However, as of yet, no national-level Democratic candidates have linked their progressivism explicitly to secularism (recall that even Sanders, who while admitting his nonreligiosity, vehemently denies that he is an atheist). There has yet to be a "secular McGovern" within the ranks of ambitious Democrats. Will a time come when some politicians see it in their strategic interest to plainly make that link? Time will tell, but with so many candidates now occupying the "progressive" lane in the Democratic Party, it is certainly possible that some may try to separate themselves from the crowd and appeal directly to the Secularist sensibilities of so many active Democrats.

We readily concede that it is unclear whether Secularists could ever be mobilized by an appeal to their worldview. In particular, the major challenge in mobilizing Secularists is their lack of distinctively secular organizational infrastructure at the grassroots. The most effective and sustained political mobilization has frequently come through preexisting organizations such as religious congregations. Even with the restrictions placed on political endorsements by nonprofit groups, many congregations have been conduits of political mobilization, on both the left and the right. In particular, the Religious Right has capitalized on the vast number of churches that have a theological stance consistent with the politics of their movement (Wilcox and Robinson 2010). Clergy appear with candidates on the campaign trail, candidates speak at religious services, and congregations distribute ostensibly nonpartisan voter guides that do not leave much doubt about which candidates are favored.

Congregations are thus prime organizations for political mobilization. If you are a candidate seeking the support of religious voters, you know where to find them. They meet regularly at a given time in a given place, in a setting where members are used to persuasive appeals. Furthermore, congregations involve a lot of their members in collective action, meaning that there is often an organizational structure already in place to get things done. In sharp contrast, Secularists do not have a comparable set of organizations. While the number of secular organizations is growing, with some even having church-like characteristics, they are still few and far between and, where they do exist, hard to sustain (Cragun, Fazzino, and Manning 2017; Hill 2019). Outside of formal organizations, we also find little evidence that people, even self-identified Secularists, engage in much consciously Secularist behavior. If you are a candidate seeking to rally Secularist voters behind you, it would be a challenge to mobilize them through a preexisting organizational network.

We stress, though, that the lack of much organizational infrastructure does not *necessarily* rule out the organization of Secularists for political ends. If a Secular Left were to emerge, it would likely be through virtual organizing. We are in the brave new world of political activity catalyzed by social media, as evidenced by highly effective online movements such as #MeToo. While the jury is still out on whether a political movement can be sustained through virtual channels, the Secular Left would be a good test case. As a group that skews young and educated, Secularists are often tech-savvy; there are myriad online forums where members of the secular population can find like-minded compatriots (Cimino and Smith 2014). In a qualitative study of Secularists, Aislinn Addington found that two aspects of their online activity stood out: "the [i]nternet as a mechanism for finding and strengthening community, and social media as a tool for secular activism and outreach" (2017, 136). Furthermore, Secularists are often comfortable with expressing their political views online. Data from our 2017 Secular America Study shows that people high in personal secularism were more likely to post political content on social media than other Americans.[6] Just as Republican candidates innovated in their ways of reaching evangelicals in their pews, perhaps one or more Democratic candidates will innovate by findings ways to mobilize Secularists through their phones.

THE SECULAR SURGE AND POLARIZATION

Will there be a Secular Left movement? We are either too smart – or not smart enough – to make a specific prediction. However, even if an effective movement analogous to the Religious Right never emerges, a secularism fault line will no doubt continue to increase in importance. There may or may not be a political earthquake, but the fault line can still cause tremors. Specifically, we point to how secularism contributes to political polarization. Not only does secularism drive political views, but politics can drive secularism – a feedback loop pulling

---

[6] Specifically, 39 percent of Secularists and 40 percent of Religious Secularists (both high in personal secularism) report posting about a political candidate over the last twelve months. Only 21 percent of Non-Religionists and 30 percent of Religionists report doing the same.

Secularist and Religionist Americans farther and farther apart from one another, both within and between the two major political parties.

Such a trend may presage a shift toward a confessional party system in the United States, in which the parties are identified as either explicitly religious or secular. Such confessional parties are found around the world, in nations as different as Germany, India, and Israel. We leave it to others to determine whether such systems successfully accommodate religious–secular divisions. But here in the United States, the two-party system makes it more likely to aggravate such divisions. Rather than accommodation, the two-party system in recent years has encouraged a zero-sum clash of worldviews (Hunter 1991). Having explicitly secular and religious parties might only add fuel to the smoldering fire of partisan polarization in American government, driving the parties farther apart ideologically, creating even greater hostility between the Democratic and Republican parties in government, and thus exacerbating gridlock and policy inaction.

The AHA activists provide some illustrative evidence. They have highly favorable views of nonreligious interest groups closely aligned with the Democratic Party, including the National Organization of Women (78 percent favorable) and AFL-CIO (62 percent), but little favorability toward nonreligious interest groups closely linked to the GOP, such as the Chamber of Commerce (19 percent) and the National Rifle Association (8 percent). These numbers suggest that there is plenty of room for more polarization.

That clash of worldviews even has implications beyond party politics, as polarization has seeped into many aspects of Americans' lives. The party you prefer shapes what you buy and where you get your news, as well as where you live and even whom you marry. Thus, one especially troubling implication of the intertwining of the religious–secular fault line and partisanship is the possibility that religious and secular Americans end up in parallel worlds, rarely or never interacting with one another. If so, this would be a regrettable change from the way that Americans have, over the past fifty years or so, formed a vast web of personal relationships across religious – and secular – lines. This high degree of interreligious bridging has enabled Americans to maintain a relatively high level of religious tolerance in the face of high and growing religious diversity (Putnam and Campbell 2012). As Americans have worked alongside, lived next to, and even married people with different beliefs, their social relationships transcended those differences in spite of political divisions along religious lines. Now, we fear, those social ties may be less likely to form, because political differences are pushing Americans apart. The AHA activists provide cautionary evidence: 55 percent report that one half or more of their five closest friends hold the same "religious" beliefs as they do – compared to 81 percent that say one half or more of their five closest friends hold the same political views. The former figure could eventually match the latter, rendering these activists even more insular.

If we ended here, it would seem as though the secular surge is destined to fuel more conflict among Americans. We confess that throughout this book we have highlighted division and difference, especially between Secularists and Religionists. However, there have also been hints that people who hold different worldviews are not necessarily trapped in a vicious cycle of mutual antipathy. Like a branching decision tree, the nation could go down the path of a deep fissure between religious and secular Americans. Or it could go down a different path, in which religious and secular Americans are not uniformly at odds, and instead work together. Lest this seem quixotic, consider the fact that many religious–secular differences have political roots. If politics got us into the current state of affairs, perhaps politics can get us out of it. While political differences are often treated as a given, in reality they are malleable – political coalitions can and do change. What if instead of exploiting and expanding religious–secular divisions among Americans, politicians sought to build a coalition that includes those with both a religious and a secular worldview?

Drawing on Charles Taylor's views on secularity, one can imagine two "subtraction stories" and one "addition story" on how such bridges might be built. The first subtraction story parallels Taylor's Secularity 1, the absence of a faith-based state. Here politicians, pundits, and activists could deemphasize religious establishment controversies, especially the use of religious symbols in the public square. As we have seen, these "church and state" issues will likely divide Religionists and Secularists. But even here there is some room for cooperation. After all, some Religionists are also strict separationists, such as Americans United for the Separation of Church and State (AU). Indeed, AHA activists have highly favorable views of AU (89 percent), more than for the Freedom From Religion Foundation (68 percent).

Instead of establishment issues, politicos could focus on the free exercise of religion – specifically, the free exercise of minority religions – where, as we have seen, agreement is more likely. Or, at least, any disagreements are less likely to fall along religious–secular lines. Recall that Secularists are not particularly opposed to personal religious expression by the president. Religionists, for their part, can also be accepting of expressions of a secular worldview, as evidenced by their willingness to vote for secular candidates (albeit with limits). Also recall that few Secularists say that people are better off "without religion in their lives," belying the notion that to be secular is to be automatically hostile to religious beliefs. In addition, 72 percent of AHA activists agreed or strongly agreed with the statement "In the realm of values, good and bad rests in the individual conscience." These patterns suggest that, at a personal level, there is potential for a high degree of tolerance for both religiosity and secularity.

The second subtraction story parallels Taylor's Secularity 2 – the decline of religious faith. Here the political class could ignore the underlying justification for policy attitudes, religious or secular, and focus only on the positions taken – where people end up, not how they got there. Consider climate change. Instead of pitting secularism against religious faith, it would be possible to highlight how different belief systems lead to the same conclusion about the need to address climate change. Many religious believers are motivated to care for the earth because their faith calls them to be stewards of the earth. Many Secularists share the same environmental objectives, but based on nontheistic arguments. Likewise, many Secularists and Religionists agree on the need for a strong social safety net. Religious believers are likely to ground their beliefs in scriptural injunctions to aid the poor, while Secularists will draw on human knowledge and experience. Either way, their goals are the same, and that can motivate political cooperation.

The AHA activists once again provide some intriguing data. Not surprisingly, evangelicals elicit very low favorability from these Secularists – at 8 percent. However, Habitat for Humanity (HFH), an organization deeply rooted in evangelicalism, has high favorability among AHA members: 82 percent. The tenfold difference in favorability between evangelicals and a group inspired and led by evangelicals surely reflects the goals and achievements of HFH in providing housing to disadvantaged people. In addition, 86 percent of the AHA activists agree with the statement "People should cooperate in politics even if they disagree on religious questions." These patterns suggest the potential for a high degree of respect for religion, and secular arguments that support shared goals.

The addition story parallels Taylor's Secularity 3 – alternatives to politics rooted in faith, secular or religious. Here politicians, pundits, and activists could seek long-term governing coalitions rather than short-term electoral coalitions. Central to this approach is an emphasis on tolerance and respect for religious and secular people alike, rather than the demonization of both. Although such a possibility may seem naive, it has a practical value: the twin facts that the American electorate is both secular *and* religious suggest that a smart political strategy would be to seek support from across the secular-religious spectrum. As we have seen, there are high costs to explicitly anti-theistic *and* pro-theocratic appeals to voters, and there are benefits to a more inclusive approach. In this regard, the big political prize is backing from Non-Religionists and Religious Secularists, voters who are often found astride the secularism fault line. After all, both Hillary Clinton and Donald Trump attracted ballots from both secular *and* religious voters. It is not much of a stretch to imagine that more motivated candidates could do even better.

Is it realistic to think that Secularists, especially those who are activists, can be conciliatory and cooperate with Religionists? After all, we have seen that Secularists are often ideological purists disinclined toward compromise. However, experience has shown that people who become politically engaged, especially as party activists, often change their political style and develop a taste for pragmatism. Indeed, there is evidence that this has happened with members of the Religious Right (Layman 2010; Shields 2009) – perhaps another way that the Secular Left might end up mirroring the experience of that group. People with deeply held religious beliefs and those who hold equally sincere secular beliefs may discover that they have more in common than they think.

The United States has always had a highly secular state. It is now becoming a more secular nation. But a more secular America need not be a more divided America.

Bibliography

Abramowitz, Alan. 2010. *The Disappearing Center: Engaged Citizens, Polarization, and American Democracy*. New Haven, CT: Yale University Press.

Achen, Christopher H, and Larry M. Bartels. 2016. *Democracy for Realists: Why Elections Do Not Produce Responsive Government*. Princeton, NJ: Princeton University Press.

Addington, Aislinn. 2017. "Building Bridges in the Shadows of Steeples: Atheist Community and Identity Online." In *Organized Secularism in the United States: New Directions in Research*, edited by Ryan T. Cragun, Christel Manning, and Lori Fazzino, 135–149. Berlin: De Gruyter.

Albertson, Bethany L. 2015. "Dog-Whistle Politics: Multivocal Communication and Religious Appeals." *Political Behavior* 37 (1): 3–26.

Aldrich, John. 1983. "A Downsian Spatial Model with Party Activism." *American Political Science Review* 77: 974–990.

   1995. *Why Parties? The Origin and Transformation of Political Parties in America*. Chicago: University of Chicago Press.

Alford, John R., Peter K. Hatemi, John R. Hibbing, Nicholas G. Martin, and Lindon J. Eaves. 2011. "The Politics of Mate Choice." *Journal of Politics* 73 (2): 362–379.

Allison, Paul David. 2009. *Fixed Effects Regression Models*. Quantitative Applications in the Social Sciences 160. Los Angeles: SAGE.

Aratani, Lori. 2012. "'Godless' Rally for Recognition." *Washington Post,* March. www.washingtonpost.com/local/atheists-others-to-gather-at-reason-rally/2012/03/23/gIQAvqY2WS_story.html?utm_term=.23418754506d.

Armstrong, Karen. 1998. *A History of God: The 4000-Year Quest of Judaism, Christianity and Islam*. New York: Ballantine.

Bailey, Sarah Pulliam. 2016. "Donald Trump Almost Put Money in the Communion Plate at a Church in Iowa." *Washington Post*, February 1, sec. Acts of Faith. www.washingtonpost.com/news/acts-of-faith/wp/2016/02/01/donald-trump-accidentally-put-money-in-the-communion-plate-at-a-church-in-iowa/.

   2017. "Trump Promised to Destroy the Johnson Amendment. Congress Is Targeting It Now." *Washington Post*, July 14. www.washingtonpost.com/news/acts-of-faith/wp/2017/06/30/trump-promised-to-destroy-the-johnson-amendment-congress-is-targeting-it-now/?utm_term=.4826863d6882.

Baker, Joseph O., and Buster G. Smith. 2015. *American Secularism: Cultural Contours of Nonreligious Belief Systems*. Religion and Social Transformation. New York: New York University Press.

Baker, Joseph O., and A. L. Whitehead. 2016. "Gendering (Non) Religion: Politics, Education, and Gender Gaps in Secularity in the United States." *Social Forces* 94 (4): 1623–1645.

Barker, David C., and Christopher Jan Carman. 2000. "The Spirit of Capitalism? Religious Doctrine, Values, and Economic Attitude Constructs." *Political Behavior* 22 (1): 1–27.

Barker, David C., Jon Hurwitz, and Traci L. Nelson. 2008. "Of Crusades and Culture Wars: 'Messianic' Militarism and Political Conflict in the US." *Journal of Politics* 70 (2): 307–322.

Barnes, Robert. 2016. "Battle Over Unions Signals Supreme Court Role at Center of Political Debate." *Washington Post*, January 9. www.washingtonpost.com/politics/courts_law/battle-over-unions-signals-supreme-court-role-at-center-of-political-debate/2016/01/09/200e9bd0-b627-11e5-9388-466021d971de_story.html?utm_term=.ce1a05b40475.

Bawn, Kathleen, Martin Cohen, David Karol, Seth Masket, Hans Noel, and John Zaller. 2012. "A Theory of Political Parties: Groups, Policy Demands and Nominations in American Politics." *Perspectives on Politics* 10 (3): 571–597.

Beinart, Peter. 2019. "Secular Democrats Are the New Normal." *The Atlantic*, March 15. www.theatlantic.com/ideas/archive/2019/03/betos-announcement-shows-triumph-secular-democrats/585001/.

Bellah, Robert N. 1988. "Civil Religion in America." *Daedalus* 117 (3): 97–118.

Bellah, Robert N., Richard Madsen, William M. Sullivan, Ann Swidler, and Steven M. Tipton. 2008. *Habits of the Heart: Individualism and Commitment in American Life*. Berkeley, CA; Los Angeles, CA; London: University of California Press.

Berelson, Bernard R., Paul F. Lazarsfeld, and William N. McPhee. 1954. *Voting: A Study of Opinion Formation in a Presidential Campaign*. Chicago: University of Chicago Press.

Bishop, Bill, and Robert G. Cushing. 2009. *The Big Sort: Why the Clustering of Like-Minded America Is Tearing Us Apart*. 1st ed. Boston: Mariner Books.

Blumberg, Antonia. 2017. "Why Secular Advocates Say Alabama GOP Senate Pick Is Dangerous." *Huffington Post*, September 27, sec. Politics. www.huffingtonpost.com/entry/why-secular-advocates-say-alabama-gop-senate-pick-is-dangerous_us_59cbe949e4b05063fe0e942b.

Bollen, Kenneth A. 1989. *Structural Equations with Latent Variables*. New York, NY: Wiley.

Booker, Ted. 2018. "Atheist Group Sets up Holiday Display in South Bend's County-City Building." *South Bend Tribune*, December 4.

Boorstein, Michelle, and Julie Zauzmer. 2016. "WikiLeaks: Democratic Party Officials Appear to Discuss Using Sanders's Faith Against Him." *Washington Post*, July 22. www.washingtonpost.com/news/acts-of-faith/wp/2016/07/22/wikileaks-democratic-party-officials-appear-to-discuss-using-sanderss-faith-against-him/?utm_term=.0915390a06fb.

Bowen, John Richard. 2008. *Why the French Don't Like Headscarves: Islam, The State, and Public Space*. Princeton, NJ: Princeton University Press.

Brady, Henry E., and Paul M. Sniderman. 1985. "Attitude Attribution: A Group Basis for Political Reasoning." *American Political Science Review* 79 (4): 1061–1078.

Brenner, Philip S. 2011. "Identity Importance and the Overreporting of Religious Service Attendance: Multiple Imputation of Religious Attendance Using the American Time Use Study and the General Social Survey." *Journal for the Scientific Study of Religion* 50 (1): 103–115.

Brewer, Mark, and Jeffrey Stonecash. 2001. "Class, Race Issues, and Declining White Support for the Democratic Party in the South." *Political Behavior* 23 (2): 131–155.

Brockway, Mark. 2017. "Home on Sunday, Home on Tuesday? Secular Political Participation in the United States." *Politics and Religion* 11 (2): 1–30.

   2019. *Secular Activism in American Party Politics*. Notre Dame, IN: University of Notre Dame.

Bruce, Steve. 2011. *Secularization: In Defence of an Unfashionable Theory*. Oxford: Oxford University Press.

Bulger, Matthew. 2012. "Unelectable Atheists: US States That Prohibit Godless Americans From Holding Public Office." *TheHumanist.Com*, May 25. https://thehumanist.com/news/national/unelectable-atheists-u-s-states-that-prohibit-godless-americans-from-holding-public-office.

Burge, Ryan. 2013. "Using Matching to Investigate the Relationship between Religion and Tolerance." *Politics and Religion* 6 (2): 264–281.

Burke, Daniel. 2016. "The Public and Private Faith of Hillary Clinton." *CNN Politics*, October 31. www.cnn.com/2016/10/30/politics/clinton-faith-private/index.html.

Burke, Edmund. 2009. *Reflections on the Revolution in France*. Translated by L. G. Mitchell. Oxford World's Classics. Oxford; New York: Oxford University Press.

Burnette, Daarel. 2017. "Partisan School Board Elections a Source of Anxiety for North Carolina." *Education Week*, December 12. www.edweek.org/ew/articles/2017/12/13/shift-to-partisan-school-board-elections-looms.html.

Calhoun, Craig J., Mark Juergensmeyer, and Jonathan VanAntwerpen, eds. 2011. *Rethinking Secularism*. Oxford; New York: Oxford University Press.

Campbell, Angus, Philip E. Converse, Warren E. Miller, and Donald E. Stokes. 1960. *The American Voter*. New York: Wiley.

Campbell, David. 2016. "How Trump's 'Mormon Problem' Could Mean He Loses Utah to Evan McMullin." *The Conversation*, November 3. http://theconversation.com/how-trumps-mormon-problem-could-mean-he-loses-utah-to-evan-mcmullin-67898.

Campbell, David E. 2006. *Why We Vote: How Schools and Communities Shape Our Civic Life*. Princeton, NJ: Princeton University Press.

Campbell, David E., John C. Green, and Geoffrey C. Layman. 2011. "The Party Faithful: Partisan Image, Candidate Religion, and the Electoral Impact of Party Identification." *American Journal of Political Science* 55 (1): 42–58.

Campbell, David E., John Clifford Green, and J. Quin Monson. 2014. *Seeking the Promised Land: Mormons and American Politics*. Cambridge Studies in Social Theory, Religion and Politics. New York: Cambridge University Press.

Campbell, David E., and Geoffrey C. Layman. 2017. "The Politics of Secularism in the United States." In *Emerging Trends in the Social and Behavioral Sciences*, edited by Robert Scott and Marlis Buchmann. Hoboken, NJ: John Wiley and Sons.

Campbell, David E., Geoffrey C. Layman, John C. Green, and Nathanael Sumaktoyo. 2018. "Putting Politics First: The Impact of Politics on American Religious and Secular Orientations." *American Journal of Political Science* 62 (3): 551–565.

Carmines, Edward G. 1991. "The Logic of Party Alignments." *Journal of Theoretical Politics* 3: 65–85.

Carmines, Edward G., and James A. Stimson. 1990. *Issue Evolution: Race and the Transformation of American Politics*. Princeton, NJ: Princeton University Press.

Casanova, José. 1994. *Public Religions in the Modern World*. Chicago: University of Chicago Press.

Castle, Jeremiah J. 2015. "The Electoral Impact of Public Opinion on Religious Establishment." *Journal for the Scientific Study of Religion* 54 (4): 814–832.

   2017. "Authoritarianism and Public Opinion on Church and State in the United States." *Politics and Religion* 10 (1): 57–81.

Castle, Jeremiah J., Geoffrey C. Layman, David E. Campbell, and John C. Green. 2017. "Survey Experiments on Candidate Religiosity, Political Attitudes, and Vote Choice." *Journal for the Scientific Study of Religion* 56 (1): 143–161.

Christina, Greta. 2012. *Why Are You Atheists So Angry? 99 Things That Piss Off the Godless*. Amazon Digital Services: Dirty Heathen Publishing.

Cimino, Richard P., and Christopher Smith. 2014. *Atheist Awakening: Secular Activism and Community in America*. New York: Oxford University Press.

Cirilli, Kevin. 2012. "Atheists Bummed by Dems' God Flip." *Politico*, September 5. www.politico.com/story/2012/09/atheists-bummed-by-dems-god-flip-080797.

Claassen, Ryan. 2015. *Godless Democrats and Pious Republicans? Party Activists, Party Capture, and the "God Gap."* New York, NY: Cambridge University Press.

Cohen, Marty, David Karol, Hans Noel, and John Zaller. 2008. *The Party Decides: Presidential Nominations Before and After Reform*. Chicago Studies in American Politics. Chicago: University of Chicago Press.

Coleman, James S. 1988. "Social Capital in the Creation of Human Capital." *American Journal of Sociology* 94 (Supplement: Organizations and Institutions: Sociological and Economic Approaches to the Analysis of Social Structure): S95–120.

   1990. *Foundations of Social Theory*. Cambridge, MA: Belknap Press of Harvard University Press.

Collette, Jessica, and Omar Lizardo. 2009. "A Power-Control Theory of Gender and Religiosity." *Journal for the Scientific Study of Religion* 48 (2): 213–231.

Conger, Kimberly H., Rosalyn Cooperman, Gregory Shufeldt, Geoffrey C. Layman, Kerem Ozan Kalkan, Richard Herrera, and John C. Green. 2019. "Group Commitment Among US Party Factions: A Perspective from Democratic and Republican National Convention Delegates." *American Politics Research* 47 (6): 1376–1408.

Converse, Philip E. 1964. "The Nature of Belief Systems in Mass Publics." In *Ideology and Discontent*, edited by David Apter, 206–261. New York: Free Press.

Cook, Corey L., Florette Cohen, and Sheldon Solomon. 2015. "What If They're Right About the Afterlife? Evidence of the Role of Existential Threat on Anti-Atheist Prejudice." *Social Psychological and Personality Science* 6 (7): 840–846.

Coontz, Stephanie. 2016. "2016 Election: Why the White Working Class Ditched Clinton – CNN." November 11. www.cnn.com/2016/11/10/opinions/how-clinton-lost-the-working-class-coontz/index.html.

Coulter, Ann H. 2007. *Godless: The Church of Liberalism*. 1st ed. New York: Three Rivers Press.

Cox, Daniel, and Robert P. Jones. 2017. "America's Changing Religious Identity." *Public Religion Research Institute*. www.prri.org/research/american-religious-landscape-christian-religiously-unaffiliated/.

Cox, Daniel, and Joanna Piacenza. 2015. "Is America a Christian Nation? Majority of Americans Don't Think So." *Public Religion Research Institute*. www.prri.org /spotlight/is-america-a-christian-nation-nearly-half-of-americans-no-longer-think-so/.

Cragun, Ryan T., Lori Fazzino, and Christel J. Manning. 2017. *Organized Secularism in the United States*. Boston, MA: De Gruyter.

Cragun, Ryan T., Barry A. Kosmin, Ariela Keysar, Joseph H. Hammer, and Michael Neilson. 2012. "On the Receiving End: Discrimination toward the Non-Religious in the United States." *Journal of Contemporary Religion* 27 (1): 105–127.

D'Antonio, William V., Michele Dillon, and Mary L. Gautier. 2013. *American Catholics in Transition: Persisting and Changing*. Lanham, MD: Rowman & Littlefield.

Dawkins, Richard. 2006. *The God Delusion*. Boston, MA: Houghton Mifflin Co.

Dean, John W. 2006. *Conservatives Without Conscience*. New York: Viking Press.

Delli Carpini, Michael X, and Scott Keeter. 1996. *What Americans Know About Politics and Why It Matters*. New Haven, CT: Yale University Press.

Dewey, John. 2013. *A Common Faith*. 2nd ed. The Terry Lectures. New Haven, CT: Yale University Press.

Dias, Elizabeth. 2018. "'God Is Going to Have to Forgive Me': Young Evangelicals Speak Out." *The New York Times*, November 1. sec. US. www.nytimes.com/2018/ 11/01/us/young-evangelicals-politics-midterms.html.

Djupe, Paul A., and Ryan P. Burge. 2018. "Regular Churchgoing Doesn't Make Trump Voters More Moderate. It Makes Them More Enthusiastic for Trump." *Washington Post*. October 9. www.washingtonpost.com/news/monkey-cage/wp/ 2018/10/09/regular-churchgoing-doesnt-make-trump-voters-more-moderate-it-makes-them-more-enthusiastic-for-trump/.

Djupe, Paul A., and Christopher P Gilbert. 2009. *The Political Influence of Churches*. Cambridge, UK; New York: Cambridge University Press.

Djupe, Paul A., Jacob R. Neiheisel, and Kimberly H. Conger. 2018. "Are the Politics of the Christian Right Linked to State Rates of the Nonreligious? The Importance of Salient Controversy." *Political Research Quarterly*, April, 1065912918771 52.

Djupe, Paul A., Jacob R. Neiheisel, and Anand E. Sokhey. 2018. "Reconsidering the Role of Politics in Leaving Religion: The Importance of Affiliation." *American Journal of Political Science* 62 (1): 161–175.

Downs, Anthony. 1957. *An Economic Theory of Democracy*. New York: Harper and Row.

Edgell, Penny, Jacqui Frost, and Evan Stewart. 2017. "From Existential to Social Understandings of Risk: Explaining Gender Differences in Non-Religion." *Social Currents* 4 (6).

Edgell, Penny, Joseph Gerteis, and Douglas Hartmann. 2007. "Atheists as 'Other': Cultural Boundaries and Cultural Membership in the United States." *American Sociological Review* 71 (2): 211–234.

Edgell, Penny, Douglas Hartmann, Evan Stewart, and Joseph Gerteis. 2016a. "Atheists and Other Cultural Outsiders: Moral Boundaries and the Non-Religious in the United States." *Social Forces* 95 (2): 607–638.

2016b. "Atheists and Other Cultural Outsiders: Moral Boundaries and the Non-Religious in the United States." *Social Forces* 95 (2): 607–638.

Ekins, Emily. 2017. "The Five Types of Trump Voters." *Democracy Fund, Voter Study Group*. www.voterstudygroup.org/publication/the-five-types-trump-voters.

2018. "The Liberalism of the Religious Right." *New York Times*, September 19. www .nytimes.com/2018/09/19/opinion/liberalism-religious-right.html.

Elk Grove Unified School District v. *Newdow*. 2004. 542. US.

Ellis, Richard J. 2005. *To the Flag: The Unlikely History of the Pledge of Allegiance.* Lawrence, KS: University Press of Kansas.

Feldman, Linda. 2015. "Bernie Sanders: 'I'm Proud to Be Jewish.'" *Christian Science Monitor*, June 11. www.csmonitor.com/USA/Politics/monitor_breakfast/2015/ 0611/Bernie-Sanders-I-m-proud-to-be-Jewish.

Feldman, Stanley, and Marco R. Steenbergen. 2001. "The Humanitarian Foundation of Public Support for Social Welfare." *American Journal of Political Science* 45 (3): 658–677.

Finke, Roger, and Rodney Stark. 2005. *The Churching of America, 1776–2005: Winners and Losers in Our Religious Economy.* 2nd ed. New Brunswick, NJ: Rutgers University Press.

Finkel, Steven E. 1995. *Causal Analysis with Panel Data.* Thousand Oaks, CA: Sage Publications.

Fiorina, Morris P., Samuel J. Abrams, and Jeremy Pope. 2011. *Culture War? The Myth of a Polarized America.* New York: Longman.

Flock, Elizabeth. 2013. "First Member of Congress Describes Religion as 'None.'" *US News & World Report*, January 3. www.usnews.com/news/blogs/washington-whispers/2013/01/03/first-member-of-congress-describes-religion-as-none.

Foer, Franklin. 2003. "Beyond Belief." *The New Republic*, December 29. https:// newrepublic.com/article/67301/beyond-belief-religion-howard-dean.

Fox, Jonathan. 2015. *Political Secularism, Religion, and the State: A Time Series Analysis of Worldwide Data.* Cambridge Studies in Social Theory, Religion and Politics. New York, NY: Cambridge University Press.

Fox News. 2012. "Convention Floor Erupts as Dems Restore References to God, Jerusalem in Platform," *Fox News*, September 5. www.foxnews.com/politics/ 2012/09/05/democrats-restore-references-to-god-jerusalem-in-platform.html.

Francis, L. J. 1997. "The Psychology of Gender Differences in Religion: A Review of Empirical Research." *Religion* 27 (1): 81–96.

Franks, Andrew. 2017. "Improving the Electability of Atheists in the United States: A Preliminary Examination." *Politics and Religion* 10 (3): 597–621.

Franks, Andrew S., and Kyle C. Scherr. 2014. "A Sociofunctional Approach to Prejudice at the Polls: Are Atheists More Politically Disadvantaged than Gays and Blacks? Anti-Atheist Prejudice at the Polls." *Journal of Applied Social Psychology* 44 (10): 681–691.

Freedom From Religion Foundation. 2018. "FFRF Debuts Solstice Display in N. H. Capital – Freedom From Religion Foundation." *FFRF*. December 1. https:// ffrf.org/news/news-releases/item/33746-ffrf-debuts-solstice-display-in-n-h-capital.

Freeman, Jo. 1986. "The Political Culture of the Democratic and Republican Parties." *Social Science Quarterly* 101 (3): 327–356.

Frey, William H. 2017. "Census Shows Pervasive Decline in 2016 Minority Voter Turnout." *Brookings Institution*. www.brookings.edu/blog/the-avenue/2017/05/18/census-shows-pervasive-decline-in-2016-minority-voter-turnout/.

Frost, Jacqui, and Penny Edgell. 2018. "Rescuing Nones From the Reference Category: Civic Engagement Among the Nonreligious in America." *Nonprofit and Voluntary Sector Quarterly* 47 (2): 417–438.

Frymer, Paul. 2010. *Uneasy Alliances: Race and Party Competition in America*. Princeton, NJ; Woodstock: Princeton University Press.

Fuller, Robert C. 2001. *Spiritual, But Not Religious: Understanding Unchurched America*. New York: Oxford University Press.

Gage, John. 2019. "DNC Passes Resolution Criticizing 'Religious Liberty' and Praising the 'Religiously Unaffiliated.'" *Washington Examiner*, August 30. www.washingtonexaminer.com/news/dnc-passes-resolution-criticizing-religious-liberty-and-praising-the-religiously-unaffiliated.

Gallup. 2016. "Five Key Findings on Religion in the US." *Gallup.Com*. http://news.gallup.com/poll/200186/five-key-findings-religion.aspx.

Gass, Nick. 2015. "Carson Warns Liberty Students About 'Secular Progressives.'" *Politico*, November 11. www.politico.com/story/2015/11/ben-carson-liberty-university-215760.

Gerson, Michael. 2018. "Trump and the Evangelical Temptation." *The Atlantic*. www.theatlantic.com/magazine/archive/2018/04/the-last-temptation/554066/.

Gerson, Michael, Carl Cannon, and Michael Cromartie. 2004. *"Religion, Rhetoric, and the Presidency: A Conversation with Michael Gerson."* Key West, Florida. *Pew Forum on Religion and Public Life and the Ethics and Public Policy Center*. www.pewforum.org/2004/12/06/religion-rhetoric-and-the-presidency-a-conversation-with-michael-gerson/.

Gervais, Will M. 2011. "Finding the Faithless: Perceived Atheist Prevalence Reduces Anti-Atheist Prejudice." *Personality and Social Psychology Bulletin* 37 (4): 543–556.

2013. "In Godlessness We Distrust: Using Social Psychology to Solve the Puzzle of Anti-Atheist Prejudice." *Social and Personality Psychology Compass* 7 (6): 366–377.

2014. "Everything Is Permitted? People Intuitively Judge Immorality as Representative of Atheists." *PloS One* 9 (4): 1–9.

Gervais, Will M., Azim F. Shariff, and Ara Norenzayan. 2011. "Do You Believe in Atheists? Distrust Is Central to Anti-Atheist Prejudice." *Journal of Personality and Social Psychology* 101 (6): 1189–1206.

Golshan, Tara. 2019. "Bernie Sanders's Real Base Is Diverse – and Very Young." *Vox*. March 7. www.vox.com/2019/3/7/18216899/bernie-sanders-bro-base-polling-2020-president.

Gore, Leada. 2017. "Kayla Moore Posts Support from 50 Pastors; 4 Ask for Their Names to Be Removed." *AL.Com*, November 13. www.al.com/news/index.ssf/2017/11/53_pastors_sign_letter_of_supp.html.

Graham, David A. 2013. "North Carolina's Proposed State Religion Isn't as Unprecedented as It Sounds." *The Atlantic*, April 3. www.theatlantic.com

/politics/archive/2013/04/north-carolinas-proposed-state-religion-isnt-as-unprecedented-as-it-sounds/274646/.

Green, Donald P., and Jack Citrin. 1994. "Measurement Error and the Structure of Attitudes: Are Positive and Negative Judgments Opposites?" *American Journal of Political Science* 38 (1): 256–281.

Green, Donald P., Bradley Palmquist, and Eric Schickler. 2002. *Partisan Hearts and Minds: Political Parties and the Social Identities of Voters.* New Haven, CT: Yale University Press.

Green, Emma. 2018. "Poll Shows Activism Highest Among Nonreligious Democrats – The Atlantic." *The Atlantic,* October 11. www.theatlantic.com/politics/archive/2018/10/poll-shows-activism-highest-among-non-religious-democrats/572674/.

Green, John C. 2007. *The Faith Factor: How Religion Influences American Elections.* Westport, CT: Greenwood Publishing Group.

2018. "The Evangelical Consolidation." In *The Evangelical Crackup? The Future of the Evangelical-Republican Coalition,* edited by Paul Djupe and Ryan Claassen, 264–272. Philadelphia: Temple University Press.

Green, Joshua. 2005. "Roy and His Rock." *The Atlantic.* www.theatlantic.com/magazine/archive/2005/10/roy-and-his-rock/304264/.

Greene, Steven H. 1999. "Understanding Party Identification: A Social Identity Approach." *Political Psychology* 20 (2): 393–403.

Groppe, Maureen. 2018. "Religious Right Blessed by Trump-Pence." *USA Today,* January 22.

Grothe, D. J. 2009. "At Inaugural, Obama Includes Nonbelievers, Pledges to Restore Science." *Center for Inquiry* (blog). January 20. www.centerforinquiry.net/blogs/entry/at_inaugural_obama_includes_nonbelievers_and_science/.

Guth, James L. 2009. "Religion and American Public Opinion: Foreign Policy Issues." In *Oxford Handbook of Religion and American Politics,* edited by Corwin E. Smidt, Lyman A. Kellstedt, and James L. Guth, 243–265. New York: Oxford University Press.

Guth, James L., and John C. Green. 1996. "Balance Wheels: Minor Party Activists in the Two-Party System." In *The State of the Parties,* edited by Daniel Shea and John C. Green. 2nd ed., 256–269. Lanham, MD: Rowman & Littlefield.

Guth, James L., John C. Green, Lyman A. Kellstedt, and Corwin E. Smidt. 1995. "Faith and the Environment: Religious Beliefs and Attitudes on Environmental Policy." *American Journal of Political Science* 39 (2): 364–382.

Hadaway, C. Kirk, Penny Long Marler, and Mark Chaves. 1993. "What the Polls Don't Show: A Closer Look at US Church Attendance." *American Sociological Review* 58 (6): 741–752.

Halpern, David. 2005. *Social Capital.* Cambridge, UK; Malden, MA: Polity.

Hamaker, Ellen L., Rebecca M. Kuiper, and Raoul P. P. P. Grasman. 2015. "A Critique of the Cross-Lagged Panel Model." *Psychological Methods* 20 (1): 102–116.

Hamburger, Philip. 2002. *Separation of Church and State.* Cambridge, MA: Harvard University Press.

Hammer, Joseph H., Ryan T. Cragun, Karen Hwang, and Jesse M. Smith. 2012. "Forms, Frequency, and Correlates of Perceived Anti-Atheist Discrimination." *Secularism and Nonreligion* 1: 43–67.

Hansen, Susan B. 2011. *Religion and Reaction: The Secular Political Challenge to the Religious Right.* Lanham, MD: Rowman & Littlefield.

Harris, Sam. 2005. *The End of Faith: Religion, Terror, and the Future of Reason.* 1st ed. New York: W.W. Norton & Co.

———. 2008. *Letter to a Christian Nation.* 1st ed. New York: Vintage Books.

Haught, James A. 2018. "Secular Surge." *Free Inquiry* 38 (4): 15.

Hershey, Marjorie. 2013. *Party Politics in America.* 15th ed. New York: Longman.

Hetherington, Marc J., and Jonathan Daniel Weiler. 2009. *Authoritarianism and Polarization in American Politics.* New York: Cambridge University Press.

Hill, Faith. 2019. "They Tried to Start a Church Without God. For a While, It Worked." *The Atlantic.* July 21. www.theatlantic.com/ideas/archive/2019/07/secular-churches-rethink-their-sales-pitch/594109/.

Hitchens, Christopher. 2007. *God Is Not Great: How Religion Poisons Everything.* 1st ed. New York: Twelve.

Holyoake, George Jacob. 1871. *The Principles of Secularism.* N.p.: Project Gutenberg.

Hout, Michael. 2017. "Religious Ambivalence, Liminality, and the Increase of No Religious Preference in the United States, 2006–2014." *Journal for the Scientific Study of Religion* 56 (1): 52–63.

Hout, Michael, and Claude S. Fischer. 2002. "Why More Americans Have No Religious Preference: Politics and Generations." *American Sociological Review* 67 (2): 165–190.

———. 2014. "Explaining Why More Americans Have No Religious Preference: Political Backlash and Generational Succession, 1987–2012." *Sociological Science* 1 (October): 423–447.

Huddy, Leonie. 2003. "Group Identity and Political Cohesion." In *Oxford Handbook of Political Psychology*, edited by David O. Sears, Leonie Huddy, and Robert Jervis, 511–558. New York: Oxford University Press.

Hume, David. 2014. *A Treatise of Human Nature.* N.p.: Create Space Independent Publishing Platform.

Hunsberger, Bruce E., and Bob Altemeyer. 2006. *Atheists: A Groundbreaking Study of America's Nonbelievers.* Amherst, NY: Prometheus Books.

Hunter, James Davison. 1991. *Culture Wars: The Struggle to Define America.* New York: Basic Books.

Hutchison, William R. 1992. *The Modernist Impulse in American Protestantism.* Durham, NC: Duke University Press.

Inglehart, Ronald. 1977. *The Silent Revolution: Changing Values and Political Styles Among Western Publics.* Princeton, NJ: Princeton University Press.

Iyengar, Shanto, and Sean J. Westwood. 2015. "Fear and Loathing across Party Lines: New Evidence on Group Polarization." *American Journal of Political Science* 59 (3): 690–707.

Jacobs, Carly M., and Elizabeth Theiss-Morse. 2013. "Belonging In a 'Christian Nation': The Explicit and Implicit Associations between Religion and National Group Membership." *Politics and Religion* 6 (02): 373–401.

Jacoby, Susan. 2004. *Freethinkers: A History of American Secularism.* New York: Metropolitan Books.

Jelen, Ted G. 2009. "Religion and American Public Opinion: Social Issues." In *Oxford Handbook of Religion and American Politics*, edited by Corwin E. Smidt, Lyman A. Kellstedt, and James L. Guth, 217–242. New York, NY: Oxford University Press.

———. 2010. *To Serve God and Mammon: Church-State Relations in American Politics.* 2nd ed. Religion and Politics Series. Washington, DC: Georgetown University Press.

Jelen, Ted G., and Clyde Wilcox. 1995. *Public Attitudes Toward Church and State*. American Political Institutions and Public Policy. Armonk, NY: M. E. Sharpe.

Jones, Robert P. 2017. *The End of White Christian America*. 1st ed. New York: Simon & Schuster Paperbacks.

Kant, Immanuel. 1999. *Critique of Pure Reason*. Translated by Paul Guyer, Allen W. Wood. In *The Cambridge Edition of the Works of Immanuel Kant*, general eds. Paul Guyer and Allen W. Wood. Cambridge, UK: Cambridge University Press.

Karol, David. 2009. *Party Position Change in American Politics*. New York: Cambridge University Press.

Kaufmann, Eric P. 2010. *Shall the Religious Inherit the Earth? Demography and Politics in the Twenty-First Century*. London: Profile.

Kellstedt, Lyman A. 2008. "Seculars and the American Presidency." In *Religion, Race, and the American Presidency*, edited by Gaston Espinosa, 81–100. Lanham, MD: Rowman & Littlefield.

Kellstedt, Lyman A., John C. Green, James L. Guth, and Corwin E. Smidt. 1996. "Grasping the Essentials: The Social Embodiment of Religion and Political Behavior." In *Religion and the Culture Wars*, edited by John C. Green, James L. Guth, Corwin E. Smidt, and Lyman A. Kellstedt, 174–192. Lanham, MD: Rowman & Littlefield.

Keneally, Meghan. 2017. "Donald Trump's Past Statements About LGBT Rights." *ABC News*, July 26. https://abcnews.go.com/Politics/donald-trumps-past-statements-lgbt-rights/story?id=48858527.

Keneally, Meghan, and John Parkinson. 2017. "What Roy Moore's 8 Accusers Have Said and His Responses." ABC News. November 15. http://abcnews.go.com/US/roy-moores-accusers-responses/story?id=51138718.

Kettell, S. 2013. "Faithless: The Politics of New Atheism." *Secularism and Nonreligion* 2: 61–72.

Kinder, Donald R., and Nathan P. Kalmoe. 2017. *Neither Liberal Nor Conservative: Ideological Innocence in the American Public*. Chicago: University of Illinois Press.

Kinder, Donald R., and Cindy D. Kam. 2009. *Us Against Them: Ethnocentric Foundations of American Opinion*. Chicago Studies in American Politics. Chicago: University of Chicago Press.

Kinder, Donald R., and David O. Sears. 1981. "Prejudice and Politics: Symbolic Racism Versus Racial Threats to the Good Life." *Journal of Personality and Social Psychology* 40 (3): 414–431.

Kirkpatrick, Jeane J. 1976. *The New Presidential Elite*. New York: Sage.

Knoll, Benjamin R. 2009. "'And Who Is My Neighbor?' Religion and Immigration Policy Attitudes." *Journal for the Scientific Study of Religion* 48 (2): 313–331.

Kurtz, Paul. 1973. *Humanist Manifestos I and II*. Amherst, NY: Prometheus Books. 2000. *Humanist Manifesto 2000*. Amherst, NY.

Kurtz, Paul, Vern L. Bullough, and Tim Madigan. 1993. *Toward a New Enlightenment: The Theory and Practice of Paul Kurtz*. New Brunswick, NJ: Transaction Publishers.

Kuru, Ahmet T. 2009. *Secularism and State Policies Toward Religion: The United States, France, and Turkey*. Cambridge Studies in Social Theory, Religion, and Politics. Cambridge, UK: Cambridge University Press.

Landler, Mark. 2012. "Pushed by Obama, Democrats Alter Platform Over Jerusalem." *New York Times*, September 5. www.nytimes.com/2012/09/06/us/politics/pushed-by-obama-democrats-alter-platform-over-jerusalem.html.

Layman, Geoffrey C. 2001. *The Great Divide: Religious and Cultural Conflict in American Party Politics*. New York: Columbia University Press.

2010. "Religion and Party Activists: A 'Perfect Storm' of Polarization or a Recipe for Pragmatism?" In *Religion and Democracy in the United States: Danger or Opportunity?*, edited by Alan Wolfe and Ira Katznelson, 212–254. Princeton, NJ; Thousand Oaks, CA: Princeton University Press and Russell Sage.

2014. "Party Activists." In *Guide to US Political Parties*, edited by Marjorie Hershey, Barry C. Burden, and Christina Wolbrecht, 209–221. Washington, DC: CQ Press.

2016. "Where Is Trump's Evangelical Base? Not in Church." *Monkey Cage: Washington Post,* March 29. www.washingtonpost.com/news/monkey-cage/wp/2016/03/29/where-is-trumps-evangelical-base-not-in-church/?utm_term=.a7168558ae42.

Layman, Geoffrey C., and Mark Brockway. 2018. "Evangelical Activists in the GOP: Still the Life of the Party?" In *Evangelical Crackup: Will the Evangelical-Republican Coalition Last?*, edited by Paul Djupe and Ryan Claassen, 32–48. Philadelphia: Temple University Press.

Layman, Geoffrey C., and Thomas M. Carsey. 2002. "Party Polarization and 'Conflict Extension' in the American Electorate." *American Journal of Political Science* 46 (4): 786–802.

Layman, Geoffrey C., Thomas M. Carsey, John C. Green, Richard Herrera, and Rosalyn Cooperman. 2010. "Activists and Conflict Extension in American Party Politics." *American Political Science Review* 104 (2): 324–346.

Layman, Geoffrey C., Thomas M. Carsey, and Juliana Menasce Horowitz. 2006. "Party Polarization in American Politics: Characteristics, Causes, and Consequences." *Annual Review of Political Science* 9: 83–110.

Layman, Geoffrey C., and John C. Green. 2006. "Wars and Rumours of Wars: The Contexts of Cultural Conflict in American Political Behaviour." *British Journal of Political Science* 36 (1): 61–89.

Layman, Geoffrey C., and Christopher Weaver. 2016. "Religion and Secularism among American Party Activists." *Politics and Religion* 9 (2): 271–295.

Lazarsfeld, Paul, Bernard Berelson, and Hazel Gaudet. 1948. *The People's Choice*. New York: Columbia University Press.

Lee, Lois. 2017. *Recognizing the Non-Religious: Reimagining the Secular*. Oxford, UK: Oxford University Press.

Levendusky, Matthew. 2010. *The Partisan Sort: How Liberals Became Democrats and Conservatives Became Republicans*. Chicago: University of Chicago Press.

Levin, Yuval. 2017. *The Fractured Republic: Renewing America's Social Contract in the Age of Individualism*. New York, NY: Basic Books.

Lewis-Beck, Michael S., ed. 2008. *The American Voter Revisited*. Ann Arbor, MI: University of Michigan Press.

Lim, Chaeyoon, Carol Ann MacGregor, and Robert D. Putnam. 2010. "Secular and Liminal: Discovering Heterogeneity Among Religious Nones." *Journal for the Scientific Study of Religion* 49 (4): 596–618.

Lipka, Michael. 2017. "Supreme Court Same-Sex Wedding Cake Case Reflects Split among American Public." *Pew Research Center* (blog), December 5. www.pewresearch.org/fact-tank/2017/12/05/supreme-court-same-sex-wedding-cake-case-reflects-split-among-american-public/.

2019. "10 Facts about Atheists." *Pew Research Center* (blog), December 6. www
.pewresearch.org/fact-tank/2019/12/06/10-facts-about-atheists/.

Lippmann, Walter. 1982. *A Preface to Morals*. Social Science Classics Series. New
Brunswick, NJ: Transaction Books.

Londoño, Ernesto. 2019. "Pride Flags and Foreign Policy: US Diplomats See Shift on
Gay Rights." *The New York Times*, June 10, sec. World. www.nytimes.com/2019/
06/09/world/americas/pride-flags-us-embassies.html.

Luo, Michael. 2017. "The Private Faith of Hillary Clinton." *New Yorker*, September 9.
www.newyorker.com/news/news-desk/the-private-faith-of-hillary-clinton.

Lynn, Barry W. 2006. *Piety and Politics: The Right-Wing Assault on Religious Freedom*.
1st ed. New York: Harmony Books.

Mahlamaki, Tiina. 2012. "Religion and Atheism from a Gender Perspective."
Approaching Religion 2: 58–65.

Manchester, Julia. 2018. "Dem Lawmakers Launch 'Freethought' Congressional
Caucus." *The Hill*, April 30. https://thehill.com/homenews/house/385573-dem-
reps-launch-congressional-freethought-caucus.

Margolis, Michele F. 2018a. *From Politics to the Pews: How Partisanship and the
Political Environment Shape Religious Identity*. Chicago Studies in American
Politics. Chicago: The University of Chicago Press.

2018b. "How Politics Affects Religion: Partisanship, Socialization, and Religiosity in
America." *The Journal of Politics* 80 (1): 30–43.

2019. "Who Wants to Make America Great Again? Understanding Evangelical
Support for Donald Trump." *Politics and Religion*, July: 1–30.

Martherus, James L., Andres G. Martinez, Paul K. Piff, and Alexander G. Theodoridis.
2019. "Party Animals? Extreme Partisan Polarization and Dehumanization."
Political Behavior. https://doi.org/10.1007/s11109-019-09559-4

Martinez, Jessica, and Gregory A. Smith. 2016. "Trump Has Benefited from
Evangelicals' Support, But He's Not the First Choice of the Most Committed."
Pew Research Center (blog), April 4. www.pewresearch.org/fact-tank/2016/04/04/
trump-has-benefited-from-evangelicals-support-but-hes-not-the-first-choice-of-the
-most-committed/.

Mason, Lilliana. 2018. *Uncivil Agreement: How Politics Became Our Identity*. Chicago:
University of Chicago Press.

Masterpiece Cakeshop, Ltd. et al. v. Colorado Civil Rights Commission et al. 2018.
584. US.

Mayer, William. 1996. *The Divided Democrats: Ideological Unity, Party Reform, and
Presidential Elections*. Boulder, CO: Westview Press.

McClosky, Herbert, and John Zaller. 1987. *American Ethos: Public Attitudes Toward
Capitalism and Democracy*. Cambridge, MA: Harvard University Press.

McCreary County v. ACLU. 2005. 545 844. US.

McCrummen, Stephanie, Beth Reinhard, and Alice Crites. 2017. "Woman Says Roy
Moore Initiated Sexual Encounter When She Was 14, He Was 32." *Washington
Post*, November 9, sec. Investigations. www.washingtonpost.com/investigations/
woman-says-roy-moore-initiated-sexual-encounter-when-she-was-14-he-was-32/
2017/11/09/1f495878-c293-11e7-afe9-4f60b5a6c4a0_story.html.

McDaniel, Eric L. 2008. *Politics in the Pews: The Political Mobilization of Black
Churches*. The Politics of Race and Ethnicity. Ann Arbor, MI: University of
Michigan Press.

Mehta, Hemant. 2018. "The Libertarian Party Now Has a Secular Caucus Led by an Atheist State Rep." *Friendly Atheist* (blog), July 23. https://friendlyatheist.patheos.com/2018/07/23/the-libertarian-party-now-has-a-secular-caucus-led-by-an-atheist-state-rep/.

Mellen, Ruby. 2016. "Thousands of Atheists Gather in DC for 'Reason Rally.'" *CNN*, June 4. www.cnn.com/2016/06/02/politics/atheist-reason-rally/index.html.

Milkis, Sidney M., and Daniel J. Tichenor. 2018. "Building a Movement Party." *Miller Center*, September 18. https://millercenter.org/rivalry-and-reform/building-movement-party.

Miller, Arthur H., Christopher Wlezien, and Ann Hildreth. 1991. "A Reference Group Theory of Partisan Coalitions." *Journal of Politics* 53 (4): 1134–1149.

Miller, A. S., and T. Nakamura. 2002. "Gender and Religiousness: Can Socialization Explanations Be Saved?" *American Journal of Sociology* 107 (6): 1399–1423.

Miller, Gary, and Norman Schofield. 2003. "Activists and Partisan Realignment in the United States." *American Political Science Review* 97: 245–260.

Miller, Warren E., and M. Kent Jennings. 1986. *Parties in Transition: A Longitudinal Study of Party Elites and Party Supporters*. New York: Sage.

Miller, Warren E., and J. Merrill Shanks. 1996. *The New American Voter*. Cambridge, MA: Harvard University Press.

Mockabee, Stephen T. 2007. "A Question of Authority: Religion and Cultural Conflict in the 2004 Election." *Political Behavior* 29 (2): 221–248.

Moore, R. Laurence, and Isaac Kramnick. 2018. *Godless Citizens in a Godly Republic: Atheists in American Public Life*. 1st ed. New York: W. W. Norton & Company.

Mora, G. Cristina. 2014. *Making Hispanics: How Activists, Bureaucrats, and Media Constructed a New American*. Chicago; London: The University of Chicago Press.

Mosca, Gaetano. 1939. *The Ruling Class*. New York: McGraw Hill.

Moyer, Justin Wm, and Jenny Starrs. 2016. "Trump Says Very Curious Things About God, Church and the Bible." *Washington Post*, January 19, sec. Morning Mix. www.washingtonpost.com/news/morning-mix/wp/2016/01/19/trump-says-very-curious-things-about-god-church-and-the-bible/.

Murashko, Alex. 2012. "DNC: Christian Leaders Comment on Night 'Dems Booed God.'" *Christian Post*, September 7. www.christianpost.com/news/dnc-christian-leaders-comment-on-night-dems-booed-god-81234/.

Mutz, Diana Carole. 2006. *Hearing the Other Side: Deliberative Versus Participatory Democracy*. New York: Cambridge University Press.

Neil, Shane Paul. 2016. "Soccer Is Here, for Real This Time." *Huffington Post* (blog). April 20. www.huffingtonpost.com/shane-paul-neil/soccer-is-here-for-real-t_b_9730440.html.

Nicholson, Stephen P., Chelsea Coe, Jason Emory, and Anna V. Song. 2016. "The Politics of Beauty: The Effects of Partisan Bias on Physical Attractiveness." *Political Behavior* 38 (4): 883–898.

Nie, Norman H., Jane Junn, and Kenneth Stehlik-Barry. 1996. *Education and Democratic Citizenship in America*. Chicago: University of Chicago Press.

Niose, David. 2013. *Nonbeliever Nation: The Rise of Secular Americans*. New York: Palgrave Macmillan.

2014. "Secular-Progressive? You're Probably a Humanist." *Psychology Today* (blog). www.psychologytoday.com/blog/our-humanity-naturally/201403/secular-progressive-youre-probably-humanist.

2015. "Humanist Egalitarianism Puts People First." *Patheos* (blog), November 18. www.patheos.com/topics/consumerism/humanist-egalitarianism-puts-people-first-david-niose-11-18-2015.

Norpoth, Helmut. 2019. "America's Largest Denomination: None." *PS: Political Science & Politics*, August, 1–7.

Norris, Pippa, and Ronald Inglehart. 2011. *Sacred and Secular: Religion and Politics Worldwide*. Cambridge, UK: Cambridge University Press.

Obama, Barack. 2009. "Barack Obama's Inaugural Address." *New York Times*, January 20. www.nytimes.com/2009/01/20/us/politics/20text-obama.html?mcubz=1.

O'Hair, Madalyn Murray. 1972. *What On Earth Is an Atheist!* New York: Arno Press.

Oldfield, Duane. 1996. *The Right and the Righteous*. Lanham, MD: Rowman & Littlefield.

Oppenheimer, Mark. 2012. "Politicians Who Reject Labels Based on Religion." *New York Times,* November 9. www.nytimes.com/2012/11/10/us/politics/politicians-who-speak-of-religion-in-unaccustomed-ways.html.

O'Reilly, Bill. 2006. *Culture Warrior*. New York: Random House.

Patrikios, Stratos. 2008. "American Republican Religion?" *Political Behavior* 30 (3): 367–389.

Pew Research Center. 2007. "US as a Christian Nation." *Fact Tank* (blog). July 21. www.pewresearch.org/fact-tank/2007/07/21/u-s-as-a-christian-nation/.

2010. "US Religious Knowledge Survey." *Pew Research Center*. www.pewforum.org/2010/09/28/u-s-religious-knowledge-survey/.

2015. "America's Changing Religious Landscape." *Pew Research Center*. www.pewforum.org/2015/05/12/americas-changing-religious-landscape/.

2017. "US Muslims Concerned About Their Place in Society, but Continue to Believe in the American Dream." *Pew Research Center*. www.pewforum.org/2017/07/26/findings-from-pew-research-centers-2017-survey-of-us-muslims/.

2018. "US Adults Are More Religious than Western Europeans." *Pew Research Center* (blog). www.pewresearch.org/fact-tank/2018/09/05/u-s-adults-are-more-religious-than-western-europeans/.

2019. "Religion's Relationship to Happiness, Civic Engagement and Health." *Pew Research Center*. www.pewforum.org/2019/01/31/religions-relationship-to-happiness-civic-engagement-and-health-around-the-world/.

Philpott, Daniel. 2009. "Has the Study of Global Politics Found Religion?" *Annual Review of Political Science* 12: 183–202.

Powers, Kristen. 2019. "Mayor Pete Buttigieg's Countercultural Approach to Christianity Is What America Needs Now." *USA Today*, April 3. www.usatoday.com/story/opinion/2019/04/03/mayor-pete-buttigieg-christian-right-2020-democratic-primary-trump-column/3342767002/.

Pruyser, Paul W. 1974. "Problems of Definition and Conception in the Psychological Study of Religious Unbelief." In *Changing Perspectives in the Scientific Study of Religion*, edited by Allan Eister, 185–200. New York: Wiley.

Putnam, Robert D. 1994. *Making Democracy Work: Civic Traditions in Modern Italy*. 1st ed. Princeton, NJ: Princeton University Press.

2001. *Bowling Alone: The Collapse and Revival of American Community*. New York, NY: Simon & Schuster.

Putnam, Robert D., and David E. Campbell. 2012. *American Grace: How Religion Divides and Unites Us (Paperback, with New Epilogue)*. New York, NY: Simon & Schuster.

Rapoport, Ronald B., Alan Abramowitz, and John McGlennon. 1986. *The Life of the Parties: Activists in Presidential Politics*. Lexington, KY: University Press of Kentucky.

Reicher, S., R. Spears, and S. A. Haslam. 2010. "The Social Identity Approach in Social Psychology." In *The Sage Handbook of Identities*, edited by M. S. Wetherell and C. T. Mohanty. London: Sage.

Riley, Naomi Schaefer. 2013. *'Til Faith Do Us Part: How Interfaith Marriage Is Transforming America*. Oxford, UK; New York: Oxford University Press.

Ritter, Ryan S., and Jesse Lee Preston. 2011. "Gross Gods and Icky Atheism: Disgust Responses to Rejected Religious Beliefs." *Journal of Experimental Social Psychology* 47 (6): 1225–1230.

Roth, L. M., and J. C. Kroll. 2007. "Risky Business: Assessing Risk Preference Explanations for Gender Differences in Religiosity." *American Sociological Review* 72 (2): 205–220.

Rowe, William L. 1998. "Atheism." In *Routledge Encyclopedia of Philosophy*, edited by Edward Craig. London: Taylor and Francis.

"Sanders: 'I'm Not Atheist … It's an Outrage.'" 2016. *State of the Union with Jake Tapper* (blog), July 24. http://cnnpressroom.blogs.cnn.com/2016/07/24/sanders-im-not-atheist-its-an-outrage/.

Sandstrom, Aleksandra. 2017a. "Faith on the Hill: The Religious Composition of the 115th Congress." *Pew Research Center*. www.pewforum.org/2017/01/03/faith-on-the-hill-115/.

2017b. "God or the Divine Is Referenced in Every State Constitution." *Pew Research Center*. www.pewresearch.org/fact-tank/2017/08/17/god-or-the-divine-is-referenced-in-every-state-constitution/.

Schlesinger, Joseph A. 1991. *Political Parties and the Winning of Office*. Ann Arbor, MI: University of Michigan Press.

Schnabel, L. 2015. "How Religious Are American Women and Men? Gender Differences and Similarities." *Journal for the Scientific Study of Religion* 54 (3): 616–622.

Schnabel, L., M. Facciani, A. Sincoff-Yedid, and L. L. Fazzino. 2016. "Gender and Atheism: Paradoxes, Contradictions, and an Agenda for Future Research." *Annual Review of Sociology*, 75–97.

Schnabel, Landon, and Sean Bock. 2017. "The Persistent and Exceptional Intensity of American Religion: A Response to Recent Research." *Sociological Science* 4: 686–700.

2018. "The Continuing Persistence of Intense Religion in the United States: Rejoinder." *Sociological Science* 5: 711–721.

Secular Coalition for America. 2019. "Nebraska Democratic Party Joins National Trend, Unanimously Adopts Secular Caucus." Secular Coalition for America. April 2. https://secular.org/2019/04/nebraska-democratic-party-adopts-secular-caucus/.

Sellers, Frances Stead, and John Wagner. 2016. "Why Bernie Sanders Doesn't Participate in Organized Religion." *Washington Post*, January 27. www.washingtonpost.com/politics/bernie-sanders-finally-answers-the-god-question/2016/01/26/83429390-bfb0-11e5-bcda-62a36b394160_story.html?utm_term=.0cab1b2346dc.

Sessions, Jeff. 2018. "Attorney General Sessions Delivers Remarks at the Department of Justice's Religious Liberty Summit." Speech presented at the Department of Justice Religious Liberty Summit, Washington, DC. July 31.

Shields, Jon A. 2009. *The Democratic Virtues of the Christian Right*. Princeton, NJ: Princeton University Press.

Sides, John, Michael Tesler, and Lynn Vavreck. 2018. *Identity Crisis: The 2016 Presidential Campaign and the Battle for the Meaning of America*. Princeton, NJ: Princeton University Press.

Simmons, Tracy. 2019. "Portland Bans Discrimination against Atheists, Other Nonbelievers." *The Salt Lake Tribune*, March 12. www.sltrib.com/religion/2019/03/04/portland-bans/.

Smidt, Corwin E., ed. 2003. *Religion as Social Capital: Producing the Common Good*. Waco, TX: Baylor University Press.

Smidt, Corwin E., Kevin R. den Dulk, James M. Penning, Stephen V. Monsma, and Douglas L. Koopman. 2008. *Pews, Prayers, and Participation: Religion and Civic Responsibility in America*. Religion and Politics Series. Washington, DC: Georgetown University Press.

Smidt, Corwin E., Lyman A. Kellstedt, and James L. Guth. 2009. "The Role of Religion in American Politics: Explanatory Theories and Associated Analytical and Measurement Issues." In *The Oxford Handbook of Religion and American Politics*, edited by Corwin E. Smidt, Lyman A. Kellstedt, and James L. Guth, 3–42. New York: Oxford University Press.

Smith, Christian, ed. 2003. *The Secular Revolution: Power, Interests, and Conflict in the Secularization of American Public Life*. Berkeley, CA: University of California Press.

Smith, Jesse M. 2011. "Becoming an Atheist in America: Constructing Identity and Meaning from the Rejection of Theism." *Sociology of Religion* 72 (2): 215–237.

2013. "Creating a Godless Community: The Collective Identity Work of Contemporary American Atheists." *Journal for the Scientific Study of Religion* 52 (1): 80–99.

Smith, Lavendrick. 2017. "Franklin Graham Blasted Roy Moore's Critics. That Didn't Go Over Well on Twitter." *Charlotte Observer*, November 18.

Smith, Mark A. 2015. *Secular Faith: How Culture Has Trumped Religion in American Politics*. Chicago; London: University of Chicago Press.

Soule, John W., and James W. Clarke. 1970. "Amateurs and Professionals: A Study of Delegates to the 1968 Democratic National Convention." *American Political Science Review* 64: 888–898.

Steensland, Brian, Jerry Z. Park, Mark D. Regnerus, et al. 2000. "The Measure of American Religion: Toward Improving the State of the Art." *Social Forces* 79 (1): 291–318.

Stolz, Jorg. 2019. "GlobalPlus: Secularism in the West." *The ARDA | Global Plus* (blog). http://globalplus.thearda.com/globalplus-secularism-in-the-west/.

Stolz, Jörg, Judith Konemann, Mallory Schneuwly Purdie, Thomas Englberger, and Michael Kruggeler. 2015. *(Un)Believing in Modern Society: Religion, Spirituality, and Religious-Secular Competition*. Burlington, VT: Ashgate.

Stone, Walter J., and Alan Abramowitz. 1983. "Winning May Not Be Everything, But It's More Than We Thought." *American Political Science Review* 77 (4): 945–956.

Stonecash, Jeffrey. 2000. *Class and Party in American Politics*. Boulder, CO: Westview Press.

Stouffer, Samuel Andrew. 1992. *Communism, Conformity, and Civil Liberties: A Cross-Section of the Nation Speaks Its Mind*. New Brunswick, NJ: Transaction Publishers.

Sullivan, Amy. 2012. "Debunking the 'Democrats Hate God' Lie." *New Republic*, September 6. https://newrepublic.com/article/106966/debunking-democrats-hate-god-lie.

Sullivan, John Lawrence, James Piereson, and George E. Marcus. 1993. *Political Tolerance and American Democracy*. Chicago; London: University of Chicago Press.

Sundquist, James. 1983. *Dynamics of the Party System: Alignment and Realignment of Political Parties in the United States*. Washington, DC: Brookings Institution Press.

Swan, Lawton K., and Martin Heesacker. 2012. "Anti-Atheist Bias in the United States: Testing Two Critical Assumptions." *Secularism and Nonreligion* 1 (February): 32.

Taber, Henry. 1897. *Faith or Fact*. New York: Peter Eckler.

Tackett, Michael. 2019. "Trump Fulfills His Promises on Abortion, and to Evangelicals." *The New York Times*, May 17, sec. US. www.nytimes.com/2019/05/16/us/politics/trump-abortion-evangelicals-2020.html.

Tarman, Christopher, and David O. Sears. 2005. "The Conceptualization and Measurement of Symbolic Racism." *The Journal of Politics* 67 (3): 731–761.

Taylor, Charles. 2007. *A Secular Age*. Cambridge, MA: Belknap Press of Harvard University Press.

Tillett, Emily. 2017. "Alabama Religious Leaders Stand Behind Roy Moore Against Allegations – As It Happened." *CBS News*, November 16. www.cbsnews.com/live-news/alabama-religious-leaders-stand-behind-roy-moore-against-allegations-live-updates/.

Tocqueville, Alexis de. 1995. *Democracy in America*. Edited by J. P. Mayer. Translated by George Lawrence. 1st ed. New York, NY: HarperPerennial.

Town of Greece, New York v. *Galloway et al.* 2014. 572. US.

Trump, Donald J. 2018. "Remarks by President Trump at Dinner with Evangelical Leaders." The White House. August 27. www.whitehouse.gov/briefings-statements/remarks-president-trump-dinner-evangelical-leaders/.

Van Orden v. *Perry*. 2005. 545 677. US.

Vance, J. D. 2016. *Hillbilly Elegy: A Memoir of a Family and Culture in Crisis*. 1st ed. New York: Harper.

Vandermaas-Peer, Alex, Daniel Cox, Molly Fisch-Friedman, Rob Griffin, and Robert P. Jones. 2018. "Emerging Consensus on LGBT Issues: Findings from the 2017 American Values Atlas." *PRRI* (blog). www.prri.org/research/emerging-consensus-on-lgbt-issues-findings-from-the-2017-american-values-atlas/.

Vaus, D. da, and I. McAllister. 1987. "Gender Differences in Religion: A Test of the Structural Location Theory." *American Sociological Review* 52 (4): 472–481.

Verba, Sidney, Kay Lehman Schlozman, and Henry E. Brady. 1995. *Voice and Equality: Civic Voluntarism in American Politics*. Cambridge, MA: Harvard University Press.

Voas, David, and Mark Chaves. 2016. "Is the United States a Counterexample to the Secularization Thesis?" *American Journal of Sociology* 121 (5): 1517–1556.

Wald, Kenneth D. 2019. *The Foundations of American Jewish Liberalism*. New York: Cambridge University Press.

Wald, Kenneth D., and Allison Calhoun-Brown. 2018. *Religion and Politics in the United States*. 8th ed. Lanham, MD: Rowman & Littlefield.

Waldman, Steven. 2009. "Obama Touches the Untouchables: Non-Believers." *Huffington Post* (blog). January 20. www.huffingtonpost.com/steven-waldman /obama-touches-the-untouch_b_159538.html.

Warikoo, Niraj. 2015. "Muslim Women Fight for Right to Wear Islamic Headscarf." *USA TODAY*, July 1. www.usatoday.com/story/news/nation/2015/07/01/hijab-muslim-headscarf-lawsuits/29565005/.

Warner, Michael, Jonathan VanAntwerpen, and Craig Calhoun, eds. 2010. "Editors' Introduction." In *Varieties of Secularism in a Secular Age*, edited by Michael Warner, Jonathan VanAntwerpen, and Craig Calhoun, 1–31. Cambridge, MA: Harvard University Press.

Wehner, Peter. 2017. "Opinion | Why I Can No Longer Call Myself an Evangelical Republican." *The New York Times*, December 9, sec. Opinion. www.nytimes.com /2017/12/09/opinion/sunday/wehner-evangelical-republicans.html.

Weiland, Noah. 2018. "Evangelicals, Having Backed Trump, Find White House 'Front Door Is Open.'" *The New York Times*, February 7, sec. Politics. www.nytimes.com /2018/02/07/us/politics/trump-evangelicals-national-prayer-breakfast.html.

Weisberg, Herbert. 2005. "The Structure and Effects of Moral Predispositions in Contemporary American Politics." *Journal of Politics* 67 (3): 646–668.

Whitmarsh, Tim. 2016. *Battling the Gods: Atheism in the Ancient World*. New York: Vintage.

Wilcox, Clyde, and Carin Robinson. 2010. *Onward Christian Soldiers? The Religious Right in American Politics*. Boulder, CO: Westview Press.

Wilcox, W. Bradford, Andrew J. Cherlin, Jeremy E. Uecker, and Matthew Messel. 2012. "No Money, No Honey, No Church: The Deinstitutionalization of Religious Life Among the White Working Class." In *Research in the Sociology of Work*, edited by Lisa A. Keister, John McCarthy, and Roger Finke, 23: 227–250. Bingley, UK: Emerald Group Publishing Limited.

Wildavsky, Aaron. 1965. "The Goldwater Phenomenon: Purists, Politicians, and the Two-Party System." *Review of Politics* 27: 393–399.

Wiley, David E., and James A. Wiley. 1970. "The Estimation of Measurement Error in Panel Data." *American Sociological Review* 35 (1): 112–117.

Wills, Garry. 1992. *Under God: Religion and American Politics*. New York: Simon & Schuster.

Wilson, Edwin H. 1995. *The Genesis of the Humanist Manifesto*. Washington, DC: Humanist Press.

Wilson, J. Matthew. 2009. "Religion and American Public Opinion: Economic Issues." In *Oxford Handbook of Religion and American Politics*, edited by Corwin E. Smidt, Lyman A. Kellstedt, and James L. Guth, 191–216. New York: Oxford University Press.

Wilson, James Q. 1962. *The Amateur Democrat*. Chicago: University of Chicago Press.

Wolbrecht, Christina. 2000. *The Politics of Women's Rights: Parties, Positions, and Change*. Princeton, NJ: Princeton University Press.

Wolpe, David. 2011. "Why Are Atheists So Angry?" *Huffington Post*, May 25. www .huffpost.com/entry/why-are-atheists-so-angry_b_833662?guccounter=1.

Wuthnow, Robert. 1989. *The Restructuring of American Religion: Society and Faith Since World War II*. 1st ed. Studies in Church and State. Princeton, NJ: Princeton University Press.

2015. *Inventing American Religion: Polls, Surveys, and the Tenuous Quest for a Nation's Faith*. Oxford; New York: Oxford University Press.

Zaller, John R. 1992. *The Nature and Origins of Mass Opinion*. London: Cambridge University Press.

Zuckerman, Phil, Luke Galen, and Frank Pasquale. 2016. *The Nonreligious: Understanding Secular People and Societies*. New York: Oxford University Press.

Zukin, Cliff, Scott Keeter, Molly Andolina, Krista Jenkins, and Michael X. Delli Carpini. 2006. *A New Engagement? Political Participation, Civic Life, and the Changing American Citizen*. Oxford; New York: Oxford University Press.

Index